COLLEGE LIBRARY

**Please return this book by the date stamped below
- if recalled, the loan is reduced to 10 days**

Fines are payable for late return

The Future of Leisure Services

Edited by
John Benington and Judy White

Longman

Longman Group UK Limited
Longman House, Burnt Mill, Harlow, Essex, CM20 2JE

British Library Cataloguing in Publication Data
Benington, John.
    The future of leisure services.
    1. Great Britain. Leisure services
    I. Title.   II. White, Judy
    306:48' 0941
    ISBN 0582–02637–7

    ISBN 0582-02637-7

Printed and bound in Great Britain by
Biddles Ltd, Guildford and King's Lynn

Dedication

For Jenni – who was there at the beginning
and at the end;
and for Martin, Tom and William.

Longman/ILAM
Leisure Management series

Law and leisure services management
  Michael Scott

Leisure operational management vol. 1: facilities
  Pat Badmin, Martyn Coombs and Graham Rayner

Leisure operational management vol. 2: people
  Pat Badmin

Economics of leisure services management
  Chris Gratton and Peter Taylor

Marketing tourism
  Leonard Lickorish and Alan Jefferson

The leisure services yearbook 1988/89

Contents

List of Contributors

John Benington

is currently Director of The Local Government Centre at Warwick University. From 1985 to 1988 he worked at the Institute of Local Government Studies, University of Birmingham, and prior to that was Head of the Employment Department at Sheffield City Council. He is co-editor of the journal *Local Government Policymaking*

Patrick Boylan, PhD

has worked in local government and galleries for 24 years, in Hull, Exeter, Leicester and Leicestershire, where he is now Director of Museums and Arts.

Patricia Coleman

currently Director, Libraries and Information Services, City of Sheffield, she has worked for Derbyshire County Council and Manchester City Council, as well as the British Library. She is Library Adviser to the AMA and a member of the Library and Information Services Council.

Chris Field

currently Chief Executive of the Shakespeare Globe Trust, and formerly Director of Leisure Services for the London Borough of Greenwich, entered leisure management at one of the first joint provision, multi-use, recreation centres in Nottingham. He has served on the Greater London and South East Sports Council, Play Board, the Sports and Recreation Committee of the AMA for ten years

Mike Fitzjohn

Senior Research Officer with the Sports Council, has been involved in sport and recreation and policy work for 18 years, with the GLC and the North West Regional Council for Sport and Recreation as well as the Sports Council. Most recently he has conducted the review of Sports Council Strategy, *Into the 90s.*

Ian Gill, LLB

Chief Executive, Thanet District Council, since re-organisation in 1974, has spent most of his career in local government. His current post has brought him direct knowledge of the changing state of resort tourism through responsibility for the three resorts of Broadstairs, Margate and Ramsgate. He has been Honorary Secretary of the British Resorts Association since 1979, and is a Fellow of the Tourism Society and Executive Secretary to the Council for Travel and Tourism

Ian Henry, PhD

currently Senior Lecturer in Leisure Studies and Recreation Management, in the Carnegie Department, Leeds Polytechnic, worked in local government as a sports centre manager and as head of leisure services in a metropolitan district before taking up a lecturing post at Ilkley College in 1980. His principal research interests are in the field of leisure policy. He is co-author and editor of several books concerned with leisure management planning and policy

Denys Hodson

currently Director, Arts and Recreation for the Borough of Thamesdown, began his local government career as Controller of Arts and Recreation for Swindon in 1970, after working in commerce and industry. He has served on various local and national committees, including ten years as a Governor of the British Film Institute, and spells as Chairman of the Southern Arts Association and of CORA, as well as an adviser to the ADC. He is currently a director of the Oxford Stage Company and a member of the Arts Council

David Liddle

has been Director of Community Leisure Services for the County of Avon since 1985. Before that he was Librarian and Arts Officer for Gateshead MBC. He is currently responsible for a wide range of functions including the Youth Service, Community Work, Libraries, Arts and Sports Development, and grant aid to voluntary groups

James Munn, MBE

Director of the Department of Recreation and Community Services, City of Birmingham, has a prominent record with progressive Local Authorities in England and Wales. Since the mid-60's he has been identified with the development of many neighbourhood community activities which were exceptional at that time and most relevant to the main thrust of current Government legislation in the Education and Local Authority fields

Kieron Walsh

currently Senior Lecturer in the Institute of Local Government Studies, has lectured in INLOGOV since 1975 and done research on the management of local government, falling roles in education and central/local relations. His most recent research has considered the impact of competitive tendering in local government, and his most recent book is concerned with Marketing in Local Government

Judy White, PhD

Lecturer, Centre for Urban and Regional Studies, School of Public Policy, University of Birmingham, has been concerned with public leisure policy for over fifteen years. In that time she has completed numerous research and consultancy projects for a wide range of leisure interests. She also undertakes management development and training programmes for managers in leisure and other services in local government. She is currently chair of the Leisure Studies Association

Preface

This volume of collected papers is concerned with the future of the public leisure service. It is the outcome from work originally commissioned as part of a larger research project on the future role and organisation of local government. The research was sponsored by the Association of County Councils, the Association of District Councils, the Association of Metropolitan Authorities, and the Institute of Local Government Studies. The research took the form of a review with two main aims:

   1 to provide local government with an opportunity to analyse and consider the major changes with which it will be involved in the years to the end of the century;
   2 to put forward for discussion various options for the future shape and scope of local government.

The review ran for about eighteen months, from mid 1985 to early 1987. The first phase was primarily concerned with establishing and reviewing the existing functions of local government, followed by discussion of alternative ways of carrying out these functions. The functions explored were: education; community and social services; planning and transportation; public protection; economic development; and leisure. The second phase examined organisational consequences in terms of structure, leadership and management, central – local relations, and finance. One of the original outputs from this review was a series of 'green papers' on the major issues facing local government. These papers identified and analysed options, rather than argued for particular solutions. The paper on the leisure function was prepared by the two of us. The ideas and arguments it propounded were widely publicised, and we undertook a series of presentations and took part in several seminars organised by and for different parts of the public leisure service (eg the Chief Leisure Officers Association, the Sports Council, the Association of London Authorities). We also organised several one-day seminars and heard a variety of responses and views from the local government councillors and officers attending. These forums were important.

They helped us to test and explain our ideas. They gave space and time to others to examine and criticise these ideas and develop alternatives or refinements of their own. They generated lively debate by practitioners and policymakers about the fundamental rationale for the public leisure service in a way which was quite rare. As they continued into 1987 and 1988, these forums have also acted as a sounding board for further changes as they are taking place. They have helped to examine the potential impact of changes like compulsory competitive tendering on the leisure service. They have also helped us to amend and develop our thinking about strategies.

The public platforms we have occupied and the discussions we have been part of have indicated the rapid raising of the profile of leisure as a political issue. The current legislative changes centred on sport management and libraries have confirmed this. This makes the development and broadening of the debate even more important. By updating our 'green paper' and publicising these ideas even more widely, we hope to reinforce the conviction that leisure remains a fundamental service in local government.

The other contributions to this volume discuss the shape of future development in specific parts of the leisure service. Most of these contributors were involved in the earlier stage of the review. We commissioned them to write working papers which discussed key areas of the leisure service, and analysed their specific challenges and opportunites in the changing environment of local government. These working papers were subsequently updated and amended for this book and two further chapters were written.

This collection is neither comprehensive nor exhaustive in its coverage. Instead it aims to highlight the most salient issues. The authors and their argument are authoritatitive in their particular field. They exemplify the multiplicity of perspectives which exist in the different parts of the leisure service. This highlights some of the problems of diversity, as increasingly stark choices have to be made about priorities between different parts of the service.

Each chapter stands on its own and can be read as an issue paper considering the place of that part of the service in its own right. The book starts with our overview of the key issues and critical choices facing the public leisure services over the next decade. Kieron Walsh contributes an important chapter on the impact of compulsory competitive tendering on leisure services. Detailed chapters on sport, the arts, libraries and information services, museums, tourism and entertainment and community leisure then follow. Most of these are written by leading practitioners and therefore reflect their assessment of the realities of change in their organisations. The chapter by Ian Henry develops a theoretical framework to try and analyse some of the contextual factors likely to influence local government form and structure. The final chapter argues the need for local government to take a lead in developing a strategic vision for leisure services into the twenty-first century.

The appendix is a discussion of the views of a group of chief leisure services officers about the future of the service. This gives a pertinent insight into the strength, weaknesses, problems and challenges of working in an unstable and unpredictable environment. It is also a rare attempt to analyse some of the attitudes of senior managers to their service and to their roles.

The speed with which the Government is reviewing and res- tructuring policy in relation to local government in general and leisure services in particular means that further changes may take place even before these chapters are published. Nevertheless, we believe that this volume will provide practitioners, policy makers, politicians, managers and researchers with stimulating and pro- vocative ideas about the challenges and choices facing the public leisure service over the next decade. There is much at stake.

John Benington and Judy White
Birmingham, August 1988

Acknowledgements

As editors of a set of papers connected by a thread of belief in a future for leisure services in the public sector, many of which were written by a group of busy practitioners, we are very aware that without the co-operation of each author, this volume would never have seen the light of the publishing day.

As colleagues, we are grateful to our other colleagues at the Institute of Local Government Studies for their stimulus in the earlier stages of this whole project; to the three local authority associations who sponsored the research; to all those in the public leisure service who contributed generously to the review, either in writing or in discussion; and to Kathy Bonehill, Lynne Dixon, Elaine Gallagher, Joan Morgan and Dot Woolley, who were left with little leisure in the typing of all this for publication.

1 Leisure services at a crossroads

John Benington and Judy White

PART 1 — INTRODUCTION

Local authority leisure services are at a major crossroads in their development. Decisions made during the next few years will determine whether leisure remains as a major sphere of public sector policy and activity – or whether it is reduced to a residual service from which the main functions have been taken over by the private commercial sector, leaving only 'unpopular' or 'uneconomic' gaps in provision to be met by local government. The choices are to do with both content and form – *what* is provided, as well as *how* it is provided.

'Leisure' is a crucible for some of the major issues facing British society as a whole (and therefore, local government) over the next decade and into the next century. Deindustrialisation, large scale unemployment, the ageing of the population and other profound economic, technological, political, social and cultural changes, are all affecting the foundations of society, and radically altering the relationships between paid employment, useful work, domestic life and leisure. A growing proportion of the population is facing the dilemma of having more time at its disposal, whilst simultaneously lacking many of the basic resources to use it as effectively as they might want. At the same time, the still growing affluence of other sections of the population is reflected in a notable increase in the volume and range of participation in leisure activities.

The leisure industries have mushroomed rapidly since the mid 1960s with consumer expenditure on leisure rising rapidly up to 1977 (when it amounted to £23 billion, more than 20 per cent of total consumer spending[1]). Since then it has grown steadily, to about £41 billion by 1983; but it is estimated to increase to £67.8 billion by

1

1989 when it will represent 23.3 per cent of all consumer expenditure[2]. It is evident from these figures that leisure industries have become a major sector of the British economy. They currently employ about 1.8 million people in some capacity – about 8 per cent of the nation's workforce[3] – and are forecast to be the fastest growing area of employment, increasing by 30 per cent by 1990[4].

This rapid growth has opened up large potential markets for the private sector, and substantial business opportunities for giant conglomerates such as Rank, Thorn/EMI, Granada, Grand Metropolitan, Allied-Lyons and Ladbroke Holdings, and for other more specialist firms who have seen the profitable possibilities in music, film, television, video, consumer electronics, sport, gambling, tourism and entertainment. Literally thousands of other smaller companies have bought stakes in the leisure industry through sponsorships or advertising.

Public sector investment in leisure has been on a smaller scale than the private sector, but nevertheless has grown substantially over the past 20 years. Central government expenditure on leisure increased five-fold between 1967 and 1977, and by 1980–81 amounted to about £750m (or £275m if broadcasting is excluded). Local authority net expenditure on leisure services doubled between 1976/77 and 1981/82 when it totalled about £851m (even excluding expenditure on libraries, adult education and youth and community services and tourism – all of which are related, to a greater or lesser degree, to leisure).

Over the next decade, major new pressures, needs and opportunities will face leisure providers and leisure users in both the public and private sectors, as a result of the continued restructuring of the Western economy. The pattern of leisure provision for the next century is therefore likely to be shaped by the following critical issues:

(i) the relative roles of the private and public sectors in responding to growth and change in leisure needs and opportunities;
(ii) the extent to which leisure needs will be met through collective services or individual consumption;
(iii) the basis for financing leisure provision and the extent to which particular facilities will be priced through the market mechanism and/or through public subsidy;
(iv) the degree of equality or inequality of access to various kinds of leisure provision by different classes or groups within the population;
(v) the extent to which the needs of diverse cultures and minority interests will be reflected within the overall spectrum of leisure provision.

There are at least four reasons why leisure services are particularly in the melting pot as far as local government is concerned;

(i) Leisure services have been one of the important frontiers of new development by local government over the past decade.

(Economic development and equal opportunities are two more recent examples.) There has been considerable innovation in leisure services and a rapid proliferation of facilities. It is also an area of organisational development, with the gradual emergence of leisure committees, leisure departments, experiments in decentralisation and public participation,and a phase of merger with other allied services (eg adult education). However, it is a service built on precarious foundations. Apart from allotments, libraries, and adult education, the whole field of leisure is non-statutory and non-mandatory. It depends at present primarily upon discretionary rate-funded expenditure by the local authorities backed up by grants from quangos, like the Sports Council and the Arts Council, for specific projects. Therefore, leisure budgets are particularly at risk when local authority resources are being cut back or curtailed by central government.

(ii) In addition to the lack of a firm statutory basis, leisure services also lack the backing of any very coherent client or consumer lobby (such as the tenants' associations or PTAs in relation to housing and education) or a well-established profession. There is thus not a very powerful lobby on their behalf in the inter-committee bargaining for resources. Many Chief Officers of leisure departments fear that at best the period of growth and development for their service is over, or that at worst facilities will be closed down or privatised. As one commentator suggested: the rising star of the 1960s and 1970s is in danger of being the sitting duck of the 1980s[5].

(iii) A further uncertainty over the future of local leisure and arts activity came with the abolition of the Metropolitan Counties in 1984 and the phasing out of the New Town Developement Corporations. Both (interestingly) have been among the leading sponsors of imaginative leisure and arts provision. There are still widespread fears that the bodies which inherit their responsibilities will not be able to give the same priority to leisure in the long-term, because of the pressure of statutory commitments on budgets and staffing. For example, the Arts Council estimated at the time that the shortfall in subsidy for the Arts, arising from abolition of the Metropolitan Counties, was £21m[6].

(iv) The Government has decided to include the management of local authority sport and leisure facilities within the ambit of those services which should be exposed to compulsory competitive tendering, under Part 1 of the Local Government Act 1988. The Government's Consultative Paper (Cm. 324, Feb 1988) on 'Financing Our Library Service', also proposes that public library authorities should increase their income by joint ventures with the private sector and by charging for specialised services.

Leisure is thus a microcosm of some of the key issues facing local government as a whole over the next decade. How should local authorities respond to issues characterised by:

- fundamental changes in context and environment;
- changing and increasing need;
- changing values and ideologies;
- absence of statutory powers or legal obligations by the local authority;
- declining resources and restrictions governing local discretion over expenditure;
- pressures to privatise and commercialise;
- organisational restructuring and uncertainty;
- opportunities for tapping voluntary initiative and user involvement or control.

Any discussion of the future role and organisation of local authority leisure services therefore confronts central questions about the future of local government itself;

(i) Whether local authorities will be restricted to carrying out basic duties, or have a more general responsibility and competence to tackle local problems and meet local needs and identify them;

(ii) Whether local authorities will be providers of last resort, providing minimum services as a safety net to fill gaps left by the private and voluntary sectors, or providers of leadership in the community, actively searching out unmet need, developing strategies, pioneering new projects, and setting targets and standards for other agencies;

(iii) Whether local authorities will simply provide an administrative umbrella for a series of separate compartmentalised services; or whether they will be able to tackle the growing inter-relationships between issues (eg leisure, tourism, employment, education) by developing new corporate, inter-departmental, multi-disciplinary, project forms of organisation, cutting across traditional departmental divisions;

(iv) Whether local authorities will continue in their traditional role as suppliers of services to clients and users, or whether they will also develop roles as facilitators of action within the community, and/or as intervenors within the local economy;

(v) Whether local authorities will continue to finance and subsidise their services primarily through local rates and central government grants, or whether they will supplement these resources by raising charges, selling commercial services, and developing partnerships and joint ventures with other agencies.

These are the issues to be explored in the rest of this Chapter. Part 2 reviews the supply side of the leisure industry and the rapid commercialisation of leisure. Part 3 considers the impact of economic, technological and social change upon the demand side, and upon people's changing leisure needs. Part 4 then discusses the implications of these changes for the value-choices facing the leisure services and the need for a new kind of lead from the public sector.

PART 2 —
THE COMMERCIALISATION OF LEISURE: A CROSSROADS FOR THE PROVIDERS OF LEISURE

The sphere of leisure is distinctive for the range and diversity of its providers. The public sector has always been a minority provider in comparison with the voluntary sector (which ranges from personal hobbies, through family and group leisure activity, to the national and international user-controlled organisations concerned with sport and the arts). It is also a minority provider compared with the commercial leisure sector. It is the relationship between these three sectors which will be explored in this section.

Public sector involvement in leisure has evolved in a very piecemeal way, stitched together from a patchwork of unrelated fragments of legislation accumulated since the late 19th Century. The Victorian concerns for cleanliness (public baths), godliness (libraries) and improving recreation (parks) have remained a constant, if increasingly underplayed, theme in provision. The second world war showed the Government the benefits (in terms of social cohesion and morale) of public sponsorship of entertainment and the performing arts, and led to a widening of local authority permissive powers in this sector. The gradual accretion of other discretionary powers of provision and management – allotments, concert halls, golf clubs, playing fields, resort facilities, sports halls – continued through until the 1970s, and helped to fuel the rapid upsurge in expenditure on capital projects, especially sports centres, swimming pools and squash courts[7]. The 1970s also saw a series of White Papers and official reports which accepted a broader concept of leisure not just as a means to an end (eg prevention of vandalism and delinquency), but as a desirable end in itself (eg 'one of the community's everyday needs' and therefore 'part of the general fabric of the social services')[8]. However, this widespread recognition of a general governmental responsibility to meet leisure needs has not been matched by any clear legal mandate to do so.

ENGLAND: STRUCTURE OF GOVERNM

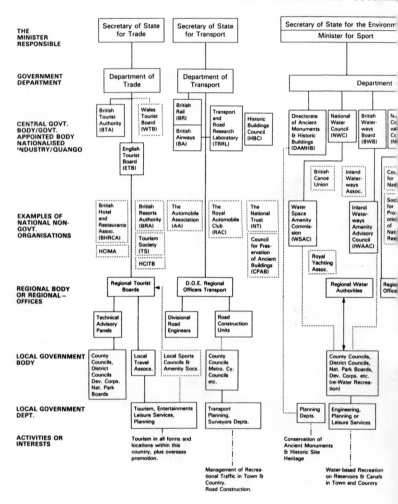

	Secretary of State for Trade	Secretary of State for Transport	Secretary of State for the Environm Minister for Sport	
THE MINISTER RESPONSIBLE				
GOVERNMENT DEPARTMENT	Department of Trade	Department of Transport	Department	
CENTRAL GOVT. BODY/GOVT. APPOINTED BODY NATIONALISED INDUSTRY/QUANGO	British Tourist Authority (BTA) / Wales Tourist Board (WTB) / English Tourist Board (ETB)	British Rail (BR) / British Airways (BA) / Transport and Road Research Laboratory (TRRL) / Historic Buildings Council (HBC)	Directorate of Ancient Monuments & Historic Buildings (DAMHB) / British Canoe Union / National Water Council (NWC) / Inland Water-ways Assoc. / British Water-ways Board (BWB)	N va Cc (N Cou for Nat Soc for Pro otio of Nat Res
EXAMPLES OF NATIONAL NON-GOVT. ORGANISATIONS	British Hotel and Restaurants Assoc. (BHRCA) / HCIMA / British Resorts Authority (BRA) / Tourism Society (TS) / HCITB	The Automobile Association (AA) / The Royal Automobile Club (RAC) / The National Trust (NT) / Council for Pres-ervation of Ancient Buildings (CPAB)	Water Space Amenity Commis-sion (WSAC) / Royal Yachting Assoc. / Inland Water-ways Amenity Advisory Council (IWAAC)	
REGIONAL BODY OR REGIONAL–OFFICES	Regional Tourist Boards	D.O.E. Regional Officers Transport	Regional Water Authorities	Regio Office
	Technical Advisory Panels	Divisional Road Engineers / Road Construction Units		
LOCAL GOVERNMENT BODY	County Councils, District Councils Dev. Corps. Nat. Park Boards	Local Travel Assocs. / Local Sports Councils & Amenity Socs. / County Councils Metro. Cy. Councils etc.	County Councils, District Councils, Nat. Park Boards, Dev. Corps. etc. (re-Water Recrea-tion)	
LOCAL GOVERNMENT DEPT.	Tourism, Entertainments Leisure Services, Planning	Transport Planning, Surveyors Depts.	Planning Depts. / Engineering, Planning or Leisure Services	
ACTIVITIES OR INTERESTS	Tourism in all forms and locations within this country, plus overseas promotion.	Management of Recrea-tional Traffic in Town & Country. Road Construction.	Conservation of Ancient Monuments & Historic Site Heritage / Water-based Recreation on Reservoirs & Canals in Town and Country	

RESTS IN LEISURE SERVICES

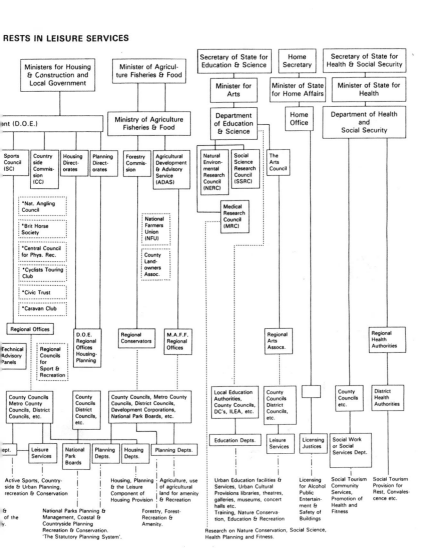

Diagram 1.1 — England: structure of government and interests in leisure services.

The piecemeal development of public leisure services, and their ambiguous status within Government policy, are reflected in their fragmented structure. For example, sport is managed through a range of 247 separate governing bodies, and a plethora of different co-ordinating bodies. (See Diagram 1.1). Despite the absence of any coherent central government strategy or statutory framework, local authorities have increasingly tried to give greater organisational co-ordination to their leisure work. There has been a widespread introduction of integrated leisure committees since 1974, spanning, in various combinations, sport and recreation, swimming pools, parks, open spaces, theatres, arts, museums, and sometimes tourism, adult education and youth services. In an increasing number of cases an overall leisure committee is paralleled by the amalgamation of separate services into a single Leisure Services Department, headed by a Director of Leisure.

This has resulted in some extremely imaginative and high quality developments, cutting across previously separate compartments within the leisure field. Examples which have come to our notice in the course of this review include:

- libraries being used as a base for computerised information services, and for the distribution of multi-media material (eg video-cassettes);
- parks being opened up as sites for open air concerts, opera under canvas, street theatre, community festivals, and play programmes;
- schools, community centres and sports centres being used as settings for a wider range of recreational and social activity (drama, yoga, aerobics, water sports, simulated rock climbing) for a wider range of groups (pensioners, the unemployed, mothers with children) for a larger part of the week and year.

However a lot of this development has been funded by specific grants for innovative projects, from sources such as the Urban Aid programme, inner city partnership programmes, Sports Council, or Regional Arts Associations. Short-term or one-off grants of this kind may be appropriate for experimental or demonstration projects, but they can sometimes distort priorities towards one-off prestige projects. A much more secure basis of funding is necessary if the lessons from pilot projects are to be translated into mainstream local government practice.

The uneven development of local leisure services, (resulting from the lack of any coherent government strategic, financial, or legislative frameworks) was revealed in the local authority questionnaire responses to our review. The nature, quality and distribution of provision varies considerably between local authorities. At worst the pattern sometimes seems to reflect the individual predilections of officers and members rather than the particularities of local need. Even at best, innovative programmes are not easily co-ordinated with the long term objectives of the service and tend to become monuments to the changing fashions of the policies of grant-giving bodies.

Co-ordination and coherence at national policy level has always been even less adequate than at local level and shows few signs of improving. Diagram 1 illustrates the confused maze of central government departments, quangos and other bodies with some involvement of interest in leisure services. In the absence of a single Minister or Department with responsibility for leisure, de-facto responsibility for policy development falls to (and between) this Kafka-like bureaucracy. Most of the quangos are appointed rather than elected bodies, and have concentrated on the planning and development of programmes within their specialist sub-area, rather than overall objectives and strategy for the leisure sector as a whole. A valuable exception to this is the discussion paper on 'Leisure Policy for the Future' published by the Chairmen's Policy Group[9].

Until recently, leisure received little or no attention in party manifestos or political debates in the UK. Increased leisure had been seen by all parties as one of the desirable fruits of economic growth and the technology revolution. Concepts like 'Sport for All' and 'The Leisure Society' have been promoted as slogans with which no-one was expected to disagree. But in the 1980s this consensus has begun to break down, as needs change and escalate (with dramatic growth in unemployment, part-time working, and shorter working weeks), and as resources contract and diversify (through public expenditure cut-backs, inflation, rate-capping, abolition, and contracting out). The choices now being faced by leisure policy makers therefore go beyond the politics of central and local government relationships. More fundamentally, they are about the nature of leisure needs, the values and objectives for leisure services, and the priorities for resource allocation.

The significance and urgency of these choices for local government is heightened by the fact that increasing pressure is coming from the private sector to accelerate the provision of leisure services within a commerical framework of values. It is therefore necessary to consider the role and direction of the commercial sector before considering the challenge for the public sector. As indicated in the introduction, the commercial sector overshadows the public sector as a supplier of leisure goods and services (in 1981/82 of the £33 billion estimated expenditure on leisure, only £851m was accounted for by the public sector). In his 1979 report for the Sports Council/SSRC John Roberts developed a useful taxonomy of leisure activities provided wholly or in part by the commercial sector[10]. Diagram 1.2 indicates the very wide range of activities covered, and also their inter-connectedness. Consumer preferences and trends in expenditure within this wide range of choices are indicated by Tables 1.1

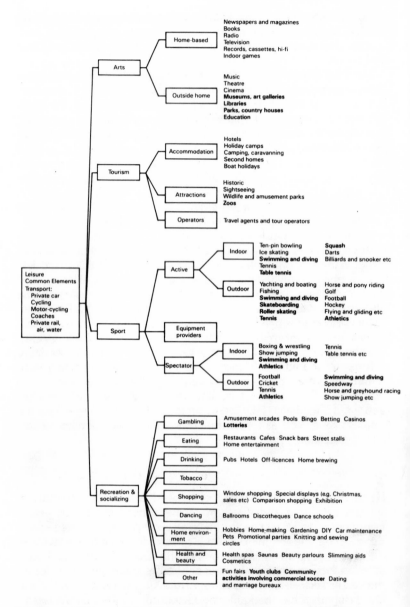

**Leisure
Common Elements
Transport:**
  Private car
  Cycling
  Motor-cycling
  Coaches
  Private rail,
   air, water

Arts
  Home-based
   Newspapers and magazines
   Books
   Radio
   Television
   Records, cassettes, hi-fi
   Indoor games
  Outside home
   Music
   Theatre
   Cinema
   Museums, art galleries
   Libraries
   Parks, country houses
   Education

Tourism
  Accommodation
   Hotels
   Holiday camps
   Camping, caravanning
   Second homes
   Boat holidays
  Attractions
   Historic
   Sightseeing
   Wildlife and amusement parks
   Zoos
  Operators
   Travel agents and tour operators

Sport
  Active
   Indoor
    Ten-pin bowling   **Squash**
    Ice skating   Darts
    Swimming and diving Billiards and snooker etc
    Tennis
    Table tennis
   Outdoor
    Yachting and boating Horse and pony riding
    Fishing   Golf
    Swimming and diving Football
    Skateboarding   Hockey
    Roller skating   Flying and gliding etc
    Tennis   **Athletics**
  Equipment providers
  Spectator
   Indoor
    Boxing & wrestling   Tennis
    Show jumping   Table tennis etc
    Swimming and diving
    Athletics
   Outdoor
    Football   **Swimming and diving**
    Cricket   Speedway
    Tennis   Horse and greyhound racing
    Athletics   Show jumping etc

Recreation & socializing
  Gambling
   Amusement arcades Pools Bingo Betting Casinos
   Lotteries
  Eating
   Restaurants Cafes Snack bars Street stalls
   Home entertainment
  Drinking
   Pubs Hotels Off-licences Home brewing
  Tobacco
  Shopping
   Window shopping Special displays (e.g. Christmas,
   sales etc) Comparison shopping Exhibition
  Dancing
   Ballrooms Discotheques Dance schools
  Home environment
   Hobbies Home-making Gardening DIY Car maintenance
   Pets Promotional parties Knitting and sewing
   circles
  Health and beauty
   Health spas Saunas Beauty parlours Slimming aids
   Cosmetics
  Other
   Fun fairs **Youth clubs Community
   activities involving commercial soccer** Dating
   and marriage bureaux

Diagram 1.2 — A taxonomy of leisure activities provided (wholly or
in part) by the commercial sector
Items in bold are marginal
Acknowledgements to John Roberts, TEST

and 1.2. These show a substantial increase in consumer expenditure on TV, computers and video, and in eating out, holidays and tourism, but a decline in expenditure on reading, cinema, and beer and spirits.

More significant than trends on the demand side of the commercial leisure market, however, are changes on the supply side. The leisure industries are rapidly becoming very big business, and they are undergoing a very intense phase of radical restructuring. Several key developments can be noted, each with considerable implications for the public sector.

Increasing Profitability

Leisure is an expanding and potentially very profitable sector of business. In the league table of the stock market's best sectors in which to have invested in 1987, leisure came seventh overall, with publishing and printing coming second. At least five leisure related firms are quoted in the top 25 of all quoted stock for 1987. These five are all at the smaller end of the leisure industry, with names like Scottish Ice Rink, Entertainment Products, Pavilion Leisure, Marina Leisure,and Black's Leisure. However, it is in the larger firms within the sector where the most substantial profitability is to be found. Big names like Grand Metropolitan, Ladbroke Group, Allied-Lyons, Trusthouse Forte, the Rank Organisation and the Granada Group all report regular annual increases of around 20 per cent to 25 per cent in turnover, pre-tax profits, and earnings per share; and in many cases more than double this. The leisure sector as a whole out-performed the main stock market by 15 per cent over 1987/88, with entertainment and catering, holidays and hotels as the fastest growing areas.

An Intensive Process of Merger, Takeover and Acquisition

The leisure industries are in a state of almost continuous flux at present, with a relentless reorganisation of portfolios taking place. The pages of the financial press and the companies' annual reports record a continuous flurry of buying and selling into and out of different parts of the leisure business. For example, Granada, des-cribed in the Press as an 'acquisition – happy leisure group', recently fended off takeover bids from both Rank and Ladbroke, and then itself bought up Electronic Rentals Group for £250m, DPCE Com-puter Maintenance for £110m and a rival bingo club chain, Essoldo, for £16.5m. In some cases the main aim of the acquisition seems to be to gain windfall profits. This was certainly the case when Mr Alan Bond the Australian media and brewing tycoon bought the ABC

Table 1.1 – Per capita spending of those participating in the activity of £p.a.

Rank		Spending	Rank		Spending
1	Alcoholic drink	435	11	TV	50.0
2	Eating out	316	12	Musical instruments	37.2
3	Holidays abroad	313.5	13	Newspapers	37.0
4	Gambling	190.6	14	Arts and crafts	32.0
5	Sport and recreation	134.3	15	Audio equipment	29.0
6	DIY	86.6	16	Gardens	26.9
7	Home computers	71.2	17	Books	18.4
8	Pets	62.5	18	Records and tapes	17.8
9	Video	57.5	19	Photography	15.0
10	Toys and games	53.2	20	Magazines	11.5
			21	Cinema	7.6

Source: Henley Centre (1985) Leisure Futures Spring 1985

Table 1.2 – Consumer expenditure at 1980 prices forecast for 1985 and 1990 £ million

		1980	1985	1990
READING	Books	451	343	325
	Newspapers	1088	1022	985
	Magazines	317	275	244
LISTENING	Audio equipment	1025	954	1083
	Records and tapes	548	588	631
SCREEN RELATED	TV rentals	893	615	495
	TV purchases	405	778	947
	Home computers	27	561	797
	Video equipment rental	66	707	1207
	Video equipment purchase	76	493	702
	Video equipment software	58	708	858
DIY & GARDENING	DIY goods	1591	1922	2202
	Gardening	517	665	734
	In home active leisure	2108	2587	2936
CREATIVE	Arts and crafts	347	394	349
	Musical instruments	108	166	199
	Photography	266	335	362
FAMILY	Pets	969	1071	1178
	Toys and games	854	921	1047
	Family activities	1823	1992	2225
FOOD & DRINK	Beer	5320	4950	4930
	Wine	1914	2740	3467
	Spirits	2720	2539	2580
	Eating out/UK residents	5427	5581	6003
	Eating out/foreign visitors	444	519	673
GAMBLING		1574	1541	1668
ENTERTAINMENT	Cinema admissions £m	147	86	84
	Other admissions	1148	1163	1519
	Recreational services	1396	1345	1702
SPORT	Sport goods	566	760	845
	Sport services	379	649	887
	Sport clothing & footwear	564	553	625
HOLIDAYS	UK resident/home holiday	2420	2185	2322
	UK resident/overseas holidays	3510	4100	4869
	Foreign visitors in UK	2961	3324	4374

Source: Henley Centre (1985) Leisure Futures Spring 1985

cinema chain and Elstree film studios from Thorn–EMI and then within a week sold them again to the American Cannon Group, at a profit of £30m. In other cases the aim is to gain access to specialist or niche markets or prestigious and profitable brand names. This seems to have been the motivation for the fierce and expensive battle between Grand Metropolitan and the Canadian spirits company Seagram to buy the French cognac house Martell. In some cases the aim is to build more robust portfolios, and to achieve market leadership. For example, Mecca's bold reverse takeover bid for the much larger Pleasurama group in August 1988 was presented as an opportunity to achieve synergy between Mecca's interests in dance halls, night clubs, holiday camps/centres and catering, on the one hand, and Pleasurama's interests in casinos, discos, amusement machine hire, coach tours, holiday hotels and theme restaurants on the other. If successful, the merger would make the Mecca/ Pleasurama group the dominant 'pure' leisure company in the sector. In other cases the reason for the acquisition is more directly to eliminate rivals and to increase market share. For example Granada's takeover of Electronic Rentals gave them an estimated 35 per cent of the TV and video rental market and put them in the same league as the market leaders Thorn–EMI who have more than 40 per cent of the market. Similarly Cannon's purchase of the ABC Cinema chain when added to their existing holdings gave them ownership of nearly 40 per cent of all UK cinema screens. In fact several of the leisure industry takeovers, mergers and acquisitions have been referred to the Office of Fair Trading to investigate the growth of monopoly control. This is part of a wider trend towards concentration in the leisure sector, which is discussed below.

Concentration of Control of the Leisure Industries

The intense process of takeover, merger and acquisition in the leisure industries is leading to a concentration of control of key sectors in the hands of fewer, larger, more powerful firms. This phenomenon is well known in the case of the newspaper industry, where Rupert Murdoch and Robert Maxwell battle it out for monopoly control. The Murdoch empire already controls two-thirds of all newspaper circulation in Australia, and has major stakes in the USA (where he recently took over the huge *Herald* and *Weekly Times* group) and in the UK (where he has bought the *News of the World,* and has designs on the *Financial Times).* A similar pattern, though with lower profile, is evident in the bookshop sector. At present the UK bookshop chains are dominated by W H Smith (which also owns Websters and Bowes and Bowes bookshops, and has about 25 per cent of the UK market); Pentos (which controls Hudsons, Dillons and

Athena shops); and the Blackwells group who now have over 75 per cent of the academic market. In the USA there are only two national bookshop chains left (Daltons and Walden Books) and it is predicted that a further process of concentration will result in the same situation in the UK before long. Similar patterns apply in other sectors. Nine firms control 95 per cent of the British paperback market; 6 film distributors control over 90 per cent of all film rental; 5 companies control over 60 per cent of the UK record market; 4 firms dominate the alcoholic and soft drinks industry, worldwide; and 2 firms control the majority of all UK cinemas[11]. Concentration is connected with another significant trend – a move towards the formation of conglomerates, operating across several sectors of the leisure industry.

The Emergence of Leisure Conglomerates

The frenetic process of takeover, merger and acquisition within the leisure industries has been accompanied by a tendency for firms to buy into several segments of the rapidly expanding leisure markets. Some of this is high risk speculative investment. For example, a firm like First Leisure focuses its long-term business interests in theatres and entertainment in London and holiday resorts (eg Blackpool Tower, Eastbourne Pier, dance halls, leisure parks), but has also got shorter-term interests in some of the more fickle fashions within leisure (eg fitness centres, bowling alleys, etc). In other cases firms go for a broad portfolio combining tried and tested but low-growth leisure activities, with faster-growing but less predictable leisure-related investments. For example, Granada's core TV and video business is matched by a mixture of faster-growth activities like computer maintenance, theme parks, motorway service areas, and specialist holidays. The predominant pattern until recently seemed to be one of very diverse portfolios, with interests spread across several different leisure-related activities. However there now seems to be a trend towards rationalisation of investments into priority business areas. There are examples of both vertical and horizontal integration and particularly attempts to inter-relate leisure products at the point of sale. Several firms have linked interests in food, drink, hotels, and holidays – an obvious set of mutually reinforcing businesses. For example, Grand Metropolitan advertised that its 25th birthday celebrations raised a number of questions: Where to hold the party? (Berni Inns, Chef and Brewer, or Pastificio?); What to Eat? (Express Foods, Eden Vale, Ski or le Soufflé?); What to Drink? (Cinzano, Le Piat d'Or, Fosters Lager, J and B Whiskey, or many more of their brands); and finally Where to Go Afterwards? (The Carlton, Cannes, The Willard, Washington DC, or the Clarendon Royal, Kent?). Brent Walker go still further with this kind of horizontal integration of leisure products, and add health, sport and fitness into the formula. They are developing the Brighton Marina as one of the largest leisure complexes in Europe. In addition to luxury hotel and housing, the marina will include moorings for 2000 boats, a health hydro, and leisure centre. Other firms, however, are choosing to divest rather than to diversify further. Guinness, in the mid-1980s, under their (then) Chief Executive Ernest Saunders, developed a management strategy which counterbalanced its brewing interests with involvements in retailing (including high street newsagents chains Lavells and Martins, and a retail chemists chain); health care (including Cranks wholefood restaurants, Natures Best dietary supplements, and several health spas); and publishing (including the Guiness Book of Records and at least 50 other titles). More recently, the new Chief Executive, Anthony Tennant, has argued for divestment of some of these businesses in order to concentrate capital and management resources on the core brewing and spirits interests. Part of his logic for this appears to be that the latter are established in international markets and that this is an increasingly important dimension of the leisure business. This is the next trend to be analysed.

Internationalisation of the Leisure Industries

Different parts of the leisure industries are at different stages in the process of internationalisation. The basic stage (the export of commodities from one country to another) is familiar in many leisure sectors. The degree of interpenetration is particularly high in the arts and entertainments spheres, with the buying and selling of films, TV programmes, live music, records and videos between countries, particularly between the UK and the USA. More bizarre examples include Granada setting up bingo halls on Indian reservations in the USA! The next stage in the process of internationalisation (the setting up of subsidiaries or joint ventures overseas) is also prevalent among the leading leisure firms. W H Smith set up 50 stores in the US and 8 Paperchase stores in Canada in 1987/88. The Rank Organisation bought Anhert Enterprises, a leading caravan park operator in America, in 1988, and also more importantly the video duplication business owned jointly by Bell and Howell, Columbia Pictures and Paramount Pictures Corporation. Rank already operates the largest video duplication business in Europe, and this American acquisition will make it the world's largest operator, producing 70 million out of the worldwide total of 190 million video cassettes. The strategy of mass distribution of the same standardised product is of course opened up in the arts and entertainment field by TV, either by export of series like Neighbours and Dallas or by simultaneous world transmission via satellite TV. The Nelson Mandela concert at Wembley in

1988 was not only international in its production (with performances from artists from several different continents), but international in its distribution and in its audience. However this process of inter-nationalisation is taken to a further stage still in some sectors, with the emergence of integrated global production for global markets. Allied-Lyons Annual Report for 1986/7 discusses their recent acquisition of a major Canadian company, Hiram Walker, for £445m in a deal in which the Gulf Canada Corporation are 49 per cent partners. The company presents this as a springboard to international business, and says that the company's strategy is to build 'a position in inter-national brands, which places us amongst the very few world operators in food and drink products. . . . Most analysts now forecast that by the 1990s the international drinks business will be controlled by just a handful of companies, each with a group of jealously guarded and highly profitable best selling brands. In specialised niches there may be room for well run smaller companies, with a special product for a limited market, but they will find the going hard. Those in the middle ground will probably be squeezed out. Only those at the top can expect to prosper. Allied Lyons has now assured itself of a seat at that top table'[12]. This seems to imply that the future of the leisure industries lies with transnational companies, integrating and co-ordinating their operations on a worldwide basis. There is, however, another trend within the leisure sector which, to some extent, counterbalances internationalisation, or at least that aspect of it associated with mass production for mass markets. This is 'flexible specialisation' – the attempt by firms to 'customise' their products in response to the fluctuating fashions, tastes and preferences of par-ticular groups of consumers or specific niches within the market.

Flexible Specialisation

Leisure is a risky business to be in, from a commercial point of view, because it is subject to many changing fads and fashions. Many of its most profitable opportunities come in activities and/or products which are at the experimental stage of their life cycle. Business can boom or slump very rapidly for leisure firms which have tried to exploit opportunities in areas like skateboarding, BMX bikes, mountain bikes, aerobics, windsurfing, tenpin bowling, or even home computers and computer games. Even with more established leisure activities like eating out, drinking, or holidays, the market is subject to quite significant shifts in consumer tastes (eg the moves towards a more health conscious diet, the increase in wine con-sumption, the reduction in smoking, the growth of activity holidays). Leisure firms have tried in several ways to invest in ways that do not tie them too rigidly to any one product or activity, or more positively which allow them to respond very rapidly and flexibly to shifting consumer preferences and specialist interests. One obvious example of this strategy is AMC's new wave of 'multiplex' cinemas, which group numerous small cinemas together in one building, to allow the simultaneous offering of a range of film choices to cater for many tastes. The multiplex also often offers restaurants, bars, creches, shopping malls and single level car parking to encourage repeat visits. AMC claim they are applying a similar formula to cinema as McDonald's have done to fast foods – convenience cinema! Another larger–scale example of flexible specialisation is emerging in the bar/restaurant retailing business. Grand Metropolitan is using the liberalisation of drinking hours to transform their pubs into all-day leisure centres focused around a particular theme or image. Victorian pubs, American diners, real ale taverns etc have all become familiar. However, Ind Coope is taking this a stage further. They are using a sophisticated computer information base, which collates information on social class, environmental characteristics, consumption patterns and turnover for different items on sale, to help them develop the specific marketing strategy and image for each of their 'pubs'. Modern information technology (often linked directly into cash registers and tills at the point of sale) now allows leisure firms continuously to monitor changing tastes and preferences within different segments of their market and to respond rapidly with 'customised' products tailor-made for that specific niche. The new technologies in effect allow firms to combine the economics of scale traditionally associated with mass production, with the flexibility and responsiveness to fluctuations in the market normally associated with small-batch production. The aim of many leading leisure firms is therefore to standardise production and marketing of a limited range of basic products or services but to package and present them in a variety of ways designed to 'cater for all tastes'.

Commodification

The next trend to be noted in the commercial leisure sector can be called 'commodification'. This rather inelegant jargon is meant to describe the attempt by leisure firms to enter into areas of leisure need which have traditionally been met *outside* the market, and to develop leisure products or services which can then be sold as commodities to supply that need. In some cases this is a matter of 'commodifying' areas of human experience which have been kept alive through family and community networks, cultural traditions or through public sector services. For example, some of the commercial sector's recent investments in heritage can be seen as the manufacture of leisure commodities out of the raw material of history which was previously in the public domain. In some cases (like the sophisticated presentation of Warwick Castle by Madame Tussaud's Group) the commercial investment has helped to preserve the heritage and may in some ways have enhanced it. In other examples, however, the commodification of heritage has distorted the reality. For example, the packaging of rural and industrial trades in commercial ventures like working mines and working farms sometimes promotes very utopian images of work and society as cohesive and conflict-free. Another indication of the commodification of leisure is the manufacture of timeshare schemes in the countryside. For example, 'the exclusive Langdale private estate offers unrivalled amenities in 35 wooded acres of of privileged seclusion in the Lake District National Park'. The benefits for members include 'membership of the £3m Pillar Club, an all-weather leisure oasis with its tropical pool, squash, hydro-spa, gym, beauty salon, real-ale pub, and gourmet restaurant'. This illustrates the way in which commodification transforms both the nature of the leisure activity concerned (Langdale Timeshare is clearly a different experience from the YHA in the same area!), and the range of potential users (Langdale Timeshare is beyond the means of the majority of users of the national park, even if they preferred it).

Commercial sponsorship

One further trend to be noted is the growth in sponsorship of leisure activities by commercial firms. The Howell Report estimated that in the sports sector alone this had doubled from about £50m in 1979 to over £100m by 1983[13]. By 1988 the Minister of Sport, Colin Moynihan, was quoting a total of £150–£200m a year in commercial sponsorship of sporting events and sporting bodies. The growth has taken place not only in the value of sponsorships, but also in the number of firms involved. 200 companies signed sponsorship deals for the first time in 1987[14]. Business sponsorship of the arts is at a much lower level than for sport, but has also been on the increase. It has risen from about £15m in 1984 to £30m in 1988. This has partly been encouraged by the Government's Business Sponsorship Incentive Scheme, but also reflects a clear commercial logic. Record companies are reputed to generate almost as much income from their sponsorship deals with beer and lager firms, as from their own sales campaigns. (Live rock performances are heavily dependent upon sponsorship by brewers). In most cases commercial firms sponsor leisure activities not so much for the direct sales involved (as in the rock concert example above) as for the marketing image, or for the advertising opportunities. For example, Mobil spends about £300,000 a year on arts sponsorship, 'purely for business reasons' according to their sponsorship manager Mr David Charlton – 'We like to link our name with excellence and quality'[15]. A more controversial example is the heavy sponsorship of sport by drink and cigarette firms (which together account for 20 per cent of the total sports sponsorship of £146m).

Such a high proportion of all commercial sponsorship deals are focused on sports, arts and other leisure activities partly because of their positive images, and partly because leisure gets such wide television coverage. It has been calculated that Embassy's £2m sponsorship of the world snooker championships gave them 81 hours TV exposure to an audience of up to 10.8m people. At normal TV advertising rates this might have cost them £68m!

Apart from the obvious concern about the promotion of alcohol and tobacco by their linkage, on television, with sport and sporting heroes, there are several other problems with commercial sponsorship of leisure activities. Funding tends to go to the élite end of the leisure spectrum, and reinforces inequalities. For example, of the £17m of commercial sponsorship of football, £10.6m goes to the 1st Division, £1.8m to the second division, £1.3m to the 3rd division, and £0.7m to the 4th division. The contrast in priorities with the public sector is illustrated amusingly by Lewisham Borough Council's sponsorship of Millwall to the tune of £70,000 per year. This supports provision of a creche at the ground, the training of a women's football team, and visits by players to local schools as part of an anti-racist and anti-sexist programme. Commercial sponsorship tends to be biased towards activities with large TV audiences like snooker, rather than, for example, squash, which has not been found so photogenic. Furthermore, commercial sponsorship can prove to be short-lived and firms may withdraw their funding at very short notice. More fundamentally, commercial sponsorship may tend to influence the pattern of leisure activity and distort priorities. The Director of the Theatre Royal (which gets no commercial sponsorship because its East End based plays are seen as too controversial) is quoted as saying that 'Commercial people's judgement is now influencing the arts far more dangerously than government interference has ever done'[16]. The reality of the relationship between commercial sponsors and the leisure services is made clear in the comment by a business consultant that 'sponsorship is not a lifebelt – it is business collaboration to create a favourable environment in which to trade'[17].

The risks of commercialisation

There is growing evidence that commercial firms see leisure markets expanding considerably over the next decade, partly as a result of demographic and socio-economic changes; partly as a result of privatisation or contracting-out of public sector leisure services; and partly through the international mass markets and audiences opened up through satellite television and the newer telecommunications systems. Such developments should be welcomed in so far as they extend and cheapen access to leisure opportunities for a broader range of the public, and in terms of jobs they may create. But there are also grounds for concern about the direction in which this could take leisure services.

Several of the responses we received from consultation with local authorities expressed concern that the commercialisation and mass production and marketing of leisure run the following risks:

(i) a reduction in the quality of services as the preoccupation with quantity increases (for example, the growth in the number of commercial cable TV channels in the USA seems to have led to a lowering of the quality of transmissions);

(ii) standardisation and homogenisation of cultural and leisure provision as a result of mass production; a loss of cultural diversity as firms exploit the economies of scale possible through distribution of the same leisure product or service throughout the world (for example, bulk purchasing and mass distribution of books by book clubs may lead to the promotion of titles with mass-market appeal at the expense of specialised or minority interests).

(iii) further pressure towards passive consumption of pre-packaged leisure, as a spectator, as opposed to active participation in live arts, sports etc, The effects of TV and home video upon attendances at live theatre, cinema, football etc have been well documented. However there are also some indications of a popular swing back towards active participation (eg mass marathons; arts festivals).

(iv) increased pressure towards privatised, individualistic consumption of leisure in the home, as opposed to shared social and group activity in the community (eg the growth in sales of home gymnasium equipment, 'entertainment robots' and other leisure gadgetry)[18]. There is certainly some evidence that leisure firms are gearing up to promote the sale of leisure hardware into the home. In some cases this involves substituting home-based commodities for services previously provided outside the home, either by theprivate sector (eg videos in place of cinemas), or by the public sector (eg the promotion of home-based equipment for self-monitoring of health and fitness)[19].

(v) further degradation of cultural values, and reinforcement of the 'sex and violence' and 'space invader' mentality already associated with parts of the commercial leisure industries.

The implications of developments within the commercial sector for the public sector cannot be ignored. The closely inter-twined nature of leisure provision is reflected in the problems of trying to dissect the different roles of the providers. But the differences between the commercial, public and voluntary sectors are clearly not just a question of boundaries, finance, and organisation. There are also deeper questions of values, objectives and priorities. What functions does (and should) leisure perform within a changing society? Bread and circuses for the (unemployed) masses? A means of transmitting the cultural heritage from one generation to another? A means of diverting/replenishing people for the world of work? Are some forms of leisure activity to be valued more than others? Participative rather than passive? Collective rather than individualistic? Live rather than 'canned'? Should the public sector take up – and be seen to take up – a leadership role in relation to these issues, and help to define and plan directions and standards for the whole community, or should its role be limited to offering a range of complementary alternatives to leisure users, while leaving the dominant role to the commercial sector? Should it be restricted to gap filling, picking up the leisure needs unmet or deemed unworkable by other sectors, or can the public sector be a catalyst and facilitator, creating a strategic framework within which the commercial, voluntary and community organisations can operate to fulfil leisure needs?

These choices are all the more urgent because of the fundamental structural changes taking place in the environment which will dramatically intensify and increase leisure needs over the next decade. The implications of these changes for the demand side of leisure provision will be discussed in the next section, before we move onto consider the value-choices facing the leisure service.

PART 3 – THE CHANGING SOCIETY: THE IMPLICATIONS OF ECONOMIC, TECHNOLOGICAL AND SOCIAL CHANGE FOR LEISURE NEEDS

The changes facing British society (and therefore government) over the next decade could be as profound as any this century. The restructuring of our economic, technological and social systems is so fundamental that some have described it as nothing less than the death throes of the second industrial revolution (based around iron and steel) and the birth pangs of a third industrial revolution (based around micro-electronics and computers). These changes imply that Britain will be facing crucial choices as we move towards the end of the second millennium. Leisure services will not only be affected deeply by the outcome of these changes; they also have an opportunity to assist the process of choice, and the direction of change. Many of the features of structural change have been documented elsewhere[20]. The aim here is to summarise those changes thought most likely to have an impact on local government's role and organisation in relation to leisure. Some of the changes are relatively certain and known, and can be described statistically; others are much less certain, and can only be discussed in terms of possible scenarios for the future.

Fundamental economic, social and political changes bearing on leisure are likely to include:

(i) Further restructuring of manufacturing industry (particularly in the run-up to completion of the European market by 1992) mainly in the traditional 'smokestack' industries, but also increasingly in the distributive, retail and related service sectors.

(ii) A new wave of technological automation affecting the service sector in particular (offices, banking, retail etc) and replacing paper based information systems with time- and labour-saving computer and telecommunications systems.

(iii) Major demographic and social changes leading to a substantial ageing of the population; shifts in the relative roles of women and men; and a decline in the prevalence of the traditional nuclear family.

(iv) Further cutbacks in the Welfare State and radical restructuring of the relationships between the public and the private sectors at local level.

(v) Changes in cultural values and ideologies, involving new concepts of work, leisure and creativity.

Economic and technological changes

The severest changes from the point of view of leisure services undoubtedly come from the restructuring of traditional industries and jobs, technological and skill changes and the growth of mass unemployment.

It is now clear that the restructuring of British industry is:

- not a temporary, but long-term phenomenon;
- not cyclical, but a structural problem;
- not limited to the manufacturing sector, but now also transforming the service sector;
- not restricted to 'lame duck' firms and inefficiently run enterprises, but also characteristic of some of the biggest and most successful firms;
- not peculiar to the UK, but part of a wider western world problem;
- not simply the result of a world recession or the oil crisis, but part of a more fundamental restructuring of production (involving increased concentration of ownership and control, transnational planning and co-ordination of 'global factories', and new forms of 'flexible specialisation' made possible by the new technologies.

One of the most far-reaching aspects of the restructuring of the economy is the rapid introduction of new technologies into both products and processes. As in previous epochs of technological change (the stone age, the bronze age, the steel age) the new tools that are now being developed open up the opportunity for fundamental changes in society – not only in work life, but also in the patterns of communication, human settlement, domestic life and leisure. While there may be differing views about the precise impact of the changes over the next decade, the new generation of technologies undoubtedly represents more than just another incremental change; it is more like a quantum leap into a new era. This is because of the *linking up* of three technologies:

- *computing* (with the ability to process vast amounts of information at enormous speed);
- *micro-electronics* (with its extraordinary possibilities for miniaturisation and dramatic reductions in cost);
- *telecommunications* (which can open up remote access to, and interaction with, computing and micro-electronics across international networks).

These three technologies when linked together open up entirely new possibilities for the automation of:

- mental functions as well as manual processes;
- office, design, and managerial work as well as shopfloor work;
- small-batch production as well as mass production;
- the whole factory management system (including planning and co-ordination) as well as individual parts of the production process.
- the distribution system (with rapid feedback from consumers and the market) as well as the production system.

The impact of computer technology on jobs and skills in manufacturing industry is well advanced and well documented. Much less is understood and documented about the service sector, but it seems likely that this will be the focus of the technological revolution over the next decade, with the widespread replacement of paper-based information systems by computer and telecommunication-based systems. Some detailed studies by employers, trade unions and government agencies estimate the impact on service sector employment to range from 20 per cent to 40 per cent job loss, by 1995. Siemens of West Germany suggest that 40 per cent of present office work could be carried out by computer systems by 1990. The International Federation of Employees (FIET) has estimated that by 1990 between 20 per cent and 25 per cent of the current 15 million office jobs in the EEC will have been affected by the new technologies; 30 per cent of banking, and 20 per cent of retail jobs could also be affected.

One of the more obvious implications is that the UK economy is unlikely to return to (full-time, paid) full employment within the next decade, if at all. A recent study for the OECD forecast a further loss of 0.86 million manufacturing jobs in the UK by 1995, on an optimistic set of assumptions, and a further loss of 1.97 million jobs by 1995 if 1970s growth rates prevail[22].

The implications of all this for leisure services can begin to be seen more sharply when some of the most likely patterns in the distribution of unemployment and employment, and in the skills required for the future, are also highlighted:

(i) a deepening division between, on the one hand, the North and Midlands (where high rates of unemployment may persist as restructuring of primary and traditional metal-based industries continues), and, on the other hand, the South East and South West (where an intense cycle of investment and growth may be kept in motion by the high tech and financial sectors attracted to the region);

(ii) continued heavy concentrations of the unemployed in the inner-city areas, and particularly within the black and ethnic minority communities (where unemployment is already frequently above 50 per cent);

(iii) particularly high incidence of unemployment among the under-25s and the over 55s;

(iv) growth in the number and proportion of those out of work for over one year and of the very long-term unemployed (over two years);

(v) an increase in the proportion of the population whose skills are at risk of redundancy, or who will require substantial re-training to remain employable. This is already extending into the commercial and service sectors – banking, insurance, office, retail etc – and into white-collar and managerial occupations.

(vi) an increase in the pattern of home-based working (currently 7.2 per cent of the labour force) as large enterprises exploit the opportunities provided by cable and other new communication systems to decentralise and/or subcontract parts of their operations[23].

However, it is not just in straightforward job and skill losses and changes that economic and technological restructuring will have impacts on leisure; the effects on patterns of communication and social interaction will also be enormous. The further development of current experiments in 'telematics' – the linking of computer, telephone and television – will result in a big upsurge over the next decade in home banking, home-shopping, self-help education, home health-care, electronic mail and facsimile transmission, and other forms of instant, inter-active services. When combined with further growth in cable television and video, this will amount to strong pressure toward more leisure time and leisure-consumption being focused on the home. These trends raise important questions about the content and quality of the leisure commodities being promoted, and about the implications of the further 'privatisation' of leisure activity within the nuclear family.

Demographic and social change

Four particularly important changes in demography and social structures will impinge on leisure need can be identified:

(i) the numbers of people over 65 will stabilise, but the numbers over 75 will continue to grow as a percentage of the total population. The proportion of those over retirement age within the population is forecast to rise from 14.9 per cent in 1981 to 18.2 per cent in 1991, and levelling off at 17.9 by 2001. The change in elderly population is most dramatic amongst those aged 85 and over, who are expected to constitute 12 per cent of the UK population in 2001, compared with 8 per cent in 1983. More people will be living longer, in better health, and with increasingly high expectations of a fulfilled later life. There will be an increasing division between those with the finances to meet some of those expectations, and those trying to survive on state benefits;
(ii) the current 'bulges' in the teenage population will become 'bulges' in young parents by the early 1990s, and middle-aged parents by the late 1990s. Many of these parents may be without traditional jobs and incomes and living in relative poverty and insecurity; whilst those still in employment will be relatively affluent and could become major consumers of commercial leisure goods and services;
(iii) the average size of households will continue to shrink. Age

structures have a significant relationship to the size of households, and it is apparent that trends which have been evident in the past fifteen years will continue – and become more central. Already, there are 4 million one-person households of which two thirds are pensioners; this will accentuate as the 'very old' and 'young singles' both increase. It is more difficult to estimate the rate and direction of change in the number of single parent families, as there are few clear indications as to whether the re-marriage rate will go up or down over the short term;

(iv) the relationship between the roles of women and men will continue to change significantly. This will affect attitudes to work; to child bearing and rearing; and to women's freedom to develop leisure life styles outside the home and significant (nuclear) family, which have been much more constrained in the past than most men's. An increasing number and proportion of women will be in, or seeking, employment (forecast to rise from 9.2 million in 1981 to 9.6 million in 1990). With the continued decrease in the number of men in employment, this will mean women will make up nearly half the workforce by the 1990s. A high proportion of their jobs will be part-time however, (rising from 17 per cent of total jobs in 1985 to 22 per cent in 1990)[24]. This will contribute further pressure towards reductions in the length of the working week and more flexible patterns of working-time and time off work (school holidays, maternity/paternity leave etc).

The implications for leisure needs and services

The implications of the above changes for both public and private sector leisure services are far-reaching. Two contrasting scenarios can be envisaged:

(i) A smaller proportion of the population will be in traditional paid employment; and those that are, are likely to be in it for a smaller proportion of their time, (with a shorter working week, year and life, but with an increasing requirement for shift-working, flexible hours, retraining and job-mobility). This group will be concentrated in the age-band 25–50, and will look to leisure as a complement/alternative/antidote to the world of work. They will have the resources (finance, transport) to satisfy many of their leisure needs through the private market, and the motivation to engage actively in voluntary leisure activity.

(ii) A larger proportion of the population will be excluded from, or otherwise remain outside, the world of full-time paid employment and the rewards and status which this generally confers in our society. This group will include the unemployed, the elderly, the early-retired, the redundant, and those whose work is temporary, seasonal, casual, part-time, or home-based. They will be primarily in the age-bands under 20 and over 50, and will look to leisure as a substitute for work satisfaction. They will not be short of time but may lack the other resources (money, transport, motivation, social skills) to satisfy their leisure needs through clubs, and other collective facilities. They will be under pressure to retreat into passive, home-based, individualised leisure activity, (not least because the relative cost of home-based leisure goods will fall as a result of mass production and mass marketing).

It is obviously over-simplistic to polarise future leisure-needs into the two catagories above. However it has the advantage of focusing questions about the priorities for the leisure provision. Without prejudging the discussion of the roles of the private and public sectors in the next section, it seems reasonable to assume at this stage that local authorities would need to give high priority in policy-making to the second category identified in the previous paragraph: the growing population of the unemployed, the under-employed, the low-waged, the elderly, and those outside mainstream full-time paid employment. The problem is that these are the very categories least well provided for by many parts of the leisure service at present. A recent study of indoor sports facilities in the UK found that the professional and managerial classes were over-represented among the users, while the semi-skilled and unskilled manual groups were only 14 per cent of the population yet make up only 13 per cent of users; while the upper socio-economic groups who were only 14 per cent of the population make up 24 per cent of the users[25]. The survey also found a serious under-representation of women and of older people (where only 8 per cent of public sector indoor facilities were over 45 years old, while they constituted 47 per cent of the population). The question for local authorities is not simply one of participation rates, but the need for clear targeting of priorities, the relevance of the leisure programmes and facilities on offer, the availability of support services (eg creches for young children), the scheduling and pricing of activities etc.

If local authority leisure services are to keep pace with the growth and change in leisure needs, and the new challenges posed by the economic, technological, social and demographic changes discussed in this section, they clearly cannot remain as a 'passive' or responsive buildings-based service (responding to those who choose to come and use a particular facility). Instead they must become a more pro-active and strategic service (actively identifying unmet and latent leisure needs in the community, analysing trends, deciding priorities for resource-allocation and then developing strategic plans and programmes for targeted groups). This has significant implications for the future role, and value-base, of public leisure services, which will be discussed in the final section.

PART 4 – THE VALUE-CHOICES FACING THE LEISURE SERVICE

The final section of this chapter focuses on the value-choices which face the leisure service over the next decade. Previous sections have argued that choice is inescapable; that leisure services face a major crossroads in their development; that powerful pressures for change are coming from both the 'demand' and the 'supply' side. These structural changes bring to the surface profound choices about the values which are to guide leisure services in the future.

Our argument, in summary, has been that on the demand side there is likely to be an unprecedented upsurge in the volume, range, and intensity of leisure needs. Economic, technological, social and demographic changes will result in continued increase in the numbers and proportions of the elderly, the unemployed, the redundant, deskilled, part-time, home-based, temporary and casual workers, and others outside the formal economy. This group, which by the year 2001 could make up a substantial proportion of the whole population, will be concentrated among the under 25s and the over 50s. They will have more time on their hands, less money in their pockets and be more isolated from the main social networks. On the supply side, the competition from (and between) the commercial leisure firms will intensify as they exploit the opportunities, provided by the new technologies, for mass production and mass marketing of leisure commodities largely for consumption in the home. This has raised fears, in many quarters, of further standardisation and homogenisation of leisure provision, degradation of cultural values and quality, and pressures towards passive 'spectatorship' rather than active participation in leisure.

These twin pressures for change (together with the Government's plans to expose several parts of the public leisure service to compulory competitive tendering) will dramatically alter the nature and pattern of leisure provision in this country. They will pose not only new questions about roles, relationships and resource allocation between the public, commercial and voluntary sectors but also much deeper choices about values. Local government will be forced to make conscious choices about the response it makes, on the one hand, to the needs of the new (unwaged) leisure priority groups, and, on the other hand, to the value questions raised by the further commercialisation of leisure. In other words the future role and organisation of local government in the field of leisure cannot be discussed in purely managerial, technical and administrative terms. The basic value choices have to be clarified before going on to consider the options for strategy roles, and organisation.

Value choices in leisure

Throughout this chapter we have suggested that current trends are felt by many in the public sector to threaten some of the traditional (though often unspoken) values associated with leisure. It is now necessary to draw these out more explicitly and to examine what assumptions lie behind them. At this stage the issues can be identified simply by contrasting some of the public 'ideals' implicity associated with leisure, against the words and images associated with the 'commercialisation' of leisure.

'Ideals' associated with leisure in the public domain	**Images associated with 'commercialisation' of leisure'**
1. Creative/craft production of leisure	Mass produced leisure
2. Active participation in leisure	Passive consumption of leisure
3. Communal, shared experiences	Individualistic, privatised experience
4. Varied and rich experience	Standardised & homogenised
5. Live music, art etc.	'Canned' synthetic, dubbed music, art etc.
6. Judged by quality (eg canons of excellence)	Measured by quantity (eg audience ratings)
7. Priorities dictated by needs, standards	Priorities dictated by commercial criteria
8. Encourages 'actors' and 'participants'	Encourages 'spectator' roles

The polarisation of opposites in this way is not intended to imply an over-simple split between the commercial sector as 'bad' and the public sector as 'good'. Our aim, rather, is to try to draw it out, for discussion, some of the implicit assumptions and values which seem to underlie the arguments for leisure as a central sphere for public sector involvement. Leisure is clearly felt by many, both inside and outside local government to be something more than a random collection of services to be administered efficiently. The ways in which it is discussed is more reminiscent of the education service or the personal social services than, say, refuse collection or even housing management. There is a sense of a moral imperative as well as a managerial administrative task – a sense in which the public leisure service is felt to be a repository of (a 'carrier' for) a wider set of societal values and meanings. These values are not very well defined, but they seem to include notions of re-creation, refreshment, renewal, stimulus, creativity, personal development, self-fulfilment, cultural heritage, and communal enrichment. It is 'ideals' of this kind which are felt to be under threat from the intrusion of 'big business' values.

The ideals associated with leisure clearly go well beyond the sphere of leisure itself. It is almost as if leisure functions as a kind of 'metaphor' for ideals about the society as a whole. This is not altogether surprising, as the meanings and functions ascribed to leisure are almost always defined in relation to (or in contrast to) the other central metaphor for differing ideals about society – the world of work. It is perhaps because leisure is often used to convey ideals about a society based on alternative or opposite values to those associated with the world of work, that the 'commercialisation' of leisure is felt to be such a fundamental threat.

In considering the future role and organisation of local government in the field of leisure, therefore, one is inevitably caught up in choices between alternative or competing ideals for society as a whole. We will look briefly at some of these competing 'metaphors' or 'archetypes' for leisure, before going on to consider alternative models for the future role of local government in this field:

(i) Leisure as a reward for, or an antidote to, hard work: the compensation for hard (often alienating) wage-labour; the refreshment necessary for the regeneration of the workforce; a separate sphere of personal development and self fulfilment; the incentive for the Protestant work ethic.

(ii) Leisure as a substitute for paid work: an alternative to employment for the unwaged; a safe outlet for untapped energies; bread and circuses for the unemployed masses; 'sport for all', instead of 'work for all'?

(iii) Leisure as an alternative to the work ethic: an expression of the post-industrial society, in which less status and time would be given to paid employment, and more opportunity for personal development, social interaction, and communal creative activity.

(iv) Leisure as the means of reproduction of cultural values: a channel for the transmission and reinforcement of shared ideas and meanings from one generation to the next; an expression of the 'great tradition' of cultural and social values which are constantly being reworked and reshaped.

(v) Leisure as a commodity: a product to be manufactured and sold alongside other commodities, to those who can pay the market price; leisure as a growth industry exploiting the opportunities, created both by greater wealth on the one hand and increasing employment on the other, to open up profitable new markets for goods and services.

The above clusters do not represent separate self-contained alternatives. They are simply different strands within a complex web of competing ideas and values. At different times one or other definition may predominate. For example in the optimistic climate of the 60s, leisure tended to be used as a symbol for the ideals of the post industrial society, providing an alternative model to the Protestant work ethic which had dominated since the war. With deindustrialisation and the growth of unemployment in the 70s, the model of leisure which began to predominate was that of a substitute for paid employment. And in the 80s with the breakdown of the post-war consensus, leisure has become the site for a battle of competing ideas about the relationship between work and unemployment, between economic and social policies. The implication of this discussion of some of the values and assumptions which lie behind different conceptions of leisure, is that, in considering the future role and organisation of local government in this field, one is inevitably drawn into a much deeper set of choices between different models of society, the policy and the economy.

Alternative roles for local government in the field of leisure

In Chapter 9 Ian Henry distinguishes five alternative models for local government, related to differing ideological positions and political and economic conditions. These are developed as 'ideal types' rather than realistic scenarios, but they help to clarify some of the choices facing local government, in the field of leisure.

Contract management – provider of last resort

Under this model (characteristic of a neo-liberal or monetarist ideology) leisure is provided as far as possible, like any other commodity, through the private market. The role of government is consciously kept at a minimal level, providing only:

- those services which the commercial leisure industry needs in order to function (eg the public infrastructure necessary for tourism to prosper);

- those public goods (eg urban open space) where it is not possible for a commercial market to function;

- those leisure programmes considered necessary to stave off threats to law and order (eg special youth programmes to counteract disorder, vandalism etc in inner-city areas).

Under this scenario, as many public sector leisure services as possible would be privatised or contracted out to commercial firms; the role of the local authority would be limited to the administration of such contracts. The voluntary sector would be encouraged as part of a philosophy of self-help and individual entrepreneurship. But outside the sphere of self-help, the commercial market would determine leisure needs and prices etc.

Financial stringency – manager of contracting resources

Under this model (characteristic of traditional, one-nation, 'wet' conservatism, and of some forms of social democracy) leisure services are seen as part of a mixed economy between the private and public sectors. The commercial and voluntary sectors are encouraged as the main providers, but the public sector is expected to fill in any gaps in provision, and to meet the needs of minorities, and disadvantaged groups who cannot afford the market price. Charges and other means of increasing revenue are used as a way of reducing public sector subsidies, and public expenditure in general is cut back and controlled.

Keynesianism – manager of expanding resources

Under this model (characteristic of traditional middle-of-the-road Labour governments, and some kinds of social democratic coalition) public sector expenditure and services are actively promoted as beneficial, in both social and economic terms. Government expenditure is not conceived as of parasitic, but as a stimulus to demand within the economy. Planned increases in both capital and revenue expenditures on leisure are therefore seen as an investment in the social fabric of the community, as well as a means of job-creation. The public sector is seen as the main provider; the commercial and voluntary sectors are seen as having a contribution within a public sector-led plan, but it is not envisaged that they provide the real initiative. Under this model it is the commercial and voluntary sectors which are left to fill in any gaps in provision left by the public sector.

Post-industrial idealism – facilitator of citizen involvement

Under this model (which is characteristic of utopian socialist and some social democratic ideologies) leisure is seen as the central sphere of the post-industrial society. High-technology is seen as reducing the overall volume of paid work necessary to create wealth within the society, thereby liberating more time for more people to enjoy leisure. The voluntary and community sectors are seen as central providers (with high levels of self-help and community participation in leisure), but with the use of capital-intensive and high-tech equipment and facilities provided by the commercial and public sector. The public sector is also expected to provide the infrastructure necessary for high-tech industries and tourism (seen as key wealth generators) to flourish, and to provide a safety net of leisure services for those who don't manage to prosper within this third industrial revolution.

Municipal socialism – active intervention to counteract the private market

Under this model (characteristic of left Labour governments) leisure is seen as part of the structure of inequality within society. The local authority role is seen as intervening actively to counteract those forces which reinforce inequalities within the leisure market, and to redistribute leisure opportunities towards the worst-off. Wherever possible, leisure services would be brought under public control; and where not there might be some attempt to gain public sector influence over private sector provision (for example, through financial investment – equity, loans or grants – in exchange for a planning agreement of some kind). The voluntary sector is likely to be supported selectively (eg those organisations felt to represent working-class rather than middle-class interests).

The need for a new kind of lead from the public sector

Ian Henry's five-fold typology is helpful in clarifying a range of alternative roles for local government in the field of leisure. But it would be unhelpful to tie these alternatives too closely to the positions of particular political parties. The options for local government don't fit neatly into existing political divisions. In many ways the challenges facing local government in relation to leisure also represent a challenge to the assumptions of the political parties. They each require a new understanding of the potential and limitations of the public, private and voluntary sectors. The stereotypes have tended to be that:

(i) the private sector is good at producing choice, diversity, innovation and cost-efficiency, but with little capacity or concern for meeting the needs of those with weak purchasing power in the market;

(ii) the public sector is associated with universality and uniformity of provision, and with particular concern for the needs of minorities and disadvantaged groups; but with little capability for maintaining choice, diversity, innovation or cost-efficiency;

(iii) the voluntary sector is associated with high commitment to user participation and responsiveness to community needs; but is seen as less good at maintaining uniformity or quality of standards of provision, or high standards of management.

These stereotypes don't match up accurately either with present realities or future requirements. In some ways the very opposite of the stereotype applies:

(i) the commercial leisure sector, as it moves increasingly under the domination of multinational and/or monopoly firms, is less and less able to present consumers with real choice and diversity. Mass production for high volume markets is in practice reducing the choices available in the commercial leisure field to many minor variations around a smaller range of themes and product-lines;

(ii) the public leisure sector (as it suffers from cut-backs in mainstream funding) has been less and less able to develop a uniform (let alone universal) standard of leisure provision. Ironically this is leading in practice to great diversity of provision across the country, and fair amount of innovation, as local authorities are driven to act entrepeneurially in the development of one-off projects;

(iii) the voluntary sector (as it becomes increasingly adept at gaining private and public sector funding for both capital and revenue projects) is developing higher and higher standards of provision, and more and more sophisticated forms of management. Ironically this then may make it harder for them to maintain their commitment to high levels of participation by users.

The search has to be for some means of maximising the strengths associated with each of the three sectors, while minimising their disadvantages. We should be looking for a leisure service which manages to combine widely accepted standards of excellence in provision with an innovative, outreaching approach designed to meet diverse leisure needs and choices (particularly the most needy and disadvantaged), while at the same time opening up opportunities for active participation by users. We have come to the conclusion that these aims and qualities can only be achieved for the leisure service of the future if the public sector takes on the leadership role. This may appear controversial and provocative coming at a time when the Government is increasingly challenging the legitimacy and the efficiency of local government. However we fear that the voluntary sector is still too fragmented and too uneven to take the lead in harnessing the efforts of other agencies to meet the challenges of the next decade; and the commercial sector is not capable of meeting or planning for the leisure needs and interests of the whole community because it is inevitably geared primarily towards the tastes of those who have purchasing power within the market.

The challenge to local government therefore is to give a new kind of lead and direction for leisure services, which are at a crossroads in their development. Subsequent chapters in this book chart some of the new territory, and explore positive ways forward.

References

1 Martin, W and Mason, S (1979), *Broad Patterns of Leisure Expenditure, London,* SSRC/Sports Council.
2 Leisure Consultants (1984), *Leisure Forecasting Overview,* Autumn 1984.
3 The Chairmen's Policy Group (1983), *Leisure Policy for the Future,* A discussion paper, London: Sports Council.
4 Institute of Employment Research (1985), *A Review of the Economy and Employment,* Vol 1, University of Warwick.
5 Respondent to questionnaire circulated to 50 Local Authority Chief Leisure Services Officers (or equivalent), May 1985.
6 *The Guardian,* 4 Sept 1985 and 15 Nov 1985.
7 The Chairmen's Policy Group (1983), *Op Cit,* p 70.
8 Department of the Environment (1975), *Sport and Recreation,* White Paper, Cmnd 6200, London: HMSO.
9 The Chairmen's Policy Group (1983), *Op Cit.*
10 John Roberts (1985), *The Commercial Sector As A Supplier of Leisure Goods and Services,* Sports Council and Social Science Research Council.
11 Greater London Enterprise Board (1985), *London Industrial Strategy: The Cultural Industries,* para 6.13, p 15, London: GLEB/GLC.
12 Allied Lyons Annual Report and Accounts 1986/7.
13 The Howell Report (1983) quoted in Gratton, C and Taylor, P (1987), *Leisure in Britain,* Leisure Publications (Letchworth) Ltd.
14 Colin Moynihan, writing in *The Observer,* Sunday 10 April 1988, p 65.
15 Quoted in *The Guardian,* Tuesday, Feb 23 1988, in article entitled 'Arts Sponsors Get Some Mixed Reviews', by Meriel Beattie.
16 *Ibid.*
17 *Ibid.*
18 For example the 'Omnibot', 'The most advanced Home Entertainment Robot', produced by Tomy and advertised as a robot who 'will fetch and carry, deliver messages, talk to friends, play your favourite cassettes, and even wake the kids up on Saturday morning'.
19 Andre Gorz (1985), *Paths to Paradise: On The Liberation From Work,* London: Pluto.
20 For example in Kenneth M Spencer (1985), *Demographic, Social and*

Economic Trends: An Overview, Institute of Local Government Studies, Birmingham University.

21 Colin Gill (1985), *Work, Unemployment and the New Technology,* Polity Press.

22 Kenneth M. Spencer (1985), *Op Cit.*

23 David Donnison (1985), *'The Rebirth of the domestic system',* Town and Country Planning, Vol 54, No 4, April.

24 Veronica Beechey (1985), *'The Shape of the Workforce to Come',* Marxism Today, August.

25 Gratton, C and Taylor, P (1985), *Sport and Recreation: An Economic Analysis,* London: Spon, p 80.

2 The consequences of competition

Kieron Walsh

Introduction

There has been a revival of the classical doctrines of political economy over the last ten to fifteen years. It has taken a number of forms, from the monetarist argument that inflation can be explained by the growth in the money supply, to the public choice theorists' focus on the interests of bureaucrats in explaining the operation of government. The British Governments of 1979 to the present have been heavily influenced by classical liberal economic ideas, which they have put into practice in a number of ways. They have sold public corporations such as British Gas and British Telecom; they have deregulated public transport; and they have attempted to re-place public servces by private investment, for example through the use of Urban Development Corporations in the inner city. In local government and the National Health Service the main impact of the new liberalism has been through the introduction of compulsory competitive tendering and, in the case of local authorities, the development of internal trading. In the National Health Service there has been a programme of compulsory tendering for catering, domestic and laundry services. In local government the Local Gov-ernment Planning and Land Act 1980 introduced competitive tendering and trading for building and highways construction and maintenance. Now the Government proposes, in the Local Gov-ernment Act 1988, to extend this regime to a range of other services. The Secretary of State for the Environment, Nicholas Ridley, has said that his ideal authority is one that meets once a year to give out the contracts and then adjourns for lunch. Such an authority may be a long way off, but the potential for the extention of competition to other services is great.

The declared purpose of introducing competitive tendering is to bring the disciplines of the market to the public sector. It will also reduce the power of local authorities and of public sector unions, which the Government sees as having been used to distort the workings of markets, and particularly of the labour market. Even if the local authority wins the contract in competition, or is simply allocated the contract because there is no competition, there will still be market disciplines because local authorities will be forced to establish internal trading systems. Whether the authority wins tenders or not it will have to operate on a quasi-commercial basis. The local authority will be forced to divide its activities into client and contractor roles, which will, at least to some degree, have different and possibly opposed interests.

It is difficult to get beyond the rhetoric when discussing competition. From the right – expressing the classical doctrines of liberalism – come arguments for the universal and unequivocal benefits of the market, while from the left come claims that competition always and everywhere leads to poorer standards of service, lower wages and worse conditions of service, and loss of jobs. Most of the claims to evaluate the impacts of competition have been made by individuals or organisations concerned to promote or oppose competition and are, therefore, tendentious. Different arguments become confused, for example the question of how services should be organised becomes confused with the question of whether or not a service should be provided directly by a public organisation. The requirement on local authorities to ensure that a service is provided is assumed to require them to actually employ the staff to provide the service themselves. In fact the results of competition are likely to vary in different circumstances and the way that services can be organised can take many different forms. It is not necessarily the case that the best way of providing a service will be either by employing direct labour or through private contractors. The method that is best will depend upon the circumstances of the case. Competition will force local authorities into a radical re-appraisal of the services that they provide and the ways in which they provide them.

In this chapter I shall consider the latest development of competitive tendering as embodied in the Local Government Act 1988. I shall consider, in particular, the introduction of competitive tendering and trading in leisure and recreation services. The leisure service poses a number of special problems in tendering, which illustrate some of the political, philosophical and organisational issues involved in introducing competition in the provision of public services. The point of this chapter is not to determine whether or not competitive tendering is a good or a bad thing but to investigate the issues that it raises. In doing so I hope to provide a framework for evaluating the policy of competitive tendering and trading.

Legislative proposals

The Local Government Act 1988 defines a number of activities for which the local authority must engage in a process of competition if it wishes to carry them out by employing its own labour. The services initially classed as 'defined activities' are refuse collection, cleaning of buildings, street cleansing, catering, grounds maintenance and vehicle maintenance. The competitive process involves the local authority specifying in detail the service that it wishes to be delivered and allowing private sector firms to tender for the right to deliver it. The local authority's own work force, already employed to do the work, will only be allowed to continue to do so if they are selected in a competitive tendering process. The local authority must not treat its direct labour organisation (DLO) any differently from the private sector tenderers. In theory the authority might select the DLO to do the work even if it was not the lowest tenderer, but, in practice, it would need to have a very good reason for doing so. If the DLO does win the right to carry out the work then it must keep a trading account for that activity. The only income that can be credited to that account will be payment for work done at a previously agreed price. The trading organisation – the DLO – will be governed by a special accounting code of practice. It will not be possible to cross-subsidise one trading account with another, though it will be possible to do so within an account. Thus local authorities will not be allowed to subsidise losses in catering with surpluses in grounds maintenance but it would be possible to subsidise losses at one leisure centre with surpluses at another. The trading account will be required to meet a financial target which will be laid down by the Secretary of State. For all activities except cleaning the target is to be a rate of return on capital employed of five per cent; cleaning of buildings, which makes very little use of capital, is to be required simply to break even. The local authority must make an annual report on the performance of the DLO which is to be certified by the auditor and sent to the Secretary of State.

The Secretary of State has taken a large number of powers to create and change rules, for example on the length and size of contracts, the nature of accounts and annual reports, financial objectives and the nature of the tender process. Rules can be created and changed by the Secretary of State for individual authorities as well as categories of authorities. The legislation also includes a requirement that local authorities shall not behave in such a way as to 'restrict, distort or prevent competition'. This very general constraint will limit local authorities' freedom considerably and will provide the private sector with a strong lever to control the action of the authority. In every decision that it makes and action that it takes, the authority will need to ensure that it cannot be accused of restricting, distorting or preventing competition. It will, therefore need to have thought out and recorded justifications for its decisions.

The Secretary of State is not likely to lay down detailed regulations on the way that local authorities are to put work out to tender. The minimum and maximum lengths of contracts will be specified, probably at three and seven years respectively, but varying for different activities. The code of accounting practice to govern how local authorities are to run trading accounts will be produced by the Chartered Institute of Public Finance and Accountancy. Detailed regulations are not thought to be needed because the requirement on local authorities not to act in such a way as to restrict distort or prevent competition can be relied upon to prevent authorities avoiding the impact of the legislation. Private contractors and trade associations can be relied upon to police the actions of the local authorities. The Secretary of State can always make or change rules at a later date, as has frequently been done in the case of highways and building construction and maintenance under the Local Government Planning and Land Act 1980.

The leisure and recreation provision of local authorities was bound to be affected by the requirement to compete for catering, cleaning and, especially, grounds maintenance. But in November 1987 the Government issued a consultative paper which proposed to extend the provisions of the legislation to the management of sports and leisure facilities. There is obviously overlap between these two requirements because grounds maintenance includes the laying out and maintaining of sports pitches, and cleaning and catering are necessary in leisure centres. Arts, libraries and museums do not yet fall under the provisions of the legislation, probably for no better reason than that they do not fall within the remit of the Department of the Environment. The requirement to compete could well be extended to these services in the future, and the Government has already produced a paper discussing the possibility of extending competition in the library service[1]. There has been speculation, for example, on the possibility of requiring competition for the management of branch libraries.

The consultative paper on sports and leisure services proposes that the legislation should be extended to the following activies:

- Sports centres
- Leisure centres
- Swimming pools
- Golf courses
- Bowling greens
- Putting greens
- Tennis courts

- Athletics tracks
- Pitches for team and other games
- Cycle tracks
- Water sports facilities
- Artificial ski slopes
- Skating rinks
- Indoor bowling greens
- Beaches

It is not precisely clear to what each of these categories refers (for example beaches). The definition of sports and leisure centres may also cause confusion because they are often integrated with other community provision. The division into sports activities and others is not clear in some cases. But, in general terms, the activities that fall under the definition are relatively straightforward. The broad principle that sports activities should be the subject of competition is clear.

The consultation paper proposes that local authorities be required to engage in competitive tendering for the management of these services, which would include the following functions:

- Taking bookings
- Collection of, and accounting for, fees and charges
- Cleaning and maintaining buildings, grounds, sports surfaces, plant and equipment
- Supervising activities, eg lifeguards at swimming pools
- Providing instruction in the sport and recreation activities offered
- Catering and the provision of refreshments
- Provision and hire of sports and other equipment
- Paying for heating lighting and other service charges
- Securing the premises

The consultative paper presents two possible alternatives for dealing with pricing, admissions and opening hours. Either the local authority should retain control, delegating the responsibility to the private sector if it saw fit, or, as the consultative paper says:

The present discretionary powers should be amended to target more specifically on those members of the community who may not be able to pay the full market rate to use sport and leisure facilities but who clearly should retain the opportunity to make use of such facilities – for example the unemployed, the elderly, school groups. This would give the private sector managers the freedom to decide their own policies on pricing, admittance, and opening hours for most users of facilities but would allow the local authorities, if they so wished, to control the policies in respect of certain disadvantaged groups.

The government has now decided that authorities should be allowed to set prices and opening hours, though change is still possible. The question of who should set prices is crucial, both because of its policy implications and because of its effects on the way that contracts can be written. The more contractors or DLOs control prices, the more they are likely to use that power to pursue their own advantage. Local authorities are not likely to be able to pursue their social and welfare objectives if they cannot control the price of services at least to some degree. But control over or influence on prices will not be sufficient for it will not allow authorities to influence the nature of the services offered.

The definitions in the consultative paper present some difficulty, notably in the area of the overlap between education and leisure. Facilities which 'form an integral part of educational establishments and which are provided principally for the use of pupils/students at those establishments' are to be exempt. But it will not always be easy to decide where education ends and where instruction in sport begins. There will be considerable difficulty in determining the respective responsibilities of education and recreation departments in the case of joint use of facilities, a problem which will be considerably enhanced when schools have devolved budgets as required by the Education Reform Bill, leading to much more flexibility in schools' use of leisure facilities. It is not clear what the financial target will be for the leisure DLO but since tendering is to be required for the management of the service not the service itself – though this is a fine and, as yet, obscure distinction – little capital would be used. A rate of return on capital would be inappropriate. A requirement to break even, or to make a small return on turnover, would be more sensible.

The decision to add leisure services to the list of defined services for tendering has now been taken. The requirement to introduce competitive tendering and trading for grounds maintenance and for cleaning and catering will also have an immediate impact upon the leisure service. A number of authorities have already contracted out the management of leisure centres, and others are likely to do so even before the requirement to tender is introduced. One authority has formed its own company to deliver leisure services. The future is likely to be one of more varied forms of service delivery.

In essence, then, the proposed legislation will require two processes for grounds maintenance and the management of sports leisure services – competitive tendering and internal trading. In the immediate future the major impact will come from the requirement to tender, but in the longer term it is the requirement to trade that will change the way that leisure services, and, indeed, the rest of the authority operate. Internal trading will change relationships and the nature of management within the local authority. Competitive tendering and internal trading will pose a number of questions and dilemmas for the authority, notably:

- How can the local authority retain control of leisure service policy if it is contracted out?
- What sort of contracts and specifications should the authority use?
- How should the local authority set standards and monitor contracts?
- How should the local authority organise itself if it wins the right to provide leisure services by direct labour?

These problems can be best understood if we place them in a theoretical context. Before going on to discuss the questions stated above I shall outline one particular theoretical approach that has been developed by Williamson to attempt to understand the value of different approaches to organising contracts.

Internal or external?

The question we are concerned with is when is it better to organise the production or provision of goods and services through direct employment and when they are most efficiently bought on the market. It is the 'make or buy' decision that faces all organisations. Some firms will stick close to their core activity buying whatever materials and support services they need on the market; others will want to control the goods and services that contribute to the final product as closely as possible and will engage in vertical or horizontal integration. Oliver Williamson, in an extended series of books and articles, notably *Markets and Hierarchies* and *The Economic Institutions of Capitalism*[2], has considered this problem, and the ideas and theories he develops are valuable in helping us to analyse the question of tendering and internal trading. Williamson argues that whether the market – buying what is needed from outside the organisation – or hierarchy – internal organisation of the production of what is needed by the organisation – is the most efficient means of obtaining goods or services will depend upon three factors, 'bounded rationality', 'opportunism', and 'asset specificity'.

Bounded rationality refers to the fact that it is not possible to know everything; there will always be uncertainty however much we may study a situation. The capacity of individuals and organisations to analyse and describe the goods and services it needs will also be limited by the fact that there will be a high cost for the collection of information. Even if it were possible to discover everything the cost of doing so would be too great to be practical. Opportunism refers to the fact that individuals will, everything else being equal, attempt to forward their own interests at the expense of those of the organisation, for example through concealing information that might yield an advantage or might be damaging to them. Similarly one must assume that a private supplier or contractor, or a DLO, will behave opportunistically given the chance. Competition is not compatible with altruism. Asset specificity refers to the fact that certain assets may be used for a wide range of purposes, whereas others are limited to highly specific uses. The concept of assets may refer either to capital equipment or to specific skills possessed by staff. An office can be used to carry on a whole range of businesses. A swimming pool or a leisure centre is much less adaptable. Typing or secretarial skills are readily transferrable from one setting to another, abilities in sports instruction are not.

Williamson then goes on to argue that the cost of transactions will vary with the extent of uncertainty, opportunism and asset specificity. A transaction involves the transfer of goods or services across 'a technologically separate interface'[3]. Transactions always involve costs, whether they be financial, or involve time or other resources. The purpose of economic institutions is to economise on transaction costs. Whether an organisation buys what it needs on the market or produces it internally by employing its own staff – whether it makes or buys – will depend upon which is the most economically efficient method.

Williamson's transaction cost analysis can be understood more clearly if we consider the implications for organising contracts if one of the factors, bounded rationality, opportunism or asset specificity, is absent while the other two are present. If there is no bounded rationality, and the cost of gathering information is low, but there is asset specificity and opportunism then it is possible to operate on the basis of planning, because one can make provision for any contingency before it happens. Total knowledge can compensate for other difficulties. If there is no opportunism but only bounded rationality and asset specificity then we can rely upon 'promise' because we can be certain that people will keep their words and not pursue self-interest at the expense of others. Only the loosest form of contract is then necessary, because the contract does not have to deal with what should be done to accommodate changed circumstances. We can rely upon people's goodwill. There will be little need to police the contract since contractors will not be trying to gain advantage. If there is no asset specificity, but only uncertainty and opportunism, then we can rely upon the market because neither party will have a continuing dependence upon each other. The buyer can readily move to another supplier when problems arise. Suppliers can, equally, move to other markets. As Williamson argues:

> Each of the three devices fails when bounded rationality, opportunism, and asset specificity are joined. Planning is necessarily incomplete (because of bounded rationality), promise predictably breaks down (because of opportunism), and the pairwise identification of the parties now matters (because of asset specificity[4]).

In these circumstances, argues Williamson, the most efficient approach is to organise on a hierarchical basis. The fact that staff are employed by an organisation to provide a service makes it easier to respond to events by changing patterns of work and job descriptions. Motivation and sanctions can be used to generate and maintain commitment, and the organisation is not at the mercy of the limited market for highly specific assets. The less there is bounded rationality, opportunism and uncertainty in any given case, the more efficient it will be to use the market as a means of procuring goods and services.

The transaction cost analysis makes clear the fact that neither the market or internal production are likely to be the most appropriate method in all circumstances, and, therefore, the make or buy decision will be one that all organisations will have to make, and continually to review as circumstances change. In practice it will not be a matter of a wholly market-based or a wholly internal pattern of provision. It will be more appropriate to supply some services by direct labour and others by spot or continuing contracts on the market, but in many cases a mixed form of provision will be most appropriate.

Williamson concentrates upon efficiency as the explanation of institutional structure. Organisations will purchase on the market or produce internally depending on which approach is the more economically efficient. But power will also be important. Groups and individuals may be able to maintain or create an institutional structure that favours their interests if they are sufficiently powerful, whatever may be the most efficient approach. A dominant retailer does not need to produce, for it can impose its preferences on the manufacturer. A dominant union can maintain a pattern of organisation against the preferences of a weak employer. The choice between markets and hierarchy will also vary over time. The history of the motor industry, for example, has developed from a high degree of vertical integration to flexible specialisation with a high percentage of inputs bought in. The institutional structure that prevails at any time will depend, partly, upon the power of individuals and groups and the circumstances faced. In considering how local authorities will be affected by the introduction of competitive tendering and trading it is necessary to consider efficiency and power and the changed circumstances that now prevail.

The policy dilemma

The local authority will obviously want to maintain control of leisure policy whether the contract is won by an internal DLO or by a private sector contractor. Leisure is unlike the other services to be subject to competition because of the complexity of the policy involved. In the case of refuse collection, catering or cleaning the policy decisions are not especially complex. The leisure service is different for three reasons. First it has links to many other policy areas. Leisure policy will have an impact on education, especially if there is joint provision. A number of authorities have made extensive investment in joint education and leisure facilities involving cooperation between counties and districts. Authorities will be concerned that leisure provision fits in with wider social aims such as provision for the elderly, people with disabilities, women or the unemployed. The involvement of a number of private providers would make this difficult. Leisure and recreation policies may be linked to the authority's policy on economic development and tourism. Developing and maintaining corporate policy will be more difficult the more organisations are involved and the less they are under the control of the local authority.

The second reason is that leisure provision must be subject to change if it is to meet changing needs and demand. Patterns of leisure change rapidly and the local authority must be able to respond. Social and economic change are likely to increase the rate of change in the future (see chapter 1). The more the authority is tied into a specific long term contract, the more difficult it will be to change policy and practice to respond to circumstances. A major reason for internally organised provision is the greater possibility of varying the pattern of service.

The third reason is that it is difficult to divorce policy and the setting of standards from the actual provision. Pricing, admissions and opening hours are crucial to the policy of the authority, not ancillary matters. The contracting out of leisure assumes that policy is made separately from implementation, but the two cannot so easily be separated. The policy that is actually pursued is the one that is implemented, not the one that the authority would like to think is being implemented. Furthermore many authorities are now emphasising closer relations with the public as a part of policy development and are therefore concerned to see their policy expressed and implemented in detail.

The policy dilemma will be expressed in problems that the authority will face in tendering for leisure services. If the need to ensure collaboration with other services and to adapt to change is to be met, there will be a need to write detailed contracts with clauses to deal with contingencies. Such contracts will be difficult and costly to write. Change is likely to lead to contractual disputes and problems of negotiating with contractors. Even if the authority has contracted out the service, it will still want close involvement, for example to maintain links with the rest of the authority's services. The client role in the leisure service is more difficult than in the other services that are subject to competition and will need more development.

Contracts and specifications

Williamson's transaction costs analysis is valuable in pointing to the factors that need to be considered in deciding how to write contracts and specifications, when putting leisure, or any other service, out to competitive tender. It suggests that writing contracts and specifications will be harder the greater is bounded rationality, opportunism and asset specificity. In the case of leisure services each factor is likely to be high. Rationality is bounded because future leisure demands and patterns of activity are difficult to predict. The rate of innovation in the leisure industry is also high, partly driven by and partly driving the form of provision. It is relatively easy to know what the future patterns of refuse collection or cleaning will be. Leisure is much more difficult to predict. There will be differences within the leisure and recreation service in the extent to which the future can be predicted. Grounds maintenance will be subject to less uncertainty than the pattern of provision in leisure centres and can be specified more closely. But, generally, writing contracts and specifications for leisure and recreation will be more difficult than for the other services that are to be subject to competitive tendering.

The chances for opportunism in leisure and recreation are great because it involves a wide range of activities that are difficult to monitor. A leisure centre will provide, perhaps, a number of different sports, swimming, bar and refreshment facilities, and the sale of various sporting and other goods. The leisure centre may also provide space for a whole range of other community activities. Many of these services will involve variable levels of provision or sale, depending on demand. Opportunism is possible in a wide variety of ways, both in the types of service provided and in the approach to pricing. The local authority will need to decide how much freedom it will allow to contractors, and, by implication, to its own internal trading operation, on the setting of prices or the actual pattern of provision. This decision will be crucial since the contractor may hope to make profit by a different form of provision rather than greater efficiency in providing the same services. A private sector provider might, therefore, lay more emphasis on the sale of goods or income from bars or restaurants than the authority might wish.

The assets that are used in the leisure services are relatively specific and cannot easily be transferred to other uses. This is true of staff and capital resources. In grounds maintenance there will certainly be relatively unskilled labour but there will also be highly specific skills in horticulture or arboriculture. Indeed, the specificity of the skills is likely to mean that there will not be a great deal of competition in the first place. In leisure provision it is likely to be the equipment and buildings that are specific to the services being provided. A swimming pool, for example, cannot immediately be converted to a wide range of other uses, but will require some conversion work. A leisure centre will have been designed with a very specific use in mind, and, unlike an office block, cannot be used to house almost any business. Leisure centres involve a considerable capital investment and the private sector is likely to see the advantage of management contracts allowing them to reap the benefits without having to take the risk of capital investment. The less convertible the asset the less the private contractor will want to invest in it. Power will influence the degree to which an asset is specific to its use, for example the public may resist the transfer of a particular sports or leisure facility to another use, thereby limiting its alternative use.

It will be necessary to write contracts in a way that takes account of the relatively high level of bounded rationality, opportunism and asset specificity in leisure services. There will be a number of specific decisions to be made, the most important of which are

- The size of the contract that should be let, for example whether to let all the leisure services of the authority in one contract or to break the work up into smaller packages;
- The length of the contract;
- Whether to combine different types of activities together or to have separate contracts for different aspects of the service;
- The form of contract to be used, particularly whether to use a bill of quantities or a schedule of rates, and how to deal with income.

The future is not at all easy to predict. In attempting to ensure flexibility, the local authority will have two possible approaches open to it. The first approach is to limit the length of the contract, so that the local authority can adapt to new circumstances as it changes contracts, say every year. But there are several problems with this approach. It is likely to lead to greater cost, both because tenderers faced with future uncertainty are likely to put in higher prices, and because of the cost of the tender process itself. It will also create uncertainty for the authority's own DLO which will have to compete more frequently. Very short contracts are likely to be looked upon unfavourably by the Government because of being seen as "restricting, distorting or preventing competition" which is specifically forbidden by the act. Private firms will want longer contracts. The second approach is to write into the contract the right of the authority to alter the pattern of provision during the contract period in order to deal with changed patterns of demand. Such a clause might be general, allowing the authority to change the pattern of provision as and when it saw fit, or it might involve review at regular intervals, say annually. Contractors tendering for such contract would, again, be likely to put in a higher price than they would otherwise do because of the relative uncertainty that they would face. Both approaches would create the possibility of many claims for variation, and plenty of occasion for argument between the authority and the contractor, which means that there will need to be a well constructed arbitration clause. The more flexible the contract the more attention and time the authority will have to devote to contract management.

The contract will need to be constructed in such a way as to prevent opportunism so far as is possible. This will present the authority with a number of dilemmas, particularly in relation to the income from the provision of leisure. If the authority sets strict limitations on the contractor's freedom over the setting of entrance charges, in order to ensure that its social policies are fulfilled, then the contractor may concentrate on those areas of provision in which it can make profit. It may concentrate on the sale of dry goods or on bars or refreshments. Generally the contractor will always have an incentive to concentrate on those areas of the service that are likely to create profit and where it is possible to increase income. It will be almost impossible to prevent DLOs and contractors selecting the levels of effort they make in different aspects of provision to match their interests. Contracts and work specifications are also systems of incentives.

Authorities will also need to consider the size of the contracts that they let. They may wish to let all sports leisure facilities or grounds maintenance as a single contract. However, this is unwise for at least five reasons:

1 They are likely to find themselves faced with great problems if that single contract should fail. Even if it should not do so they are putting a lot of power into the hands of a single contractor. Where there is only one contractor it will be very hard to resist claims for extra money in the course of the contract, or to terminate the contract, given the difficulty of making alternative provision.

2 Should the internal DLO lose in the contracting process it will have lost all its work at one go.

3 The authority will not be able to stagger the tender process, which may be important given the amount of work involved. A single large contract will create peaks of work, at the time that contracts have to be let, followed by troughs, creating planning and staffing difficulties for the authority.

4 A large contract will probably package together work that is of very different kinds. The scope of the contract may lead to inefficiency and monitoring difficulties.

5 A large contract will allow more chances for opportunism on the part of the contractor. The more facets there are to provision the more one can be neglected or emphasised at the expense of another.

Local authorities are only likely to want to create very large contracts when they are happy to hand over control of their provision to a contractor. There are also, of course, disadvantages to small contracts. Local authorities will find themselves with a large number of contracts to manage. The provision of service by the authority may become fragmented and economies of scale may be lost. The best approach is likely to involve contracts of an intermediate size, packaging together some, but not all, of the work.

The authority will normally wish to retain ownership of the leisure facilities themselves. There is nothing to stop the authority selling the facilities to the contractor, perhaps requiring them to be sold back at the end of the contract. This approach has been used for capital equipment such as vehicles but is not likely to be appropriate for land and buildings. The less control the authority has over facilities the less it will be able to bid for leisure work in the future. If a service is capital intensive then the authority is not likely to want to lose control of its capital. Another difficulty for the authority in relation to capital relates to maintenance. The consultative paper sees maintenance as one of the activities that will be subject to tender. The authority will need to ensure in its contracts that there is not an incentive either to do excessive maintenance or to let the fabric of buildings decline. The major difficulty that confronts authorities in writing contracts is to create a set of conditions that provide an incentive for the contractor to provide an efficient service and not act against the interests of the authority. The present uncertainty over the future of leisure buildings is already leading authorities to question their levels of investment and maintenance. Authorities are wary of making investments that they may have to pass over to the private sector.

Leisure services will be more difficult to specify than such services as refuse collection or cleaning because of the change in taste that is possible and the fact that take-up can vary. It is unlikely that the authority will want to try to specify exactly the pattern of leisure that is to be provided down to the last detail. But it will want to ensure that the key aspects of service and the important elements of social policy are dealt with. The authority will want to specify the parameters within which the contractor is to operate in providing leisure services. These will include objective factors, such as the opening hours of facilities or the temperature of the water in the swimming pool; policy factors, such as provision for schools or particular social groups; and service factors, such as a pleasant or safe environment. But it is very difficult to specify things that are not objective, such as that staff shall be pleasant and friendly in their dealings with the public. Hospital contracts have shown how difficult it is to specify the caring elements of service. However much detail is specified it will still be possible for the atmosphere to be unpleasant.

The contract and specification will be crucial to the success of the competitive approach. If the local authority creates too loose a contract, it will lose control of the service. Anything that is significant must be specified, because if it is not in the specification there is no guarantee that the contractor will provide it. The authority will also want to develop its own contract so as to ensure that it fits local circumstances, though it may draw on standard approaches in doing so. Preparing a good contract and specification is crucial to the future management of the contract and the service.

Monitoring the contract

The less the service can be defined in objective terms the harder it will be to monitor but, paradoxically, the more necessary it will be for the authority to ensure that a satisfactory service is delivered. A service that can be objectively defined can be monitored by the users to a great degree. Objective definitions of standards will be possible for many aspects of service, especially in the case of grounds maintenance. It is possible to specify standards for three aspects of the work that is to be put out to tender; the inputs required, the work process, and the outputs. Inputs might be specified in terms of British standards, brand names, or quality. The authority might wish to specify staff inputs either in terms of level or skill and this should be possible, despite the restrictions on contract compliance activity, as long as it is genuinely necessary to the contract. The work process can be specified, both to ensure that unacceptable methods are not used and that there are no undesirable side-effects. For example the authority will want to ensure that the grass is not cut outside schools in the middle of examination periods, or outside residential homes early in the morning.

It will clearly be to the advantage of the authority if it can specify the output that it wants from a service. In some cases this will obviously be possible, for example one can specify acceptable lengths of grass. In other cases specification of output is more difficult but still possible, for example one can specify the height to which cricket balls will bounce on a properly prepared square. Such objective tests may be difficult or expensive, and therefore, not performed on a regular basis. But their availability does give the authority a measure to fall back on in case of disputes over performance. Many aspects of the output of a service will be difficult to specify in objective terms. They will necessarily, and quite properly, be matters of judgement. It will be possible to say a great deal about the sort of provision that is made in a leisure centre, but much of the satisfaction that people get will be from the intangible 'service' elements – how the staff treat them or whether they have to wait for service. The more intangible the service the more difficult it will be to monitor. Local authorities, keen to develop a better service that is 'closer to the public', have been giving emphasis to improving the less tangible aspects of their service. They will need to monitor this aspect of provision closely.

The argument is sometimes made that, if one can specify outputs, it is unnecessary to specify inputs or work processes. This is unlikely to be so for a service that is in any way complex. It is quite possible for an output that is perfectly satisfactory to be produced by means that are not satisfactory, for example by employing under-age labour or by the use of excessively noisy or disruptive machinery. Generally the authority will want to specify in detail for inputs, work process and outputs. Such detailed specifications will allow the authority to deal with the contractor from a position of strength. It is always possible to relax a detailed specification in operation but not to make it more rigorous. It will be even more important to specify inputs and work processes when outputs are difficult to identify objectively.

The first requirement, if contracts are to be monitored adequately, is that the specification should be written in sufficient detail. If any aspect of the service matters then it should be specified as closely as possible. It may be that all that is possible is a statement that allows subjective judgement by a suitably qualified officer, but, however vague, some statement will need to be made. In theory contracts could be almost infinitely long, and the authority will need to decide at what point further specificaton would be wasteful. The decision will depend upon three factors; the cost of further specification work, whether the aspect specified could be monitored, and whether it matters. There is little point in costly work to specify matters that are of no great significance. Nor should one waste time specifying things on which it will not be possible to check. The more one expects contractors to behave opportunistically the higher the specification needs to be, but excessively detailed contracts will only serve to impose costs on the authority.

Monitoring work has two aspects; quality control and quality assurance. Quality control involves checking on work after it has been done to determine whether or not it was of an adequate standard. Quality assurance involves the development of systems to ensure that goods and services are produced to a high standard in the first place. Quality assurance involves action before the event whereas quality control takes place after the event. In manufacturing systems quality control allows the manufacturer to reject any sub-standard products. The possibilities for quality control are more limited the less physical the service. Services that are consumed at the point of production are not easily susceptible to quality control. There is little value in knowing that an unsatisfactory meal has been produced or that a swimming pool is too cold to allow swimming, because a good deal of the damage has already been done. Quality control will also be difficult when the implications of action only become apparent in the long term and are hard to reverse. Using the wrong fertiliser on bowling greens may have catastrophic effects that may not become apparent for a long time and may be difficult to reverse.

It is necessary to operate quality assurance systems if the authority is to ensure, so far as it can, that a satisfactory standard of service is delivered. Japanese industry has given a great deal of attention to the development of effective quality assurance systems, for example the use of quality circles, just-in-time supply systems, statistical process control and close relationships with suppliers. The purpose is to prevent failure happening rather than deal with it after it has happened. It is possible for local authorities to develop analogous systems. Quality assurance systems for traded services in local authorities might involve the following sorts of activities:

- Establishing a clear system of relations with the contractor involving named individuals in the authority and the contracting company who can deal with problems;
- Regular meetings between client and contractor side;
- Certification of work before payment;
- Access to contractors' premises and records where necessary;
- Detailed record systems;
- Training in dealing with contractors for all those who will have dealings with contractors;
- Clear and simple monitoring documents for all those who must monitor contracts;
- An adequate complaints procedure that will produce information on which the authority can base action.

Quality assurance is necessary if the authority is to retain control of the service as opposed to simply controlling the contract with the providing company.

Monitoring contractors is likely to be more difficult than monitoring the DLO, and is, therefore, likely to be more costly. Contractors are likely to have more incentive to be opportunistic because they can keep more of the fruits of their efforts. This is not to say that DLOs are motivated purely by commitment to public service. The experience of the building and highway maintenance DLOs after the Local Government Planning and Land Act of 1980 was that the DLO managers quickly became more commercial in their attitudes. But contractors are still likely to take a more commercial attitude because of the structure of incentives. The motivation is profit not service; as the directors of Crossland Leisure (Holdings) Ltd say, in running local authority leisure centres they would like to make their profit by:

". . .running the facility as a private members' club with full commerical fees being charged"[5]

Controlling the DLO will be different from controlling the private sector company because the structure of incentives is different and because sanctions are available that are not available against the commercial company. In the case of the company the local authority is tied into a contract, but with its own DLO there is no contract and the authority can for example change the level or type of work required. Monitoring systems are likely to be different for the DLO and the private sector.

Organising for competition

The need to keep separate trading accounts for those services that are to be subject to competitive tendering will require authorities to separate the client and contractor sides of their operations. This can be done fairly easily for services such as cleaning or catering because the two aspects of the service are relatively clear and because there is more experience. In grounds maintenance separation will be possible fairly easily, but for leisure services there is more difficulty. The problems can be understood if we consider what must be done by the client and by the internal contractor respectively.

The client side must decide policy, specify the work that is to be done, establish systems for monitoring the work and develop payment systems. The contractor side must actually provide the service. In the case of leisure services as they are presently organised there is overlap between the client and contractor functions almost throughout the department. Only at the very top of the organisation, if there, are officers working purely on the client side. The need for the service to be adaptable means that policy and executive decisions overlap, and that there has to be considerable discretion for operational managers to make what are in effect policy decisions, for example on pricing. This complexity characterises most of the service departments of a local authority, such as education or social services. Client and contractor roles are likely to be spread throughout the organisation, with schools or old people's homes being partly client and partly contractor. The overlap between client and contractor does not mean that competitive tendering and internal trading are either impossible or undesirable. Rather it means that the authority must consider carefully how to organise itself in the face of a new set of organisational imperatives.

Many local authorities have been delegating responsibility as far as they can down the organisational hierarchy, for example allowing leisure centre managers to set and vary prices. The requirement to allow private sector firms to compete may work against this move towards delegation. Authorities will be required to treat them on the same basis as the DLO, but may be unwilling to allow them the freedom that they allow their own employees. In its dealings with contractors the authority will not be able to use the sanctions that are possible in its relations with its own employees. The move to contracting out is likely to mean the retention of more centralised control.

These organisational constraints could be dealt with in a number of ways. The leisure department could adopt a "two-hatted" approach throughout so that virtually all officers had both client and contractor responsibilities. This approach would have the virtue of eliminating some duplication of function, though at the expense of confusing accountability. It is probably not possible to have a radical split between the client and contractor side of the department in organising leisure services for competition. The planning and specification of leisure services – the policy element – is more intimately involved with delivery than is the case for other competed services. But there will need to be clear separation of roles within the department as far as possible, in order to recognise the constraints of the new legislation, and to ensure that the costs of different aspects of the service are properly accounted for.

Conclusion

There are two elements to the legislation on competition – compulsory competitive tendering and internal trading. In the immediate future the requirement to compete will have the greatest effect, but in the long term it is internal trading that is more likely to change the way that organisations work. Competition is not likely to be strong at first. There are not many large firms engaged in grounds maintenance as yet. There is some evidence of amalgamation of garden centres and nurseries, but the contractors are not yet strongly organised, as they are in some of the other services that are subject to competition. There are a number of large and expanding leisure companies, such as Mecca and Granada, but it is not clear how interested they will be in competing for traditional local authority facilities such as swimming pools. There is likely to be more interest in the management of leisure centres. Crossland already has a number of local authority contracts and similar firms are likely to develop. But the development of the market is likely to be slow.

Even if they win the contracts local authorities must operate trading accounts for the management of leisure services. Internal trading will change the culture of local authorities. It will affect not only the services that are directly subject to competition, but also the central services of the authority. The trading organisation will question the charges that it is allocated from the centre for the cost of financial, legal or other services. New central services are likely to be needed such as help with business planning. Trading departments are likely to want to have a good deal of independence to deal with their own affairs.

The introduction of competitive tendering and trading into local government services means that the local authority must operate with two different and, perhaps, competing methods of organising transactions. It must operate both market and hierarchy at the same time, though that market may be internal to the organisation. It is just as likely that the authority will lose the advantages of both types of organisation as that it will gain. The major danger that local authorities face as a result of the legislation on competition is that they will become fragmented, providing a range of services with little integration or corporate perspective.

References

1 *Financing Our Library Service: Four Subjects for Debate*, London, HMSO, 1988
2 Williamson, O E *Markets and Hierarchies: Analysis and Antitrust Implications*, New York, Free Press, 1975, and *The Economic Institutions of Capitalism: Firms, Markets, Relational Contracting*, New York, Free Press, 1985.
3 Williamson, *The Economic Institutions of Capitalism*, p. 32.
4 *ibid*
5 Quoted in 'Privatization is the Leisure Dilemma', *The Times*, Nov 27, 1987.

3 The changes and challenges facing local government in the provision of library and information services over the next two decades

Patricia M Coleman

General Introduction

The first Public Libraries Act of 1850 was introduced in association with a number of other reforming measures at that time which were directed towards improving the health and welfare of the working classes. Many, although not all, of the early supporters of public libraries saw them as a means of drawing the lower classes away from frivolous pastimes, for example the patronage of gin-palaces, and into more uplifting and purposive use of their leisure time.

The early library acts simply empowered local councils to raise a rate to provide libraries. Not surprisingly, perhaps, many did not immediately see the need. The real spur to the development of local library services was not legislation but the existence of a number of wealthy benefactors who were ready to fund the building of libraries. The present library network owes a great deal to the provision made by benefactors during the latter part of the last century and the beginning of this one. The most notable individual benefactor was Andrew Carnegie who, personally before his death in 1919 and thereafter through the Carnegie United Kingdom Trust, funded the construction of over 400 library buildings in Great Britain and Northern Ireland. Many important libraries still bear the names of their benefactors, for example the Mitchell in Glasgow, the Harris in Preston and the Graves in Sheffield.

Out of an institution strongly associated with philanthropy has grown one with an image of being patronised predominantly by the middle classes. The character of the service changed after the second world war and this was principally the result of two factors: firstly, the decline and closure of private libraries which had previously served the middle and upper classes (Boots Lending Library was the last to go in the early fifties); secondly, the development of the profession of librarianship which was facilitated by the provision of grants for Higher Education in the 1944 Education Act (many of the first college-trained librarians were grant-aided ex-servicemen).

It is true to say that people from higher social classes do tend to make greater use of and have greater influence on the development of library provision but this is the case for all public services. It is equally true that people from all backgrounds use libraries and in large numbers. Up to forty per cent of the population use a public library regularly, that is, once a month or more. This must make it the local authority service with which the greatest number of people have direct personal contact.

The high level of use is a reflection of the impressive network of outlets. There are almost 4000 public library buildings in the UK, services in prisons, hospitals and schools, mobile services to the housebound and those who live at a distance from a library. In rural areas and increasingly in urban areas too, the public library may be the only public building in a community. Almost inevitably it will be the only public building open throughout the year and in the evenings and on Saturdays.

All of this represents a considerable investment in buildings, equipment, materials and staff. In fact, spending on public libraries represents a high proportion (about 60 per cent) of all public expenditure on the arts. Arts and libraries spending is generally linked together since it is all administered through the Office of Arts and Libraries by the Minister for the Arts.

This situation is responsible for a major dilemma for libraries in terms of policy development and resource provision since they are not solely an arts activity but are also concerned with education, information and leisure provision. The library service is, in fact a support service providing information, materials and other resources to support all kinds of activities which may be artistic, educational, economic, recreational etc. Only to a very limited extent is it a direct provider of these activities. It is far easier to make a case for direct spending on the activities themselves than to argue for resources to make the pursuance of activities more effective. For example it is easier to get funds to start a small business from the present government than to get funds to provide an information service which will enable existing small businesses to operate more effectively. The boundaries or limits of the area of benefit of a general support service are also more difficult to draw. Particularly at a time when resources are limited it is tempting to argue for a reduction in the area of benefit in order to achieve a higher level of service rather than to adopt the policy of providing the best possible service to the whole community within the limit of resources. If the area of benefit is reduced the crucial question is, on what basis? Inevitably, views within the profession on this question are varied.

What is the library and information service? Who provides?

In general terms the pattern of leisure provision has been affected most dramatically by the fact that ordinary people have a greater amount of leisure time and surplus income to spend on other than the basic necessities of life. The working week has gradually been shortened and people are retiring earlier. After they have housed, clothed and fed themselves and their families most people have money left to spend on themselves and their leisure time. The result has been a dramatic growth amongst commercial suppliers of leisure goods and services since there are now large profits to be made whilst public provision has also developed in response to demands for more sophisticated facilities than municipal swimming baths, parks and libraries.

Much of commercial leisure development has been directed towards persuading people to acquire a growing range of consumer durables and much of it has been technology led.

The increasing influence of television and TV related activities, eg video and home computers, reflects the dominance of passive leisure pursuits. Interest in another important area – music – is also predominantly passive and technology related as people are persuaded to acquire stereophonic/quadrophonic sound systems, personal hi-fis, compact disc players etc. This has also influenced the style of public provision.

Local government reorganisation in 1974 was an influence on public leisure provision for two main reasons. Firstly, the larger authorities which resulted were better able to contemplate and finance large scale leisure projects eg sports complexes, country parks, theatres and concert halls. Secondly, the newly created metropolitan county authorities were looking for a role. For many of them the rapidly expanding area of leisure provided an area of potential development which they could make their own without treading to a great extent on the toes of District Councils. The best examples are West Yorkshire – tourism, Greater Manchester – the arts, Merseyside – media and the arts, and of course the GLC. But most metropolitan county councils have made a significant contribution to public leisure provision in the past ten years.

Specifically in public libraries 1964 was a significant year in that they became a statutory service as a result of the Public Libraries and Museums Act which became law in that year. For the last twenty years there has been the security of knowing that the service has to be provided by local authorities. However, the Act itself is couched in such vague terms that there is a great variation in the way that individual local authorities fulfil their statutory duty. It requests local authorities to provide 'a comprehensive and efficient (library) service' for people who live, work or are educated within their boundaries. There is no consensus as to the level at which comprehensiveness and efficiency is achieved.

Local government reorganisation in 1974 also affected public libraries. Until then both county and district councils had library powers so there were some anomalous situations where county and districts were both serving the same population. In county towns the county library headquarters was often a matter of yards away from the district library headquarters but both systems would be run completely independently. In 1974 library powers given were to the shire counties and the metropolitan districts. In the earlier reorganisation in London they had been vested in the London boroughs. It is interesting to speculate whether the library service might have fared better if it had become a metropolitan county and GLC responsibility. In addition to their patronage of the arts certain metropolitan counties, eg Tyne and Wear and West Yorkshire, have been particularly keen supporters and developers of archive services, another area closely related to libraries. It is generally true that the larger authorities, whether shire counties, metropolitan districts or London boroughs are the ones making greatest input to public libraries and where the standard of service is reckoned to be higher. It is certainly easier to justify resources and to use them more effectively and efficiently for a larger population.

Until the 1960s libraries were a totally book based service. From that time onwards first gramophone records, then recorded sound cassettes, film strips and slides and, latterly, video cassettes, computer software and compact discs have extended the range of materials provided. The development of alternative media provision was the result of both demand and need. The first gramophone record libraries were commercial ones but they were a failure. There are few, if any at all in existence today. The public library service is geared to lending materials and does not have the overheads of commercial, single operation outlets. The provision of recorded music is now a recognised part of most, if not all public library services. The video revolution has not yet taken such a hold but over one third of all public library authorities now provide video lending collections. Whether commercial competition will die in the same way as with music is not yet clear but the response of the public to library video provision is that it is more efficient and of better quality than that of commercial competitors. The latter have the edge in offering longer opening hours – often 24 hours – and material unsuitable for library shelves. Public libraries, on the other hand, generally provide a far wider range of material than commercial video outlets thus offering the public greater choice in video viewing. The way in which libraries have been shown to be able to respond to demand for new materials illustrates the strength of the principle upon which they are based – that of public ownership of resources which are then made available for everyone to use.

In addition to demands for material other than in printed formats there was also the evidence of need presented by the Adult Literacy Campaign of the 1970s and during the same period the recognition of the needs of cultural and ethnic minorities who were unused to print as the dominant medium or to the use of English as their main language. Librarians were heavily involved in the Adult Literacy Campaign and many also began to take special interest in the library needs of ethnic minorities.

While most librarians like to think that libraries are now multi-media, there is a traditional section of the profession who believe that the role of the library service is simply to provide books and any concern with other materials serves only to undermine the position of the book. This dilemma is reinforced by the fact that many local authorities have refused to fund the full expansion of library services in respect of other materials provision and have insisted that provision should be partly or even wholly self-financing.

Television has had a considerable influence on the provision of library services. Initially thought to be responsible for a drop in library use, watching TV probably now does more to stimulate people to read than to deter them. Novels that have mouldered on library shelves for years are in high demand once they have been televised. The introduction that television provides into a wide range of subject areas stimulates interest which people go on to follow up through printed material. Many television programmes now specifically direct people to other materials. As well as formal educational pro-grammes, eg Open University, this is the case with many programmes on Channel 4 and increasingly on other stations too. The video-loan collections already referred to which were introduced in the main as the result of demand for feature films (the audio-visual equivalent of light fiction) are increasingly providing material on video which is particularly suited to that medium and complements rather than competes with the rest of the library's collections, eg instructional material, natural history and opera, ballet and drama.

The influence of the television medium is likely to continue with the possibilities provided by viewdata systems and cable. The former (TV and telephone) provides the potential for information stored in libraries (or in data banks elsewhere) to be made widely available in an easily accessible form which is also capable of manipulation by the user. Some library systems have been involved in such developments for a number of years but the introduction of Freedom of Information Legislation in 1986 could provide the push to local authorities to properly finance such developments. There is no doubt that many councils have been shown to be making inadequate provision for informing people about their policies and services and the development of viewdata systems which are particularly suited to locally based information which requires frequent updating offer an imaginative way forward.

If a cable network were ever fully developed in this country and viewed as a public service (like the telephone network) rather than as a vehicle for commerical gain, it could also offer the opportunity for developing information systems linked to libraries opening up a wealth of opportunities for people pursuing learning opportunities by enabling them to access material for their studies directly in their own home.

The developments in new technology in general are affecting the ways in which public libraries provide important parts of their services and the kinds of services they can offer. No longer need individual library systems be reliant on their own literature holdings or even dependent on inter-loan arrangements with other libraries in this country and abroad. It is now a simple, though somewhat costly process, to access remote data bases covering all kinds of subjects via on-line computer links. Not only does this provide access for users to a wealth of information but the on-line facility allows users to interrogate the data base and manipulate information far faster and far more thoroughly than is possible by manual means. The ramifications of this are enormous, particularly for users of information with economic value. As a result a new information industry has developed in recent years operated by information brokers. These individuals usually work independently and specialise in the manipulation of on-line links to data bases in a limited area. Because of their specialised subject knowledge, familiarity with the data and the time and effort they are able to give to a single enquiry they are able to provide clients with a special level of information or information with 'added value'. This means that the information is not simply presented as it appears in the data base but is manipulated in order to bring out its full implications.

There is no reason why public libraries could not develop a similar level of service if additional resources were made available. It could even be a self-financing service if that were felt to be appropriate. Some public libraries have the bases of such arrangements already in the form of co-operative schemes which link commercial, industrial and public libraries within a particular locality for the purpose of sharing resources in terms of materials, staff expertise, training opportunities and often providing a specialised and higher level information service to constituent members. For the benefits obtained from such an arrangement members pay an annual subscription. SINTO – the Sheffield Interchange Organisation – was the first of these schemes to be developed in the 1940's. Initially it linked the public library, on which it was based, with librarians and information officers employed by the major industries (mainly steel producers) in the city. Arising from their special needs for metals information the world metals index, an internationally important but still manual data base, was developed. SINTO is still in existence but it is a sign of the times that most of its members now represent service industries, eg banks and academic institutions, and representation from industry has rapidly declined. Similar schemes in other parts of the country are now far more vibrant and progressive, eg HERTIS based on Hertfordshire Polytechnic Library and LADSIRLAC based on Liverpool Central Library.[1]

Whatever the potential, however, this is an area of development in which the present government does not believe public libraries should be involved. Their view, clearly expressed in recent annual reports on library matters by the Minister for the Arts and in a document produced for the Cabinet by the Information Technology Advisory Panel in 1983 entitled 'Making a Business of Information' is that responsibility for developing the commercial uses of information through the utilisation of new technology should be a commercial venture undertaken by the private sector. Even amongst library and information professionals there are differences in views about this. Accepting the principle that certain kinds of information should be charged for will endanger the principle of free access to information for all. Yet the costs of accessing information via new technology applications are high and individual enquiries undertaken can be costed quite accurately. Moreover it is likely that the majority of users will be corporate users who might expect increased profits as a result of using the information or students following a formal research project for which they are being financed. So why shouldn't a charge be made? Already a number of libraries are making elaborate arrangements to ensure that individuals are able to access information on-line free of charge whilst corporate users pay the full or a subsidised cost. This is messy and at the end of the day there are important principles to be settled. The influence of new technology in public information provision can only become progressively more important.

The role of the commerical sector

The main area of commercial supply operating in the same area as
public libraries are publishers and bookshops. Bookshops and
libraries do not see themselves to be in competition. All evidence
suggests that book borrowing and book purchase are linked activities
– people who borrow books will buy books and vice versa. Public
libraries are prevented under the terms of the section of the Local
Government Act on Local Authority Trading from selling books for
profit other than their own publications and discarded library books.

Many publishers and book sellers are heavily dependent upon
their sales to public libraries and public library business is so
significant that there are a number of firms who specialise in library
supply and deal only with libraries. They operate on such a large
scale that they can command large discounts from publishers and
also provide special services to libraries in the form of labelling and
jacketing of books so they are ready for library shelves, inspection
copies of new books for librarians, and special current information
listings.

Originally library suppliers were independent and even family run
firms but in recent years a number have been the subject of takeover bids and mergers. This is illustrated by the rise of John Menzies'
library supply business. This is the firm with the nationally famous
chain of newsagents and bookshops which now also has the largest
supply business in the country. The basis of Menzies' library supply
empire was two family firms – Woolstons and Blunts who merged in
the early seventies. Throughout the seventies the company traded
under the name Woolstons & Blunts but its status changed. In the
mid-seventies it was taken over by an American company involved
in library supply in North America – Collier MacMillan Distributors
Services. A couple of years later it came into the hands of another
British based company – Lonsdale Universal who dealt in international library supply with interests in North America, North Africa
and Australia as well as dealings in technical publishing and commercial stationery. In the early eighties this company took over
another major and old established British library supply business –
Cambridge Jackson (also originally two companies). Finally in 1982
John Menzies took over the lot. In 1983 Menzies acquired John
Coutts Library Services Limited, of Canada. Library suppliers are
becoming bigger and fewer in number. W H Smith, Menzies main
rivals in the bookshop area have recently taken over the country's
largest paperback library supplier – Books for Students. They are
also said to be interested in purchasing one of the very few remaining
independent traditional library suppliers should one become
available. This interest in library supply might suggest that the commercial world foresees the sudden blossoming of public library

budgets. In fact what they are probably all interested in is not supply to libraries in this country but the supply of English books to libraries in other parts of the world – which is becoming very big business. John Menzies is now the largest library supplier in Australia.

For the most part neither bookshops nor publishers are independent but belong to large chains particularly in the case of the latter often multi-national. The last few years have seen a spate of international mergers and takeovers of publishing companies with the names of Maxwell and Murdoch frequently to the fore. British publishing is big business with a turnover of over £2 billion in 1985 and more than thirty per cent of production exported. The results of takeovers and mergers are bigger and better capitalised publishing companies offering bigger advances (eg £625,000 to Michael Holroyd in 1987 for a yet to be completed biography of George Bernard Shaw), longer term commissions and more intensive marketing. Even more books are being published – currently about 850 new titles come onto the market each week in Britain – but fewer books are being bought. Consequently in order to attract the maximum number of purchasers publishing output is becoming blander resulting, paradoxically in less choice for the reader despite an increasing number of titles. Bookselling chains have grown too, also as a result of takeovers and mergers. Between 1983 and 1987 the six major quality bookselling chains increased their shop square footage from 953,000 to 1.13m. Competition seems to be ever-increasing as chains deliberately pursue a policy of opening new shops in close proximity to their competitors. The result is that major towns and cities are usually now very well covered by major bookselling chains whilst smaller towns and villages often remain without any book shop provision. Small independent bookshops and publishers have a difficult existence as profit margins are low. The large profits made by the large publishing and bookselling chains is the result of their size and the fact that they operate more efficiently.

Books are one of the few commodities still subject to Resale Price Maintenance which limits the scope for competition. The provisions of the Net Book Agreement make it illegal to sell books at other than the published price with one or two notable exceptions which are: if they are remaindered by the publisher (ie they are the end of the print run and are no longer selling at the published price) or they are reprinted and sold through a book club. Libraries which are open to the public are able to purchase books at a discount of ten per cent on the publishers price – no more and no less – through a related agreement with the Publishers and Book Sellers Association known as the Library Licence. Supporters of the Net Book Agreement (first instituted in 1956) say that it protects the book market by ensuring that a wide range of titles is published and that publishers and booksellers are not drawn into a situation where they publish and sell only those books which will have wide popular appeal. Similar concerns were voiced when it was suggested that the Government might impose a standard rate of VAT on books. Moves within the European Community towards the harmonisation of VAT rates on individual commodities by 1991 mean that this remains a very real possibility in the not too distant future. Without testing out this theory in a practical way it is difficult to know how true the claims are. Instinctively people in the bookworld – librarians, publishers, booksellers – join together to oppose any move which might seem to undermine the important and special position of the book but it is sometimes difficult to believe that the large profits of the multi-national publishers in particular can be so vulnerable. The balance of books being published has been changing anyway without alterations to the Net Book Agreement or VAT level. More books are being published than ever but the growth is in the area of highly priced 'coffee table' books and popular fiction and non-fiction. Publishing in specialist areas – first novels, children's books – is declining. The publishing and bookselling lobby is a very powerful one, witness the strength and money behind the anti-VAT campaign, but it seems inevitable that cracks will appear in the Net Book Agreement before too long. If they do it will be the small independent bookshops and publishers who will go to the wall.

A development in recent years has been the entry into bookselling of leading chain stores. The first was Marks and Spencer who have lately been followed by Sainsbury's. Both stores sell a range of cookery books, books about home improvements and soft furnishings. Marks and Spencer have a range of general interest books and both stores sell books for children. The books are published under the stores' own brand name and usually they are unique publications. However, Sainsbury's have recently introduced a range of children's picture books which are almost identical in format and by the same author as a range published by a traditional publisher. The difference is the price – the Sainsbury's versions cost considerably less. There is a question of whether this infringes the Net Book Agreement. Sainsbury's have also begun a marketing campaign which takes the line that as well as caring for children's bodies by selling nutritious food, Sainsbury's now cares for children's minds.

The advent of aggressive marketing of books by publishers and booksellers is a phenomenon associated with the development of multi-national companies. Books are now advertised before publication on television. Pre-publication serial rights are sold to leading newspapers. More space in newspapers and magazines is devoted to reviews and advertising of books and *The Sunday Times* has recently introduced a special weekly Book Supplement. The number of programmes devoted specifically to books on radio and television is increasing. Prizes are given which attract widespread media coverage. Finalists for the Booker McConnell prize are guaranteed to be best sellers yet the prize itself is only worth £15,000. Bookshops use gimmicks to draw attention to book launches. Chains of new bookshops are being opened with an up to date modern image, lengthy opening hours into the evening, offering tea or coffee to customers whilst they browse. The Publishers Association supports a special section (formerly a semi-autonomous body known as the Book Marketing Council) whose role is to promote books in all possible ways through special posters, TV and radio coverage, articles in the press etc. All of this suggests that some books at least are big business.

Finally, there is an area of bookselling and publishing which is at the other end of the spectrum to the highly commercial profit-oriented undertakings. Radical or alternative publishers and booksellers exist to give a voice to those publications which would not normally be taken up by the commercial sector. Although their livelihood is generally insecure, some publishers which began in this area, for example Virago and the Women's Press publishing feminist material and Pluto Press specialising in publishing Left Wing political material have become commercial successes with their works now sold in established bookshops too. In Sheffield the City Council has a policy of buying from the local radical bookshop whenever possible.

It is difficult to predict where bookselling and publishing might go in the next two decades. It is likely that the commercialism attached to certain areas of the book market will develop even further. Advertising and promoting books has been shown to work, they do become best-sellers. Probably the competition between individual publishers and individual booksellers will intensify resulting in a smaller number of bigger chains and conglomerates. This can only be bad news for book production in general since the range of titles published and sold is likely to diminish although not the number of titles. It is becoming increasingly difficult for the first novel, the work of serious non-fiction, the children's book which does not have a novelty attraction, to find a publisher. The ground on which the Net Book Agreement is based is becoming progressively more shaky. If it falls the result is likely to be spiralling book prices, the close of all small independent bookshops and publishers and a further restriction in the range of titles published. If commercialism gains any more control over publishing and selling it is difficult to see how books can continue to retain their VAT-free status, particularly with the likelihood of pressure also from the EEC.

The alternative to all of this would be some form of state control of publishing or even better local authority publishing as a municipal enterprise. In this way the quality and range of published titles could be preserved. However, the traditional structure of publishing and bookselling is too well established to contemplate this scenario becoming reality.

Financing the public library service

The capital provision for the library service in Sheffield in recent years is similar to that in the rest of the country. Newly built libraries are few and far between and usually result from the existence of external funding, for example Urban Programme from central government or a property developer if the scheme is part of an overall development, (for example a shopping centre), a specific political commitment to part of a city, county or town, the need to replace an existing library building because of accident or age. Libraries have to compete with other services which may be deemed to be more politically deserving in the struggle to obtain capital funding – for example Housing and Social Services and also Sports, Arts and Museums provision. Also in recent years central government has progressively squeezed the amount of money local authorities can devote to new capital projects and increasingly too the restrictions on revenue expenditure mean that even if capital funding is available for new buildings the additional running costs are difficult if not impossible to find.

The situation is not necessarily as bleak in all parts of the country. In Manchester imaginative use has been made of Inner City Partnership Funding to build a large number of new libraries/community cultural centres and also to convert and improve many existing buildings. In some authorities money is still available from the mainline programme for large scale new build schemes, eg Derbyshire County Council have just opened a new library in Chesterfield at a cost of over £3m.

Revenue provision for the library service in Sheffield has always remained fairly stable and at an appropriate level in relation to other authorities in terms of the population it has to serve. In the mid to late seventies reductions were made in support areas of the budget, eg training, furniture and equipment and general maintenance and the accumulated effects are now being felt quite badly. The Materials Fund which is used principally to buy books has been badly affected by inflation over the last ten years. Although the general rate of inflation has been added each year books have been affected by above average inflation and during some years the rate has been as high as thirty per cent. Since 1986 the Council has been forced through the increasing restrictions on local authority finance as a result of rate capping and declining levels of the rate-support grant, to make reductions in the level of all the services it provides. Although public libraries have been reasonably well protected they have not been immune from cuts with the result that decreasing expenditure on staff has resulted in reduced hours of opening of libraries.

Nationally expenditure in libraries looks to have remained relatively stable in recent years. In fact revenue expenditure has suffered at the expense of capital and public libraries have fared worse as a result of greater expenditure on the British Library and specifically the costs of building the new British Library complex at St Pancras.

Public libraries are almost totally funded by the local authority. There is some income from users through fines for non return of books, charges for use of materials other than books, eg video and music, charges for services such as photocopying, photographic reproduction and sales of library produced publications. There is scope for achieving small amounts of grant-aid, eg from Regional Arts Associations and the British Library but this is for particular projects rather than for the day to day running of the service. Funding of certain posts through Section II of the Local Government Act of 1966 and the Urban Programme is used by many libraries and recently there appear to be some possibilities for funding to be obtained from the EEC.

Central government's view is that there is considerable scope for private sector involvement in the provision of library services either by the public sector giving up particular aspects of the service altogether (as referred to earlier) or by local authorities contracting out certain parts of the service to commercial contractors who, they believe, could supply the service at reduced costs, for example, the provision of light fiction material. Since library services are already provided very cheaply – in Sheffield a high quality service is provided at a cost of approximately £10 per head of population per year – it is difficult to see that the latter development would in fact reduce costs. In 1987 a publication entitled 'Joint enterprise: Roles and relationships of the public and private sectors in the provision of library and information services' outlined the possibilities for joint private/public sector partnerships with some actual examples, which libraries could pursue. The reaction of most librarians was that the material contained in the report described very few areas of activity that most library authorities had not been pursuing for a number of years.

The Government also believes that there is considerable scope for income generation by libraries and for obtaining sponsorship. Some libraries have indeed gone to town on the generation of income, the London Borough of Sutton being a particularly significant example. Amusement machines, eg space invaders are provided in libraries, space is sold to double-glazing salesmen and other forms of advertising are undertaken and a wide range of items such as badges, tee-shirts, novelties as well as the library's own publications are sold. Despite this the scope for income generation is considered to be limited. The public do not expect to pay to any great extent for the use of library services so there is a cut-off point beyond which it is counter-productive to raise charges for the use of services or materials other than books. Sales and advertising do not generate significant amounts of income particularly if the staff time involved in arranging such activities is costed in. These were also the conclusions reached by CIPFA when they undertook research in 1982 for the British Library on the scope for income generation by librarians. It was also the view expressed by the Library and Information Services Council (the body which advises the Minister for the Arts on Library issues) in their appendix to the report of the Minister for the Arts on Library and Information Matters during 1984.

Finally, although sponsorship or benefaction may have played a considerable part in the history of public libraries, the opportunity for obtaining all but very limited amounts are very few if not non-existent. Sponsors with large amounts of money to distribute are looking for activities which will project their names to large numbers of people through prestige and preferably televised events. There is definitely scope for large amounts of sponsorship for national and international arts and sports events but libraries are a local service and do not attract such attention.

Central government's ideas about the future financing of public libraries have been set out in a Consultation Document entitled 'Financing our Public Library Service: Four Subjects for Debate'. The premise on which the Green Paper is based is that public libraries would be able to develop their service in directions which would satisfy their clients if they were able to find ways of financing such developments other than through public expenditure. It is suggested that library authorities could raise their gross annual income from about £22m now to over £50m without damage to their basic service. There are two issues here, first the introduction of the concept of the 'basic service' which the Green Paper attempts to define, and secondly the proposed increase in income which is based on dubious figures and relates to gross rather than to net income. Even if library authorities were able to raise the suggested amount the impact would be minimal amounting to about fifteen pence per head of population nationally in return for a great deal of effort. Having said this there are also doubts about whether the measures outlined would bring in the proposed increase in income. The charges for other than the 'basic' service (largely the borrowing of books up to a certain number and excluding categories such as new fiction and biographies and the personal use of reference services) would be discretionary, it is said. The suggestion is that charges for other services, eg the loan of audio-visual materials should be at an economic rate. Joint relationships with the private sector are encouraged but, as mentioned earlier, many library authorities have already pursued initiatives in this direction. Finally possible areas of service which could be contracted out are proposed and it is here the report is probably the most flawed as it is unable to demonstrate why the particular services described have been selected or how they could be run more cheaply under contracting-out arrangements than under public control. The question of who in the private sector might choose to run them is not addressed at all. Finally the report refers to anomalies and limitations on charging for services at present which it intends to remove but the impression given is that these are merely a peg on which to hang proposals for the erosion of what has until now been a service provided virtually free at the point of use.

Organising the public library service

Sheffield City Libraries is one of the larger library authorities in Britain. The organisation employs approximately 600 people. About one hundred of these are employed on manual grades – cleaners, drivers, handymen, security attendants, the rest are professional librarians – about one hundred – library assistants and general clerical and administrative staff. Numerically these numbers are not sufficient. The use of the service has increased enormously in the last decade, particularly through people using libraries for information as opposed to simply borrowing books, but staff numbers have barely increased at all in that time. Salaries are low at all levels. One of the major reasons for this is that the majority of staff employed in libraries are female.

Eighty-eight per cent of the staff in Sheffield Libraries are women yet the majority of posts at the highest levels are occupied by men.

Working conditions tend to be poor too. Unsocial hours are worked – generally two evenings each week until eight or nine o'clock and alternate Saturdays. In some authorities there are extra payments for this but in others, like Sheffield, there are not. Job security is as reasonable as in any aspect of the public service but as in many authorities libraries are experiencing a greater share of cuts than other services this is unlikely to continue.

The numbers of people employed in public libraries both in

Sheffield and nationally has remained reasonably static in recent years although in Sheffield there has been a slight increase whilst nationally numbers have fallen slightly. Nationally, the number of professional librarians has fallen whilst numbers of (lower paid) non-professional staff have increased. The number of places at polytechnic and universities for aspiring professional librarians is also decreasing as numbers of teaching staff are reduced. A number of reviews on the provision of facilities for librarianship education and training have recommended a reduction in the number of places and the closure of several of the existing Departments of Librarianship. There are currently twenty of these in universities and polytechnics throughout the UK. Students undertake either a three year under-graduate course or a one year post-graduate course.

Until three years ago it was possible to qualify via a two year diploma course. This route was particularly suited to the less academically inclined or people wishing to enter the profession later in life when family and personal commitments make the shortest possible route to qualification attractive. However, it was the desire of the profession generally that it should become an all-graduate one. Once having acquired formal qualifications students have to undertake a minimum of two years paid, supervised employment at the end of which they are required to submit a final dissertation to the professional body, the Library Association. If this is deemed to be satisfactory they are granted the status of a Chartered Librarian.

In recent years the undergraduate route to qualification has become the most popular because of reductions in the number of bursaries available for graduates in other disciplines wishing to become librarians. There is a strongly held view that because of this the profession is losing many of the most able potential recruits. In addition, because the minimum requirement for entry to a course is the normal university or polytechnic requirement for entry to any undergraduate course many people who might make excellent professional librarians are barred. This applies particularly to candidates from ethnic minorities or disadvantaged social backgrounds. For these people and for those who wish to qualify later in life there is a growing demand for day-release opportunities and these are now being provided in some parts of the country.

As it was noted earlier, the pay levels for all staff employed in libraries are low. There are moves to improve the position of both professional and non-professional staff. Until 1984 there was a nationally agreed minimum grade within the NJC Scheme of Conditions for chartered librarians employed in professionally designated posts; this was scale 4. Following a joint investigation by the employers and the staff side it was concluded that it was no longer practical to specify a national grade since the kinds of work the professional librarians were employed to undertake varied greatly across the country. The national prescription was removed with the recommendation that there should be local negotiations to agree appropriate gradings for both professional and non-professional staff. In Sheffield it has recently been possible to agree on a grading structure which allows for a career structure for non-professional staff which takes account of length of experience, ability and at higher levels formal administrative and managerial qualifications achieved, whilst at the same time improving the gradings of lower levels of professional staff. The different roles of professional and non-professional staff have been clarified so that non-professionals are not simply seen as doing work which is less demanding and inferior to that of professionals but are seen to have vital and separate functions to pursue. For the first time higher levels of non-professional staff will be paid above the lower levels of professional staff. Almost inevitably the next two decades will see a change in the structure of employment within libraries from a two tier to a three tier system. This will allow for a technical level of expertise – people with supervisory or specialist or special skills in new areas of development, eg computers, video, arts administration – between the general routine and clerical level and the professional managerial level.

A further issue which is important for employment conditions within libraries is that of job-sharing. Particularly because of the large number of female employees but also because of the nature of the work, job-sharing is a logical development. In Sheffield, although total numbers of staff employed in the libraries department are relatively low, it has more job-sharing pairs than any other department of the council.

As far as overall trends in future decades are concerned the prediction must be that the overall numbers of professional librarians will decrease if only because the opportunities to qualify are being reduced. There is not a particularly high level of unemployment in the profession at present although there is some and numbers are rising. If numbers of library staff stay the same the trend towards employing a greater number of non-professional staff will inevitably continue. This situation will be exacerbated if current restrictions on local authority expenditure remain. Government recommendations are also for the replacement of staff in libraries by machines to enable more money to be released for the purchase of books. Although most libraries are now using technology for the routine clerical work associated with the loan of books, the further scope for this kind of development is very limited and the number of jobs that could be saved is very small. The suggestion only proves that the present government does not really understand the proper nature of a library service.

The degree of trade union organisation in libraries varies throughout the country but by and large librarians are passive by nature. The fact that they have accepted low pay levels and poor conditions of employment for so long demonstrates this. The particularly iniquitous cuts in services in some parts of the country in recent years have forced some librarians to become more militant. The Library Association has hitherto frowned upon such militancy denouncing it as politically motivated. Consequently library workers have been forced to organise outside their professional association and have set up groups called LOAF (Libraries Open and Free) and at the beginning of 1984, the national Library Campaign, which is based in Sheffield but steered by a committee of representatives from across the country, was formed. Since the establishment of the Library Campaign, strong links have been established with NALGO nationally and with some local branches and the union has been generous in financing the campaign. To put this kind of activity into perspective, however, it still only involves a small minority of library workers.

There is less universal agreement about the most important interests and aims of the profession than was the case in former years. Most librarians would point to the principle of the free library service – freedom of access for all irrespective of the ability to pay. Yet this principle has been eroded over the years by the introduction of charges for some elements of the service and is likely to be eroded further in response to the further development of information technology, and the consequences of the government's Green Paper on the future financing of libraries referred to earlier. Another value which librarians profess to hold is their neutrality or impartiality.

To some of us it seems naive to deny that libraries are themselves part of or agents of a political process. Information is not neutral so how can the collectors and providers of information profess to be? The breakdown of the principle of neutrality is more likely to occur as society becomes more polarised politically. This is not to suggest that librarians themselves will have to embrace party political policies but they will have to undertake and decide upon the relationship between the nature of the information and materials provided by their service and the political complexion of the local authority which directs their services. In recent years responses by librarians and their local authority employees to issues of censorship resulting from the News International Industrial Dispute and the Spycatcher case have brought this issue into the open.

Who uses the service? How can new users be encouraged?

Generally between thirty and forty per cent of the population are regular users of libraries. Provided that the level of resource input does not decrease much further and particularly if it were to increase, it is likely that even more people would use libraries in the future. The enormous increase in the use of libraries in Barnsley and other districts in South Yorkshire during the Miners' Strike illustrates what happens when people suddenly find themselves with unusual amounts of free time and little money. In addition to larger numbers of people without employment in the future there will be a greater proportion of elderly people in the population and they are particularly keen users of libraries.

Although people of all ages and social classes use libraries, use is heaviest amongst those who are elderly and middle class. The central focus of libraries is still the printed word and so people who are less able at reading are more likely not to be users, as are members of ethnic minorities not simply because they may be less than totally familiar with English but also because they may also be unfamiliar with the public library as an institution. Although children use libraries in substantial numbers, teenagers tend not to unless they are students. This is because libraries offer little to people in this age group and the attitude of many librarians is unsympathetic towards their behaviour, language and style of dress. In addition libraries are often targets for vandalism and disruptive behaviour often being the only public building which is open and has free entry on a winter evening. Overall libraries in middle class areas are better used than ones in working class areas though this is not always the case. The other occurrences of under use are amongst those people who for various reasons are unable to visit a library, for example the physically handicapped, the sick, those in prison or those with handicaps making it difficult for them to use libraries, for example the deaf, visually handicapped and mentally handicapped.

In 1978 the then Library Advisory Council for England and Wales published a report entitled 'The Libraries Choice' which drew attention to a number of groups (predominantly those listed above) who experienced difficulties in gaining access to a library service. The report listed examples of good practice which it encouraged all library authorities to adopt, for example providing books in their mother tongue and appropriate audio visual materials for ethnic minorities; attempting to reach inner city residents in non-traditional ways, for example by visiting youth clubs and community centres or taking specially adapted mobile libraries there. Many of these strategies are still employed but in addition, thankfully, the approach is becoming more sophisticated in some instances. One of the reasons why libraries in inner city areas are used less is because they are likely to have received the worst deal in terms of resource allocation. The buildings are likely to be older and more outdated, standards of maintenance lower, input of new books and other materials less and the gradings and experience of staff poor in comparison with colleagues in other areas. This is because until recently the prime measure of the success or failure of a library service was, and still is in some instances, the number of books a library lends. In inner city areas people are more likely to call in and sit and read in the library because it's warm and they don't have a car to drive them there and whisk them back home and the population of the library's catchment area is likely to be smaller. Issue performance (of books) when used as a guide to resource allocation began a gradually downward spiral. The policy now, in Sheffield at least, is to give priority to inner city libraries which now have the best graded staff, additional allocations for the purchase of materials, priority in terms of spending on maintenance, equipment and capital improvements.

Special provision for members of ethnic minority groups has developed beyond the provision of mother tongue materials. There is now a wide range of cultural activities which are intended not only to show members of ethnic minorities that the library service endorses and embraces their cultures but also to help to introduce the indigenous population to other cultures. An increasingly controversial area is that of the removal of racist (and also sexist) materials from libraries. There are basically three views: firstly that all racist and sexist material should be removed from library shelves; secondly, that the worst examples of sexist and racist material should be removed but the main thrust of efforts should be directed towards educating people about the best and worst aspects of material they find in libraries; thirdly, that any suggestion that any material should be removed, whatever problems there might be with it, represents censorship and should not be engaged in by a professional librarian. These viewpoints are constantly discussed and debated and different library services accordingly pursue different policies.

In addition to increasing the range of materials provided in libraries so that people who do not easily assimilate information through the printed word or find reading a relaxing and enjoyable occupation can find the medium which does appeal to them, libraries are also trying to extend the range of services and activities which are offered in order to provide a more relevant service to particular sections of the community. One of the most important areas of service development in the past decade has been that of Community Information which is usually defined as 'information which people need in the course of their everyday lives – information about their homes, their jobs and their rights': ('Community Information: What Libraries Can Do'.

Report of a Working Party on Community Information, published by the Library Association in 1980.) Traditionally libraries are places where people go to get unchanging, factual information which can be found in books, eg 'which is the longest river in Africa or the highest mountain in South America?'. Such information is not of direct relevance to people in inner city areas struggling to maintain their homes and families on low incomes. Most libraries now make efforts to provide information about welfare benefits, rights and the law etc. It is also usual for advice agencies to operate regular advice sessions from libraries. (This happens in more than half of the 38 libraries in Sheffield). A major area of controversy has been whether, when dealing with this kind of information which often does require interpretation by the provider depending on individual circumstances and an awareness of how rapidly such information changes, librarians move beyond mere information provision into the area of advice. The division is between those in the profession who say that the librarian's role is to provide information, not to interpret it or advise people about the consequences of using information and those who say that this is an unrealistic stance, that good librarians have never simply placed information in front of people but have always helped them to make the best use of it. The fact that the controversy has arisen in relation to this area of information provision has probably more to do with the fact that it is an area which some librarians feel unhappy about dealing in rather than simply problems with regard to an extension of their role. There are a number within the profession who feel that this kind of service or indeed any which positively discriminates towards disadvantaged sections of society is moving into the area of social work rather than librarianship.

Activities are also being developed in some libraries which encourage people to participate actively rather than as passive observers or consumers. Because of their network, position and facilities librarians have the potential to become community cultural centres with provision for community arts and media activities. Rather than simply providing materials for people to use, it seems obvious that libraries should also be the places where people become actively involved in the production of materials. Creative writing for example should be shown to be something that everyone has the potential for, not simply a few people who happen to have written books which appear on library shelves and video equipment and micro-computers give ordinary people the power to express themselves and realise their own creative potential. In Sheffield during recent years key staff have been appointed within the Libraries Department to work in the areas of creative writing, community arts and media.

A scheme called 'Write Back' has been developed which operates in the Central Library and increasing numbers of branch libraries in the city. Its purpose is to encourage people to write or to make public the writing they are already producing. Libraries have display boards and racks for materials people wish to display, word processors for people to produce their work on and offer cheap photocopying and a publishing programme. A range of activities such as workshops and talks by authors are provided in association with the scheme. Notably, regular workshops are now organised for and by Afro-Caribbean writers, a sampler of local women's writing has been published and financial and practical support has recently been given to publishing projects by Women Against Pit Closures Group. Two community arts workers are employed whose brief is to support the development of community arts in Sheffield by assisting groups to secure funding and venues and by introducing community arts activities in communities where there is a perceived need. These activities may be based in a library or elsewhere as appropriate; however, the library is often the chosen venue. During the past year various craft, printing, banner making, drama and mural activities have taken place. Even if the library is not the venue for the activity it does provide an exhibition space to show the rest of the community what has been achieved. The fourth appointment has been that of a Community Media worker who concentrates on raising awareness about the value of video as a community resource and means of expression. Of all four posts this is perhaps the one most logically linked with the traditional public library service. Libraries are involved with the communication process. Print, formerly the dominant medium of communication has now been overtaken by television. The public library network has tremendous potential for distributing video, not just the mainstream commercial products but the output of independent and community producers which have limited value without an audience. The Community Media worker is investigating ways in which the distribution network can be developed at the same time as encouraging groups and individuals within communities to recognise the potential of video.

The same kinds of developments are happening elsewhere. In Gateshead the library service has had a Community Arts Team for some time and has also been involved in community television projects. In Manchester, inner city partnership funding has been used to develop libraries as community cultural centres. Many new buildings have been developed which incorporate provision for a wide range of activities – community rooms, video, printing, pottery and dark room facilities, interior and exterior performance space. Older buildings have also been remodelled to provide these facilities. The GLC, although not a library authority, recognised the potential of libraries. The view was that public libraries and the broadcast media were the two most important networks for the distribution of arts and culture.

Increasingly the distinction between the library building and the rest of the community is becoming blurred. Library services are no longer seen as being provided in buildings but wherever is most appropriate in a community. Librarians are recognising the need to become involved with community organisations and use their expertise about access to and use of information for the benefit of tenants groups, pensioners, mothers with young children etc. Taking the service out into the community both through personal contact and by placing collections of materials in places where people congregate is another way of reaching people who will not, for one reason or another, visit a library building.

Finally, another area of growing importance is that of helping people to use libraries in order that they realise the benefit of them and are able to make the most use of them. There are resources available in libraries which would be of great benefit to particular groups, eg trade unionists, women's and peace groups but their existence is not widely realised. Increasingly librarians are recognising the need to direct their services at particular groups with particular needs. Rather than simply providing information and waiting for people to discover it the relationship is being seen as a more active one with librarians collecting information and materials on the basis of need and then promoting them to groups identified as having those needs. The library service with the general aim of providing a service to the general public has been seen to be less successful than it might have been simply because 'the general public' does not exist.

What are the key social changes which will affect the service?

The decline of society's traditional economic base in manufacturing industries has not yet had widespread implications for public leisure provision. Leisure provision is only slowly coming to be seen as other than peripheral to the main business of economic regeneration. The GLC is the only body which has looked at the concept of cultural and leisure industries in any detailed way and in practical terms the only schemes have been limited to token sports provision within redevelopment schemes, eg the Lower Don Valley in Sheffield and tourism projects and in this area there has probably been most success. Hebden Bridge in West Yorkshire is an example of a town which was dying after the decline of the textile industry but now has a thriving tourist industry. Wigan, a town with few outstanding features has recently renovated the main one – Wigan Pier – as both a tourist attraction and an educational facility where people can see the history of the Industrial Revolution revealed in practical terms. The glass industry of the Black Country is being rejuvenated on the basis of formerly derelict machinery and buildings and ancient skills of glass making are being revived. There is a need for more research into how a public leisure industry, far broader in scope than the present commercial leisure industry, could be developed, given that so many more people will have so much more leisure time in the future.

Within the area of the public libraries' remit reference has already been made to the possibilities in terms of state publishing (either central or local). In the previous section the potential of libraries to act as a distributive network for independent and community video producers was noted. The opportunities in respect of public input into media development are far broader than this. There is no reason why central or local government, particularly the latter, should not invest in, for example, film and TV production and distribution and music recording. The main stumbling block seems not to be whether projected developments are viable either in a strictly commercial sense or in terms of the area of benefit, but whether they are the kind of activities which ought to be publically funded.

The major problem for the development of leisure provision at the present time is that people with the greatest amount of leisure time tend, in the main, to be those with the least money. This results in two tiers of leisure provision. The private and part of the public sector is directed towards people who can afford to pay to participate in activities which will entertain them or help them to rest and recover from work whilst the remainder of public provision is having to respond to increasing numbers of people who are simply trying to occupy their time. However, many people remain at a distance from any kind of provision simply because they are unable to face the stigma attached to activities which are specifically provided or are provided at a subsidised rate for people who are unemployed. Public libraries, parks and in some though not all cases, art galleries and museums are the only facilities which are genuinely free for everyone to use and therefore do not have this stigma attached. This is a situation which public leisure providers must face whatever happens in terms of economic restructuring at either a macro- or a micro-level.

If work and economic resources were ever able to be shared on the basis of need, the demand for leisure opportunities of all kinds would increase. A leisure based society particularly of an artistic, cultural or educational nature offers a satisfying alternative future to the present economically oriented one. Personal productivity rather than economic productivity would be the key feature and the goal that people would aim for.

Specifically in relation to developments within the public library service increasing unemployment will inevitably mean increasing use probably particularly within the following areas:

1 Community Information – as people struggle to find their way through the mass of rules and regulations involved in claiming benefits.

2 Learning opportunities – both in the formal sense of attendance at classes and educational events organised by libraries but also use of library facilities to pursue independent and personal learning programmes.

3 Use of newspaper and magazine provision and the library as a place to go to sit and be with other people in a warm and social atmosphere.

4 Attendance at arts and other cultural events and activities.

Employment is a major source of friendship for people. For some who live alone it offers the only opportunity for contact with other human beings. Unemployment obviously removes this opportunity but so do some of the new technological developments which result in people working at home. Add to this the growing number of possibilities for shopping, banking or obtaining other services through use of the television and telephone and it is clear that we are moving closer towards a society where people could spend most of their time in their own homes watching a TV screen. Even access to library services can be provided very easily in this way. To prevent this scenario there must be an emphasis on providing leisure opportunities which encourage people to come together and participate.

The crucial political attitude for public libraries is the attitude to the provision of a service which is basically free at the point of use. This idea is directly contrary to the monetarist policies of the present government. In fact the Minister of Arts had been recorded as saying – with direct reference to Public Libraries – 'If a charge is made for services, then the user will appreciate what he or she is getting, use will be restricted to those who really have an interest rather than a whim and extra resources are available for the service as a whole'. However, the government seems at present to be resisting advocating direct charges for all aspects of library services.

Freedom of access to information is also the central feature of the democratic process. Any attempt to control society must begin with restrictions on the availability of information. The profession is, by and large, against the idea of charging for any aspect of the service although there are individuals who feel the service *would* be a more valued one if people had to pay to use it and charging might also provide the prospect of more resources for a service which at least in some parts of the country is struggling to exist. Generally, staff would oppose the widespread introduction of charges as they would oppose moves to privatise or contract out aspects of the service. However organisations within the profession either trade union led or otherwise may not be strong enough to withstand any such moves. Given that it would, considering the nature of funding for the service, be a local authority decision for such moves to occur, one can envisage a situation where the principle could be lost very quickly due to capitulation by a few local authorities which are traditionally known to treat the library service very badly and where the staff have no will or ability to resist.

In geographical terms public libraries could be said to be the first decentralised public service with the first steps taken to establish the branch library network in Manchester in 1857. However services within individual local authorities often remain one of the most centralised managerially and professionally. The hierarchical structure with Chief Librarian and a small group of senior staff controlling the management and direction of the service is still found although in recent years more and more libraries departments have been restructuring on the basis of teams of staff responsible for particular aspects or geographical parts of the service. This allows staff in direct contact with users or potential users to control at least the day to day business of running the service and hopefully also to participate in discussions and decisions about general policy and direction.

Until recently too the general attitude about the provision of library services was that professional librarians knew best about what the public wanted or indeed, what the public ought to have. In recent years has come the realisation that it is this attitude which has led to the traditional image of libraries and librarians so often portrayed in TV comedy shows. The keynote of progressive library services is now to implement measures which assess people's needs or, ideally, work with communities through both groups and individuals, to help them to assess their own library needs. This is quite a difficult process given that the traditional image of what a library is and what librarians do is so strong. There is undoubtedly scope for community participation in the control of library services and facilities. On a simple level this could be in respect of where the mobile library stops through to the extent of involvement in staff appointments and selection of books and other materials.

The most critical demographic change will be the continued ageing of the population. This will increase the need to deliver the service especially to people in their own homes or in elderly persons' accommodation. This is an expensive way of providing a service. In addition a library service is more than simply a delivery system for books and other materials. Time spent with elderly people in understanding their needs and ensuring that they receive intellectual stimulation in order to keep them mentally and physically healthy is extremely important as the library service is likely to be the main source of leisure activity. Bibliotherapy is an important aspect of work with geriatrics; this is extremely demanding of staff time and the continuity of staff is also important.

Other areas of service provision where the nature or extent of demand is likely to change are in respect of, firstly, the libraries' community information role. Society and relationships within society are becoming increasingly complex so that people do require help to find their way through the mass of rules and regulations which govern everyday life. In addition people are far more willing to accept that they do need information to help them cope and no longer see a request for information as admitting a personal failure to sort out a problem. Secondly libraries like many public services are likely to be affected by the continued decline of the public transport system. In many cases, but particularly in cities, the service has been planned on the basis that people would have access to public transport to help them visit libraries. In Sheffield, the Central Lending Library is one of the busiest public lending libraries in the country despite the fact that Sheffield also has a large number of branch libraries per head of population. This is because the service has been planned on the assumption that certain types of more specialised material will only be available at the Central Library rather than duplicating provision of little used material at the expense of more general provision which it is known will be needed and widely used everywhere.

The scenario of a society in which the work ethic is no longer dominant (it is progressively no longer functional already!) would provide a power base for the public leisure service in which it would be able to achieve greater political commitment and as a result a higher level of resources. Leisure would be seen as an area of importance in its own right rather than as secondary to the main concerns of housing and jobs since leisure would replace work as the main activity which most people engaged in. The development of the concept of leisure can usefully be viewed as a three stage process:

Stage I – Full or almost full employment, work ethic dominant.
Leisure = opportunities for rest and recuperation.
Stage II – Growing unemployment, cracks in the work ethic principle.
Leisure = entertainment and relief from boredom.
Stage III – Age of leisure, work ethic no longer dominant.
Leisure = personal development (including social and community development).

The 'post industrial' society or the age of leisure offers a much brighter prospect for public libraries. The service is geared to providing for the needs of the purposive user than for those seeking entertainment although a considerable amount of use comes from those who are merely seeking to be entertained.

What organisation and resource changes will aid development of the service?

Changes in finance and subsidy of library services are dependent to a considerable extent upon the political complexion of the central government of the day. This is not to suggest that as a directly funded service by local authorities public libraries do not suffer under both Conservative and Socialist administrations; however an alteration of the principles surrounding the financing of the service is more likely to occur under a Conservative central government than any other. If the present government continues along the path it has already marked out one can anticipate a revision of the 1964 Public Libraries and Museum Act to allow local authorities to charge for the use of some aspects of the service including certain elements of book provision, together with encouragement to authorities to increase private sector involvement in the provision or financing of the service.

One of the particular requests from certain local authorities for a number of years has been that the financing of major regional reference libraries which service a larger population than that contained within the immediate area of the local authority should be a central government responsibility or should at least be recognised as a reason for a special allocation within the Grant Related Expenditure Assessment for Public Libraries. The present government has so far refused to accept the argument and feels secure in doing so because other local authorities do not want to see the big cities getting more despite the fact that for many of them the propinquity of a large central reference library means they can reduce expenditure on their own reference library services. However some cities are signalling that they are approaching crisis point and if cuts in public spending continue they will no longer be able to fulfil their regional function. The ten libraries considered to fulful a regional function are: Edinburgh, Glasgow, Newcastle, Leeds, Liverpool, Manchester, Sheffield, Birmingham, Belfast and the City of London – Guildhall.

The trend in recent years has been for greater central government control over leisure funding. In some cases this has been the result of back door measures like the Arts Council's 'Glory of the Garden' strategy which through the introduction of development money which demanded matching by local authorities enabled central government to dictate to a considerable extent that local authority funding of the arts was to be in those areas of the arts that they wished to see developed, namely the prestige 'high' art areas such as opera, ballet and classical music. The abolition of the Metropolitan Counties has resulted in even greater central funding of the arts since the Arts Council is responsible for them. The amount now made available falls considerably short of that previously provided by the Metropolitan Counties and it is inadequate to develop badly needed new initiatives and new areas of activity. Metropolitan District authorities have not been in a position to take on the latter either.

Whether increased centralisation occurring in the arts will be mirrored in libraries is difficult to say. The expectation is that by increasingly placing pressure on local authorities to spend on services according to the individual GRE assessment Central Government's priorities will be forced upon libraries. Because of the way in which the GREA for public libraries is calculated all authorities, even the ones which have been cutting back the service for years, spend above the GREA. Privately, civil servants recognise the problems inherent within the formula they use but publicly do nothing to amend it.

The prospect of greater involvement by the private sector in the provision of library and information services has been dealt with earlier. Whilst the public sector retains an interest in the provision of all aspects of these services the rights of individuals to free access to information will be maintained. However if the private sector take control in any area the principle of free access will be lost. As an example, there were until recently two legal on-line information services, Eurolex and Lexis. The owners of Lexis – Butterworths – made a successful takeover bid for Eurolex and a request that this deal should be investigated by the Monopolies Commission was rejected. The costs of subscribing to the single remaining service are now far greater than either of the previous subscription costs. They have risen so sharply that few, if any local authorities will be able to justify a subscription in the present financial climate.

Expenditure on leisure activities is becoming a far more important area of expenditure for people with disposable income. The effect of this is likely to be that public as well as commercial leisure providers view leisure as an area of income generation with, at best, arrangements made for ways of subsidising use by people without the ability to pay, for example, through Passport to Leisure schemes which offer free use of facilities at less popular times of the day, or concessions or free use of services to certain categories of user, notably the elderly and unemployed. There are greater difficulties in maintaining the principle of a free service for all when some people are willing to pay. In a survey conducted by the Labour Ward Party in a middle class area of Sheffield (Nether Edge) a very high percentage of those questioned said they would be prepared to pay to use libraries yet the actual evidence is that where charges are already made, even a small charge deters a large number of people.

Local authorities must take on board the idea of planning for the 'age of leisure'. A situation whereby committees and departments are shuffled about simply to acquire a structure which looks good or satisfies the greatest number of people is not sensible. The starting point must be those areas of service which will constitute the response to leisure needs. These are – Libraries; Arts; Recreation provision encompassing sports, parks and entertainments; Adult Education; Youth Services; Museums; and special provision for Unemployed people. These services should be under the control of a single Leisure Committee. The size of the area of concern and the level of resources available should ensure that the committee would command considerable attention and importance within the local authority structure thus attracting able and powerful politicians. This tends not to be the case under present organisational arrangements where these areas of services are either split between a number of committees or where a Leisure Committee does exist but with a far more restricted remit.

Whether the individual areas of service should be organised within a single departmental structure is a different question whose answer depends on the size of authority involved. There is probably an optimum size for a single Leisure Department – probably a population size of about 300,000. Above that the communications structure becomes far too difficult for the department to be managed effectively and efficiently. Most professionals – of whatever discipline – fear the monolithic department but research and practice both show that the ability and personality of the head of service area count for far more than their position within the organisational structure. It has to be said, however, that few individuals have so far demonstrated an ability to manage and develop and implement policy across the whole of such a diverse area. In larger authorities the grouping of libraries, arts and museums or cultural services, recreation, community services/affairs seem most effective. There has recently been some controversy about the positioning of youth services away from education within either a recreation department or a community services directorate.

There is a question mark about how able library professionals are to head the new and larger departments. There are a number of examples where Chief Librarians do head large leisure directorates and have achieved the position in direct competition with professionals from other disciplines. Generally librarians are no better nor worse suited to be top managers than those with backgrounds in sports, the arts or adult education. There is a general lack of managerial expertise amongst people from all these professional disciplines and there is a need for far greater provision of training for leisure managers in local government.

Whatever the structure, the response to Leisure needs and proper planning and delivery of services will only take place if there is a corporate approach. The history of the development of public leisure provision has resulted in a situation where individual services actually see themselves as in competition. This is inevitable when resources have been limited and services are viewed as peripheral to the main and important work of the local authority. The separatist and competitive approach has also resulted in duplication of effort in certain areas.

In addition to corporate management there must also be a closer working together of staff at grass roots level so that, for example, community recreation workers do not follow community librarians who do not follow community arts workers in approaching individual communities to assess service needs. There is considerable scope for joint training programmes for staff in related disciplines which would make practical arrangements for working together far easier.

The future

The next two decades offer the Public Library Service some of the greatest challenges and most exciting possibilities than at any point in its history. New technology offers the opportunity to reach more people with more information than ever before whilst the prospect of a greater commitment to Leisure by resource providers and consumers should provide a stimulus for a far more analytical and critical look at the needs which the service should respond to and the nature of that response. The brightness of the future is, however, set against a background of public expenditure cuts and a central government determined to pursue policies which are contrary to the principle of a free public service and particularly a service which is central to the continuation of democracy. For these reasons it is difficult to predict with any confidence what changes the next two decades will produce.

In the future, the crucial influence on all leisure provision will be society's attitude towards paid employment and those who have it and those who do not. At present people's worth is measured by the jobs that they do and people without jobs are made to feel worthless. The question is how long this situation can be maintained when the reality is that full employment for all is unachievable and even many of the jobs created in the post-industrial age are so mindless and boring that they are better undertaken on a shared basis. When employment becomes less important leisure will become more important. The term leisure, instead of referring to the use of time other than work which is used for rest and recuperation or entertainment, will come to mean the opportunity for personal development. The library service will fit more happily and easily into this kind of leisure environment than the present recreation dominated one. If and when this change (revolution!) does occur it is possible to foresee emphasis on learning opportunities either formal or through support for independent learning being an important part of the Age of Leisure. It was in support of independent learning that public libraries were first developed.

References

1 HERTIS stands for Hertfordshire Technical Library and Information Service. LADSIRLAC stands for Liverpool and District Scientific Industrial and Research Library Advisory Council.

4 The arts, local authorities and the future

Denys Hodson

Government has been careful to avoid being specific in many areas of intended cost reduction and the Arts have not so far been singled out for attack. However, given the cumulative reductions in local government expenditure forming the basis for discussion on Rate Support Grant over the next few years it is hard to see how this can be seen in any other light but a planned reduction in Arts support also.

Received central government wisdom is concerned not only with limiting cash expenditure but, for reasons which are too esoteric for most people to understand, there is also a strong prejudice against direct employment. Government has 'solved' some of its own ideological conflicts by turning civil service departments into quangos (National Heritage, Countryside Commission). I suspect that in any one to one negotiation Government would therefore look with less hostility on grants to independent trusts than on local authority direct expenditure. The curious negotiations on the abolition of the GLC tend to confirm this view.

The problem facing the prophet is to guess whether the policies of the present Government will be successful in achieving a substantial, permanent reduction in local authority expenditure. The difficulty here is that the crude targeting methods of the Department of the Environment do not reflect in any proper way the relative *efficiency* of individual local authorities. Those that could maintain or increase leisure spending by vastly improving other elements of service delivery are lumped together with the Audit Commission's estimated *one-third* of authorities which already operate at very reasonable efficiency. Thus a successful reduction in the efficient authority's costs can only be achieved by a cut in services – and it's hard to see the Arts escaping at least their fair share.

Nevertheless it is so depressing to assume that much one has worked for over the last seventeen years is going to be wilfully destroyed that one must look at the alternative scenario which is that the basic ambitions, social and political, of local authorities will survive and that progress will continue albeit in the peculiar way of these things – by fits and starts, Knights' Moves at best. If this happens it is legitimate to look at what sort of changes can be anticipated in Arts policy.

Prophecy can only reasonably be built on trying to identify the way in which things are already moving, to project those movements and to put in what modifications experience and intuition may suggest. It is necessary to put in a little potted history of the way the Arts in local authorities have developed and to identify the significance in any developments which are likely to have a bearing on the future. There are certain landmarks which can be seen perhaps often more as symptomatic than causative. There are the foundation of the Committee for the Encouragement of Music and the Arts in 1940 (which turned into the Arts Council of Great Britain in 1946), the start of the Arts Centres movement (Somerset 1945, Swindon 1946), the 'sixpenny rate' power in Bevan's 1948 Act, the foundation of the Regional Arts Associations (South West 1956, Northern Arts 1960), the Maud Report on Local Government Administration (*not* reorganisation), the 1972 Local Government reorganisation legislation, the Bains report (influenced by various individually commissioned studies by Urwick Orr, PE and other consultant firms from 1968 onwards). Behind these there are even more slow moving influences – the flowering (and subsequent death) of cinema, the collapse of independent provincial theatres, the setting up of the regional repertory companies, television and the development of an unbelievable richness in recorded and broadcast music, the development of the public library service as a force in the Arts (Dudley, Scunthorpe, Swindon) and the fast rate of growth of the Regional Arts Association in the last decade.

Reduced to essentials the last forty years or so can be summarised something like this. Particular cultural/social considerations became prominent during the war – possibly due in part to the dispersal of a great many academics through the Civil Service – and these led to a situation in which the Arts became for the first time in British history an accepted area of public policy. Influenced by the Government's position local authorities and voluntary bodies through the country began a process in which *local* support for the Arts became acceptable, though far from widespread. As with many local activities much depended on the twin forces of what has felicitously been called 'burgher pride' of single-minded activists – local chairmen, officers and leaders of local clubs.

Until 1948 local government powers were vestigial. The famous 'sixpenny rate clause' was much influenced by the need to help 'tourist' authorities to support *entertainment* but nevertheless the powers were widely drawn and could be used by progressive authorities, often through their library programmes, to make real Arts progress. It was particularly significant in the fifties and sixties when the Arts Council was setting up its network of repertory theatres, occasionally in new buildings (Nottingham, Exeter), but often in old theatres which had gone or were going bankrupt under the dual influence of cinema and television. There were similar, though less dramatic movements on concert halls and number one touring theatres where a number of local authorities were encouraged to get involved in maintaining the bigger provincial theatres which could accept the revived or new opera and ballet companies. It is a small footnote in history that Covent Garden had once, I understand, been used pre-war for what was essentially a striptease show.

We entered the seventies with Arts policies largely based on the big towns and cities strongly orientated towards (i) entertainment in its broadest form; (ii) the performance arts within a broadly classical tradition; (iii) traditional museum and art gallery activities neither helped nor influenced by the Arts Council and therefore leaning towards the artistically accepted and safe.

During this time the Arts Council itself had been getting at once closer to and further away from local authorities. It had never, and has still only marginally, sought to involve local authorities as *senior* partners and knowledge of the policies and practices of all but a relatively small number was abysmal. So whilst concordats were made with the 'theatre' cities, sometimes at member level only, little constructive attention was given to the rest of the country, if only because Arts Council policy was officially one of response rather than initiative.

The Regional Arts Associations (RAAs) with their growing resources became influential from the late sixties and particularly in the seventies. Their growth was coincidental but only very loosely connected with the development of new Leisure committees, departments and officers with specific responsibilities that included Arts which started in Teesside with the appointment of John Pinches in 1968, was adopted by a few other local authorities during the next few years, became enshrined in the Bains report and was heavily supported by the Sports Council in the run up to 1974 reorganisation.

The emergence of Leisure committees with Arts responsibilities was patchy. Two classes of authority in particular were initially resistant – the rural districts which often had no major town or existing infrastructure and many of those metropolitan districts in particular which were essentially unchanged and therefore continued to exercise their Arts responsibilities through library committees and staff. In the same way the emergence of RAAs, by this time all with substantial or majority local authority presence on their controlling bodies, was marked by a wide variety of reactions among local authorities. In the North East, the political clout of the politicians and authorities which had put Northern Arts together secured immediate acceptance. Others, where the people nominated by member authorities were often the 2nd XI players, found it difficult to strike relationships with local authorities, and were looked on with suspicion by members and officers alike. A subtext which has run right through the period has been the Arts funding bodies' policy support – stemming largely from the hardening of policy in Arts Council itself – for professionals to the exclusion of amateurs and for the work of advanced contemporaries. These have proved bones of contention between the Arts 'experts' and local authorities who are likely to wish to be highly supportive of amateurs and who tend to be ill-educated in most accepted contemporary Art forms. This natural (and by no means evil) tendency in councilllors *may* have been partly reinforced by a concentration of ex parks and sports centres managers in the new Chief Leisure Officers posts created in 1974 and indeed since.

Current estimates of Arts expenditure by local authorities are suspect but it is safe to conclude that local authority Arts expenditure, excluding formal education, is now somewhat above the annual expenditure of Arts Council. The largest spending group of authorities comprise non-metropolitan districts. The highest average per capita spend is found in the larger non-metropolitan districts centred on large towns or cities and the equivalent metropolitan districts and London Boroughs. The special situation of metropolitan counties and the GLC has already received much attention and decisions, for good or ill, have been taken. RAA expenditure comes almost entirely out of the joint totals of Arts Councils and local authorities. The total expenditure of RAAs together does not exceed £25 million (not taking into account the temporary government funding in respect of the abolition of the metropolitan authorities which is currently about £7½ million).

Over the course of the next few years Arts Council's own grant is unlikely to rise even by more than the year-on-year rate of inflation. For a variety of technical reasons, in particular honouring long standing growth commitments and the relatively slow process of cutting off clients no longer in favour, this means substantial reduction in real terms for major areas of work.

RAAs and *selected* provincial centres may continue to profit, albeit marginally, by the strategy of the 'Glory of the Garden' but it has to be clear that this strategy is not designed to assist the chronic under-funding of *established* cultural initiatives. Increases in funds, such as they are, can be used only to support real growth in services and are strongly tied to equivalent *real* increases in local authority or private support. The amount of development money available locally or nationally is unlikely to rise.

The panacea put forward for all Arts ills for the eighties has been sponsorship and some steps have been taken by Government to make this more attractive. The problems of sponsorship are well-known but can be simplified as:

(i) While commercial wealth and power is concentrated in London, sponsorship will always have a strong metropolitan bias. This overwhelming concentration of wealth is not traditionally true of, for instance, the United States or West Germany;

(ii) Sponsorship under the present rules is bound to favour the artistically safe and is unlikely to be available for new, experimental or socially challenging work;

(iii) Sponsorship knows no loyalties – a board can change its policies overnight.

Although, given reasonable economic conditions, one can expect some growth in sponsorship this will, I fear, do no more than compensate in the best cases for reduced public funding. As a second plank of policy there is of course private *investment* in the Arts. This has always taken place in some branches of the Arts notably publishing, film, the West End theatre and above all television. For private investment to work there must be a reasonable return.

Now this is where I start to worry about the future. Many forms of the Arts have a long tradition of public subsidy but that tradition was not necessarily based on an overall decline in public desire. Shakespeare's Drama Company had a wealthy patron, Velasquez did all right out of Spanish state funds, every little state in Eighteenth century Germany seems to have had its Kappelmeister (mostly Bachs), but the work produced seems so far as we can judge to have been *popular*, certainly among the people who exercised *social* power – whether the city apprentices or the burghers of Hesse-Darmstadt. There was no sense in which the patrons of old felt they were *preserving* the Arts forms they patronised. Yet behind so much of present subsidy and those endless arguments which surround it *preservation* is often the game and in the act of *preservation* we may lose the general support of substantial sections of the population.

To oversimplify, cinema destroyed much of the audience for popular drama and was in turn destroyed by television. Indeed it is probably only the poverty of the British Film Institute that prevents an enormous drive to create and maintain new cinemas and to restore old ones in all directions for the *preservation* of the Art Form. Arts Council did just that in the fifties and sixties when a large network of subsidised repertory theatres was created. Now throughout this the British people have in fact been absorbing an enormous amount of drama – probably a growing amount – and the quality of that drama, however skilfully we are manipulated by cynical screen writers, is probably just as high as much current theatre and perhaps better than much of the past (is Maria Marten really any *better* than Dallas?).

I have illustrated this through drama but there are similar problems in other Art forms. The significance of any truth that lies behind the argument is that it seems to me more than possible that the ordinary voter may feel increasingly unwilling to support the preservation of Art forms which he may well see as outdated. This has particular significance for local authorities because councillors are much closer to and indeed more closely resemble their voters than Members of Parliament. This enables Parliament often to decide issues on a basis of high-minded principle, whether it is Arts Council Grant or the abolition of Capital Punishment, which would be unlikely to get through an equivalent body of local councillors (and perhaps a good thing too).

This, in conjunction with central government policy, makes it possible to wonder whether even the existing network of repertory theatres, the smaller chain of No. 1 touring dates (and with them some of the major touring companies) and some of the orchestras face much of a rosy future. Cut down subsidy in real terms and they clearly do not. Emphasising an inevitable class bias (often not as bad as some left wing politicians would have us believe but there nevertheless), will not be helpful. This is particularly so if you realise that *no-one* wants to know about the liberal-arts-orientated (if somewhat mythical) middle class which is attacked from the Left as bourgeois and from the technocrats of the New Right as irrelevant to a lean, hard, wealth-producing economy.

It seems possible to me therefore that the main thrust of traditional Arts policies over the next decade *may* be considerably weakened as central funding first stops growing and then declines and local government, forced to seek further reductions in expenditure, instead of taking over the main burden starts once more to question the whole basis of funding in terms of social policy.

Does this mean the collapse of Western Civilisation as we know it or the progressive withdrawal by local authorities from all Arts funding? Let me hasten to say that that is not my view. Whilst certain traditional fields may be under attack there is a balancing factor of great importance which is concerned with much wider responses by local authorities to social change. Even for quite a big international

athletics match at Crystal Palace there will be plenty of empty seats –
but participation in marathons and fun runs reaches *amazing* proportions. Participation rates in most leisure activities are still high and
many are growing whilst spectator figures remain on a downward
trend. The same, for good or ill, applies in some fashion to the Arts. It
is not unusual to find that the total of dancers in a community is
higher than the dance audience figures, more people may paint than
attend contemporary art exhibitions, more write poetry than attend
poetry readings. The old style Arts Council pro-professional (and
therefore inevitably anti-amateur) stance has had to be modified in
itself, has been further modified by the RAAs and yet further by
many local authorities who within the broad concept of Leisure do
not have to limit themselves to any specialised meaning of the word
'Arts'.

There has been much debate (most of it very boring for all but the
protagonists) over the last two decades on the issue of Democratisation of Culture versus Cultural Democracy. Very roughly this
can be summarised as Royal Opera for all on the one hand and
community written and produced rock opera on the other. The
expense and difficulty of making Royal Opera available and
accessible to all but a tiny minority of people is probably almost
insurmountable in both the short and middle term. Germany is one
of the most successful 'opera nations' but that success is built on the
twin planks of overwhelming subsidy and a long tradition of high
level music teaching for most of the population. Rock opera on the
other hand will not appeal to cultural purists and funding bodies will
not see it as a proper sphere of expenditure. Yet in a sense society
has moved much closer to cultural democracy and it has even began
to acquire a certain central status. The work of Peter Cheeseman at
Stoke and Ann Jellicoe in the South West are both attempts and not
unsuccessful ones to find a new and valid reason for playgoing and
playmaking where what is being offered may no longer be seen as
the *same* as T.V. drama. Ann Jellicoe in particular has put new
meaning into the process of playmaking as a good in its own right
and similar work has sprung up in other parts of the country.

Now here is something which is much more attractive to many of
the newer breed of politicians with their stress on participation, on
consultation, on the community. Running alongside these high profile activities are the Arts centres, the community arts groups, the
experimental film makers and video workers all believing at least up
to a point that the *process* of the Arts is a vital part of the product and
that in this way you can introduce Arts activities with all their life
enhancing potential to genuinely new audiences. This is especially
relevant in a time of manufacturing decline and high unemployment
since councillors are naturally and rightly concerned to make special

efforts for the unemployed and it seems inevitable that they will be that group in society which has had the least chance to develop from education or social environment the knowledge and skills which underlie so much of what we have all looked on as The Arts.

Not that this is going to make life any easier for councillors and officers. The old touchstone of accepted quality will have gone. Decisions will have to be made in a way which will involve greater dialogue between local authority 'patron' and 'client'. There may be less grand occasions with a reception in the mayor's parlour and more visits to difficult and possibly hostile young arts workers. There will be less stress on new purpose built performance spaces and more on outreach. People may live only a mile or two from present theatres or concert halls but it can be a life time's journey away and local authorities will increasingly be pushing for *local* activity with local orientation.

To summarise, I see the future of Local Authority and the Arts as:

(i) manning for some years to come with crumbling defences of the fifties and sixties Arts which will only survive in the end to the extent that the public wills them to;

(ii) a greater role in the setting up and support of arts centres or other structures serving the same purpose;

(iii) a general stress on *participation* including a growing interest in the crafts;

(iv) outreach work in the Arts to run parallel to Action Sport;

(v) a growing interest in public accessible Art such as mural painting;

(vi) support for people who wish to learn or improve skills at lower levels than the traditional – teaching young people to make better rock rather than hoping they will *all* play the oboe.

What I have written is a personal guess – not a personal wish. It is hard to assess what will be the effect of the new education measures which appear at this stage to include Art and Music in the core curriculum. It is not beyond dreams to hope that the effect could be significant. For myself I would wholeheartedly welcome much greater and better stress on Arts in formal education to counteract and eventually change the anti-Arts pressures of this most philistine society. I would like to see a country in which the popular press could not afford to take the profoundly anti-Arts stance that it does. I would like to see more people have a free cultural choice between different aspects of music or painting or writing – a choice from which they are now largely excluded. I do not welcome or relish the thought of decline in quantity or quality of opera (to which I am far from addicted) or classical dance (which I enjoy) or indeed of any of the 'Heritage' Arts. But we are offering a public service using money contributed in part by nearly all members of society including a child buying a Mars bar. Inevitably, I believe, pressure will continue to build to direct our Arts programme, as we have already begun to direct our recreational programmes, to those who are in Arts terms (and mainly in life terms) the deprived and under-privileged. Experience suggests that we will not be all that successful in statistical terms – perhaps raising participation rates by no more than a very few percentage points over a very long period – but one percentage point could be half a million people and I for one would see that as a worthwhile objective.

As a footnote our success when we achieve it will *still* come from the dedicated and powerful chairman, the community activist who won't take 'no' for an answer and from local authority employees. Employing arts *animateurs* is still at the moment comparatively rare and they certainly don't always sit easily within bureaucratic structures. My successors will have to learn the special skills of *allowing things to happen*. All too often we ourselves and the systems which we serve are better at *preventing* than *enabling* and once we move towards the policies I suggest may be coming in the future, *enabling* is the name of the game.

5 The changing world of museums and art galleries

Patrick Boylan

Introduction

Unlike the majority of services under consideration in the current review, there is no widespread understanding of or general agreement about, the nature, purpose and philosophy of museums, at least outside the (very small) museum profession, so a substantial part of this chapter is necessarily given over to a review of modern perceptions of museum as such, and in particular their (exceedingly complex) organisation in the UK in general, and England and Wales in particular.

Finally, four specific important issues that are of current concern to local authority museums, and are likely to remain so for the foreseeable future are examined.

The first of these is the challenge to, and impact on, the local authority sector of the rapid growth of the 'independent museum' movement with its claimed advantages over local government services, but which are in practice frequently heavily subsidised and supported by the public sector, and which are in many cases in a very vulnerable state.

The second is the growing involvement of local museums with environmental issues, especially research, recording and interpretation, across the whole field from geology to local oral and social history.

The third is the place of museums within local government organisation and management structures, and particularly the impact of 'generic' leisure or recreation departments on both service provision and professional standards. Whilst it is clear that museums and galleries make a major contribution to leisure-time enjoyment (far more so in statistical terms than all spectator sports including football and cricket combined, for example), a 'leisure service' model of the purpose and objectives of museums seems very inadequate and incomplete, and they ought more properly be regarded as an educational service (as indeed they were classified in the Bains Report).

Finally, finance is considered. Here, there is a long history of chronic underfunding of the local government sector, especially in comparison with the national museums, and under present Rate Support Grant policies and allocations this can only get worse rather than better, especially if local government ever began to take seriously the RSG figures and regarded them as firm targets or limits.

The museum phenomenon: national and international

Museums have not exactly been blessed with a 'good press'. In the House of Commons in 1896, John Burns MP denounced the museums of the Science and Art Department (ie the Victoria and Albert and Science Museums) as a 'nest of nepotism and a jungle of jobbery', and a dozen or so years later one of the founders of Italian Futurism, Marinetti, called on artists to destroy all libraries and museums and to start afresh, rejecting all tradition. He continued by denouncing museums as identical to cemeteries' . . . in the sinister promiscuousness of so many objects unknown to each other. Public dormitories, where one is forever slumbering beside hated and un-known beings'.

Indeed, death and decay metaphors seem to be liberally sprinkled through twentieth century comments on museums and galleries, as in the distinguished archaeologist's description of the great western archaeological museums as 'charnel houses of murdered history'. Even Jenny Lee, the nearest thing to a Continental-style Minister of Culture that Britain has ever had, seemed to base her mid-1960s policies on an implied distinction between museums and galleries on the one hand and what she termed the 'Live Arts' on the other – a distinction which survives today in British government policy on arts funding.

And yet, at a conservative estimate, at least 1 billion people a year visit the world's 30,000 or more recognisable museums, and an enormous number – certainly some hundred of thousands – must be actively involved in the museum movement on a voluntary basis, assisting as 'Friends' or volunteers with the professionally staffed museums, or helping to organise and run the tens of thousands of mainly small, local voluntary museums and preservation projects that are springing up at an astonishing rate (certainly several per day) throughout the world.

To give only two examples, in the UK the Museums Association, which has in membership virtually every professionally-staffed museum, has around 520 British Institutional members, yet a recent survey by the Association of Independent Museums has identified over 1,400 museums in the country run by voluntary organisations and individuals, of which less than a hundred are members of the Museums Association, and the preliminary work for a national Museum Data-Base Project funded by the Office of Arts and Libraries suggests that around 3,500 institutions exist within the UK that may fall within the Museums Association's definition of a museum. Even more surprising is the position in the Soviet Union, where the number of local, voluntary, community museums run by local groups attached to schools, factories, collective farms, trade union branches, etc is now thought to exceed 12,000, compared with a total of around 1,400 'official' state museums.

However, the explosive growth in museum provision is very much a twentieth century phenomenon (though, in Europe and eastern North America, it clearly had its origins in the nineteenth century), although a small proportion of the world's museums has a much longer history. The original Museum at Alexandria, founded in the third century BC, was destroyed in the third century AD, and none of the other Greek or Roman forerunners of the present-day museum survive. The oldest recognisable museum foundation surviving today is almost certainly that of the great Todaiji Temple at Nara – the ancient imperial capital of Japan near Kyoto, founded as a treasury of religious art and relics in the eigth century AD.

In the Christian world, the building up of collections of religious objects began in the Middle Ages, although it was not until the mid-18th century that these, led by the Vatican museum in around 1750, began to develop into recognisable museums, accessible to the public. Great private collections were also made available on a limited basis to the public, as in Florence, where the Medici treasures of the Uffizi were accessible from the late sixteenth century, although it is arguable whether it could be classed as a museum as early as that.

The earliest scientific museums arose in the late seventeenth century out of the growing interest in the study of nature, with a University Museum opening at Basel in 1671. Six years later, Elias Ashmole bequeathed his collection to the University of Oxford, and a museum building was specially designed to house this and earlier accumulations of collections, the new building being formally inaugurated by a Royal visit in May 1683. (Although the Ashmolean Museum itself has long since moved to a new building nearby, the original purpose-built building in Broad Street, just by the Sheldonian Theatre, still survives as a University Museum, and now houses the Museum of the History of Science).

Basel and Oxford were of course the forerunners of many thousands of University museums all over the world. The British Museum is the world's oldest national museum (excluding the special case of the Vatican Museum), and opened in 1753. Its origins and early history, however, perhaps typify the ambivalent attitude that most governments have taken to the development of museums in the United Kingdom. Under his will, Sir Hans Sloane instructed his executors to give the Government the first option to purchase his outstanding collection (mainly of natural history material) to form the basis of a national museum. Eventually, Parliament reluctantly agreed to accept the collection, but only on condition that the cost of purchasing it should be met from the proceeds of a public lottery! Once established, the British Museum remained, for many years, a national disgrace in terms of the lack of care and sheer disorder of the collections, and was almost totally inaccessible to the general public. It was open for only a few hours a week, and then only to persons presenting a letter of introduction from the Chamberlain to the Royal Household, the Archbishop of Canterbury (as an ex officio Trustee of the Museum), a Peer of the Realm, a Member of Parliament or someone of similar standing! It was not until the Museum moved into its present Bloomsbury building in the 1820s that any serious consideration was given to the possible interest of the ordinary citizen.

A far more systematic approach to the establishment of a national museum was taken by revolutionary France. Whilst Parliamentarian England, the previous century, had seized the great art collection of King Charles I in order to sell it, revolutionary France seized the collections of the Royal Family and the nobility in order to create a museum that would not only bring art and history to the ordinary citizens, but would be a proud statement of '*la gloire*'. The Palais du Louvre was similarly appropriated and used to house the sequestrated collections which were pouring into Paris from every part of France, and the Louvre was opened as a museum in 1793. Not content with a merely national role for the new museum, Napoleon later used his military conquests to internationalise the collection – bringing back treasures from as far afield as Egypt.

In a number of European countries from the mid–18th century and particularly during the nineteenth century a network of local museums was established in the major provincial cities and towns. Often these were originally established and run by local scientific or historical societies formed by the newly emerging urban middle classes. These new societies and their museums followed to a considerable extent the fashions of the day, and this inevitably led them into the world of natural history and – especially – geology, which were the key sciences of the period, at least in terms of both amateur practice and public controversy. Both as individual and as societies, therefore, those involved in this new movement began to build up collections of geological and natural history material both for reference purposes (particularly in terms of identifying new finds of rocks, minerals, fossils, etc) and in order to develop general awareness of the science. Soon, there was a demand for these collections to be developed into working museums, first for the benefit of the members of the Society, and soon for the edification and interest of the population at large.

Most of those voluntary societies have long since found the burden of maintaining an adequate (and inevitably expanding) public museum too great, and in most cases responsibility for their museums has now passed to municipal or other government authorities. However, some notable early examples of voluntary museums are still run by their founding body, for example the very important Teyler's Museum, in Haarlem, Netherlands.

The major colonial expansion of the nineteenth century also had a substantial effect on the development of museums in at least two ways. First, large numbers of items of all kinds, particularly of ethnography and natural history collected by travellers and those working in the various colonial administrations overseas, were taken back to both the national and local museums of the various colonial powers. Second, in a small number of cases, embryo museums were established in the colony itself as part of the overall transfer of European educational and cultural traditions to colonial capitals, and in such cases the museum has formed the natural nucleus of a post-independence national museum, as with, for example, the world-famous Egyptian Museum in Cairo, or the colonial period museums of Delhi, India.

However, there is no doubt at all that in numerical terms museums are very much a twentieth century phenomenon, taking a world-wide view. Although exact statistics are not available it seems clear that at least 90 per cent, and probably more than 95 per cent, of the present-day museums of the world have been established since the Second World War.

Perhaps the most spectacular growth in terms of public museums has been in the USSR which had no more than a dozen or so significant public museums at the time of the Revolution, but now has over 1,400, including major international museums such as the State Hermitage Museum in the former Winter Palace in Leningrad, as well as many historical museums dealing with different aspects of the development of the country, and large numbers of substantial new regional museums.

The USA has seen a comparable growth in voluntary museums, which include some major 'national' institutions such as the Metropolitan Museum of Art and American Museum of Natural History facing each other across Central Park, New York.

The enormous expansion in museum provision of the past 40 years or so has been so diverse in terms of geographical distribution, size or type of museum that it is very difficult indeed to summarise or even characterise in any useful way. New developments have included such diverse projects as the great aeronautical and space collections of Washington and Moscow, the outstanding National Anthropological Museum in Mexico, at least 40 new national museums in newly-independent states in all parts of the world, through to innumerable preserved and restored historic house museums, and tiny community museums.

One particularly important development, pioneered in such projects as the restoration of eighteenth century Colonial Williamsburg, in the USA, from the 1920s onwards, has been the growing interest in on-site preservation and interpretation. This has been one of the most exciting new developments of recent years for which the distinguished French museologist, Georges-Henri Riviere has coined the term 'ecomuseum' – a museum project that attempts to conserve and interpret the complete natural and/or human ecology of an area, as in the Ironbridge Gorge Museum in England, or Riviere's own lasting monument, the Museum of the Camargue in France.

However, a mere summary of the development of the world's museums over the past two centuries or more, (which is in any case far too generalised), throws comparatively little light on the motivation of their original founders and present-day supporters, and even less on their purpose and objectives.

In both professional and popular parlance, the word 'museum' is used to cover such a wide range of wildly different institutions and organisations, that one frequently wonders whether it is possible to define the basic meaning of the word, let alone identify a common purpose and objective behind the tens of thousands of museums that now exist. The 1970s in particular seem to have been the period of serious self-doubt, coupled with a more positive searching for renewal and identity, amongst the museum movement of the world.

The International Council of Museums (ICOM), is the official UNESCO non-government organisation for museums and related areas. In opening its triennial General Conference in France in 1971, the host Minister of Culture suggested that museums were facing serious difficulties in three areas: sociological, particularly in relation to youth; technological, particularly in relation to the development of audio-visual and related techniques; and cultural, in relation to the need to communicate. Later in the same meeting, the director of an unconventional, black neighbourhood museum in Washington D.C., which has been extremely successful in involving the local community in its work, argued that the basic problem is that 'museums resist progress'. A similar line was taken by the Netherlands Government's new policy for museums in 1977: 'Museums have got out of step with the realities of the present, and the demands of the future. They have been exclusively devoted to collecting and conserving cultural goods from the past. A kind of cult of the past has developed with museums as temples'.

These are harsh words indeed, but are they fair reflection of the majority of the world's museums? And, if so, why do governments and individuals around the world continue to fund museums and art galleries and enlarge their collections, and why does the world's public flock to them in ever-increasing numbers? Is it really a demonstration that 'Nostalgia Rules, OK!'? Or are museum directors really in the same boat as the apocryphal foreign tenor appearing for the first time in the San Carlo Opera House in Naples, who was euphoric when the notoriously demanding audience demanded a third encore of his first aria, until the prompter explained that the audience had every intention of insisting on him singing encore after encore until he managed to sing it right!?

The nature and purpose of museums

What, then, is a museum (or public art gallery – the word 'museum' being used to include art galleries, unless the context indicates otherwise)?

At its 1971 Conference, the International Council of Museums (ICOM) turned its attention to the definition of a museum (including the definition the public art gallery of British parlance), partly in the context of a review of its own constitution. Following widespread consultations around the world, an agreed definition was adopted at its next General Conference, held in Copenhagen in 1974, as follows:

> A museum is a non-profit making, permanent institution, in the service of society and of its development, and open to the public, which acquires, conserves, researches, communicates and exhibits, for the purposes of study, education and enjoyment, material evidence of man and his environment.

In addition ICOM recognises that a number of cognate institutions, such as historic and natural monuments and parks, and some archive centres, zoos, botanic gardens and specialist libraries exercise in part what are fundamentally museum functions and responsibilities.

A moment's reflection will confirm that the introspective stereotype portrayed by the Dutch Cultural Minister or by the use of the word 'museum' in a perjorative sense, bears little or no resemblance to the ICOM-UNESCO definition which has now been widely adopted at a national level as well. (It is now the working definition used by the Museums Association in the UK, and is incorporated in the Association's Code of Practice for Museum Authorities which it commends to its Institutional Members, ie museum governing bodies of all kinds). But the definition repays examination and analysis in much more detail since it encapsulates most if not all of progressive museum policy and thinking.

The first factor that the ICOM definition emphasises is that museums are permanent institutions, not mere temporary exhibitions, world fairs, festivals, etc. The issue of 'permanence' is of special importance in relation to the collections.

The first thing that people donating their treasures to a museum want to be sure about is that, once accepted into the collections, they will be held in trust for present and future generations of potential museum users and visitors, and that the survival of the collection will not depend on the whims of transient boards of trustees, directors, etc, nor will the town council be able to sell the museum collections in order to repair the swimming bath roof. Similarly, potential benefactors want to be sure that the institution is a charitable institution (non-profit in North American parlance).

The second phrase of the ICOM definition, asserting that the museum is 'in the service of society and its development' confronts head-on the old argument, rarely heard today, that the essential purpose of a museum or gallery is the building-up of a collection merely for the purposes of connoisseurship. Instead, museums are exhorted to find a direct role of service to the public and to the advancement of its community. Of course, very many institutions in a complex modern society have a similar fundamental objective: for example schools, universities, libraries, health services, etc. The two things that distinguish museums from these are (1) the subject matter, comprising the original (not, in normal circumstances, reproduction or replica) three-dimensional objects which are evidence of man's development or the environment in which he lives (whether a Rembrandt painting or a microscopic fossil), and (2) the kind of techniques used by the museum in order to achieve its objectives, and in particular, acquisition, conservation, research and communication. In these factors, of course, there is the closest possible professional and ethical correspondence between museums and archives.

Except for a small number of specialised museums where the collection is 'closed' for historic reasons (eg because it is the reflection of one person's activity and taste), all museums are, to some extent, involved in the development of their collections through acquisitions. Although most of the press publicity in relation to museum acquisitions seems to be focused on spectacular purchases of expensive, European paintings in the great auction houses of the world, this is a very distorted picture indeed.

For many museums, particularly those concentrating on natural history or local history and archaeology, much the greatest part of the growth in the collections may well derive from the museum's own planned programme of field research and collecting, whether of biological or geological material from the locality, or as a result of systematic archaeological investigation organised by, or in close consultation with, the museum.

Once an object has been added to the collections of the museum, for good or ill, it has to be conserved, in the broadest sense. Conservation has been one of the more spectacular growth industries within the museum world of post-war years in particular. New scientific techniques for investigating virtually every kind of museum material have led to a far better understanding of the causes and nature of both natural and artificially-induced deterioration, and, over the same period, a wide range of new materials (particularly synthetic polymer chemicals – especially adhesives) have transformed the range of laboratory techniques available for both preserving and restoring works of art and museum objects.

The ICOM basic definition of a museum also stresses that it has a research role as a fundamental characteristic and reponsibility. At its most basic level, the museum's obligation to carry out research may extend no further than the investigation of new acquisitions in order to identify and catalogue them fully. At the other extreme, the world's major natural history museums, such as the British Museum (Natural History), or the US National Museum of Natural History within the Smithsonian Institution, Washington, are, nowadays, just about the only places where large-scale fundamental research on the classification and identification of animals, etc. is carried out, and much of this work is of great economic importance, for example, in relation to insect pests. Similarly, the work of the geology departments of the major natural history museums is of fundamental importance in relation to the identification of the fossil sequence, and, hence, to much of economic geology. But, even more modest and local museums may have a substantial research role in relation to not merely their own collections but also their own environment, (see chapter 8 below).

The final element of the ICOM definition is the declaration that the museum communicates and exhibits its collections 'for the purposes of study, education and enjoyment'. One may perhaps be forgiven for thinking that it has taken a long time to reach the self-evident 'front-of-the-house' function of museums and galleries, but, in a fully developed museum, the public facilities are the tip of the iceberg. To carry this old metaphor further, it is the largely unseen fundamental base of adequate, properly conserved and fully researched, collections relevant to the museum or gallery's functions and responsibilities, that makes possible and gives stability to the public function.

The most obvious way in which a traditional museum or gallery communicates with the public is through its display galleries. In the vast majority of cases, only a small selection from the collection will be on display at any one time. There are, however, exceptions to this: the National Gallery, London, manages to show in either the primary galleries or in an area of the basement freely open to the public, the whole of its collection except for items on loan elsewhere or requiring or undergoing conservation treatment. Such an arrangement is practicable when dealing with a collection of only a little over 2,000 paintings, and some small local folklife museums also manage to have virtually the whole of their collections an public display. At the other extreme, the world's major natural history museums may have in excess of 50 million individual items each, most of which would be meaningless to the ordinary non-specialist visitor unless interpreted in some way, and in many cases of microscopic size. A display of a couple of hundred thousand small tubes containing fleas preserved in alcohol might bring home to the public the fact that the museum is involved in some odd areas of research, but would hardly be an exciting entertainment or educational experience! The great majority of museums, therefore, have to be selective in terms of what they display, and, even more important, must attempt to interpret the material to the visitor.

As soon as one talks about 'the museum visitor', the curator (and the designer, if, as is increasingly the case, there is a professional design input to the planning and execution of the display or exhibition) runs headlong into the first major problem. Unlike a teacher planning an activity for a group of eight year old children of known ability and attainment, or a playwright working on a script for a late evening TV drama production, there is rarely, if ever, a clear and unequivocably identifiable customer for a particular museum display. (The only examples that come to mind of such a clearly identifiable and homogenous museum user group are all in specialised museums that have a very restricted access, for example, a teaching museum within a University Hospital, which is open to medical students and doctors, and can have specialised displays which have been planned specifically for a medical audience). The great majority of museums are, in theory at least, totally indiscriminate in terms of the audience that they attract, and, consciously or unconsciously, have to make assumptions (or, in many cases, positive policy decisions) about the target audience of their permanent displays and temporary exhitions.

In recent years, there has been a growing interest in North America in particular, but also in the UK, in museum visitor research, using, in broad terms, opinion poll techniques, and, in the great majority of

cases, such surveys have shown a very substantial over-representation of the white, physically-fit, middle class amongst users, with a
corresponding under-representation of the socially, economically
and physically disadvantaged. There is no one, simple, explanation
of this bias. Partly, it is a reflection of the cultural tradition within the
urban middle class that was largely reponsible, as society members,
local councillors or benefactors, for the creation of our western
museum heritage in the Victorian period. Partly, too, it is a reflection
of differences in educational attainment.

So far as the disabled and frail (including the elderly) are concerned, the monumental nature of most nineteenth and earlier
twentieth century museum buildings frequently makes access and
circulation within the building virtually impossible (a problem that is,
of course, by no means unique to museums amongst public
buildings of those periods). Moreover, one can argue that the very
scale of museum buildings of that period (particularly the traditional,
imposing cathedral-like entrance hall!) can be a serious psychological
barrier which keeps out a high proportion of the population. There is
a lot of evidence to show that this pseudo-ecclesiastical atmosphere
was deliberately sought by nineteenth and early twentieth century
museum governors, curators and architects, and this is reflected in
contemporary descriptions of museums in those times in terms such
as 'a temple of knowledge'. Certainly in the case of the larger
museums able to have special staff for the purpose, a museum
education service can play a vital role in broadening the population
base from which future generations of museum users will be drawn,
quite apart from the direct benefit that children and teachers can
derive from using museums and galleries in a purposeful way.

Formal educational facilities for organised school party groups
visiting museums began to be offered by a few pioneering institutions
a century ago and in such cases many teachers at schools within easy
reach of museums quickly recognised the benefit of organised school
visits to children on a number of counts: first, in amplifying or
illustrating particular areas of the school curriculum; second, in
broadening in general terms the experience of the children; and,
third, in introducing children from families who were not museum
users to museums in general, and their local museum in particular.

In the case of the large museums, it soon became clear that special
facilities needed to be provided for the growing number of organised
school parties, and, before the end of the century, a number of major
museums had arrangements under which qualified teachers were
seconded to work with visiting groups within the museum on a
regular basis. As early as 1872, the City Museum in Liverpool, began
to experiment with the idea of lending original museum specimens to
schools for use by teachers within their own classrooms, and by the

end of the century special 'Children's Museums' were under development in the USA.

The majority of museum education services around the world still see their primary task as the provision of specialist support to teachers willing to use the facilities and resources of the museum, whether by bringing the children to the museum in an organised group, or the use of a loans service (where one is in operation). However, the old emphasis on 'guide-lecturing' parties of schoolchildren around the public galleries has all but gone. Activity rooms and other special teaching facilities are used, where these are available, and there is considerable emphasis on the handling and using of specimens or of exact replicas, where the original is too fragile or too precious to be used, in order to deepen the experience.

Programmes and activities can be tailored to the exact requirements and interests of a particular group, and there is a growing emphasis on formal and informal training courses for teachers to enable them to use the museum facilities themselves with their own students, as an integral part of their normal teaching, rather than 'take the children to the museum for a talk'. In many of the larger museums the numbers of educational parties is so great that the direct teaching by museum education staff of all the parties visiting the museum would be totally impossible. Instead, the teacher can obtain from the Education Section a wide range of resources, materials and suggestions, including 'worksheets' which he or she can use with his or her own group. Many museums also make extensive use of specially trained volunteers (often termed 'docents' in North America) to assist in the educational and guiding work of the museum.

The museum and art gallery service in the United Kingdom

Although the oldest public museum in Britain, the Ashmolean Museum of Oxford University is now more than 300 years old, in common with most of Europe, the great majority of United Kingdom museums have been founded in the present century. A detailed survey carried out by the Museums Association in 1911 identified about 350 museums in the whole of the British Isles (including the parts of Ireland which are now in the Republic). Even the most conservative, present-day estimate suggests that there has been a five-fold increase in the number of recognisable museums in the United Kingdom over the past seventy years, and the true present-day total is almost certainly well over two thousand, with new museums being established all the time.

The lack of any statistics, even at the most basic level of an estimate of the number of museums in the United Kingdom, is a sad reflection of the lack of any overall national museums policy, or even any sort of clear definition of what constitutes a museum, whether in law or in practice, in Britain. Well over a hundred museums are the direct reponsibility of central government agencies, but even these are organised and managed in a wide variety of ways, and come under many different ministries. Indeed, out of the current Cabinet of twenty-two members, only the Prime Minister, the two Treasury Ministers, the two Leaders of the two Houses and one Minister without Portfolio, appear to have no museum responsibilities at all, and at least eleven have significant ministerial responsibility for nationally funded museums – including such unlikely ministries as Energy (which is responsible for industrial history museums of the nationalised fuel industries) and the Department of Health and Social Security (responsible for the funding of a number of very important medical museums).

There is no uniformity in terms of museum provision in the local government sector either. Any local authority other than a parish or community council (or its equivalent) may establish and run museums and galleries, and about half of the county and district councils in England and Wales, together with a substantial pro-portion of Scottish councils exercise museum and art gallery powers in one form or another, and are responsible for approximately 600 local government museum services.

Since the First World War, two completely new types of local or regional museum have emerged: military museums, reflecting the history of particular army, navy or air force units (most commonly dealing with a single local Regiment), and a wide range of 'in situ' museums and monuments – usually relating to a building of historic interest or a working industrial monument, and, very frequently, the responsibility of a private individual or trust. The number of military museums has grown from zero at the end of the First World War to around 140 at the present time.

The total number of private museums of all kinds (including local 'community' historical museums established and run by voluntary groups) depends to an extent on their definition and minimum standards used, but must certainly be well over 1,000 on even the most restricted definition – although the exact number certainly changes week by week. At national level, the educational potential of local museums was recognised by the Board of Education (now the Department of Education and Science) at a comparatively early date, and, more than a hundred years ago, the Board's own museum, the South Kensington Museum (now divided into the Victoria and Albert Museum and the Science Museum) was recognised as having a positive education role, not merely in terms of the visitors to its London building, but also in terms of supporting local museums and Schools of Art in the provinces. A circulating exhibitions service was established to take examples of good modern design, etc. into provincial museums and Art Schools, and this provision brought very great benefit to many remote parts of the country, and to the majority of local museums, for over a century, until the Victoria and Albert Museum's circulating exhibition service became a victim of public expenditure reductions in the mid-70s.

However, this initial service was subsequently supplemented by a purchase grant scheme, under which provincial museums and galleries wishing to buy works of art or specimens could obtain both expert advice and, if the proposed purchase was approved and sufficient funds were available, a cash grant of up to 50 per cent of the purchase price, and this very important service (administered by the Victoria and Albert Museum in relation to art and history) continues to the present day, and is a most important channel for central government aid to local museums of all kinds.

More than fifty years ago, it was recognised that the central government's very limited assistance to provincial museums in the form of touring exhibitions and purchase grants through the Victoria and Albert Museum, valuable as they were, met only a small proportion of the needs of local museums. These services gave no help whatsoever in the vital fields of providing proper building accommodation for local museums, nor in areas such as conservation, restoration and the display of the permanent collections. As in most parts of the world the most serious problems facing the typical United Kingdom museum particularly the provincial museums of all kinds, are shortage of space and shortage of staff.

A detailed, independent report by the Government's own advisory body – the Standing Commission on Museums and Galleries (now renamed the Museums and Galleries Commission), published in 1978, estimated that the provincial museums alone needed a minimum of £100m at 1977 prices (approximately £200m at today's costs) for essential and urgent building improvements and extensions, but progress towards eliminating the deficit in facilities and the many problems identified more than ten years ago has been minimal.

So far as staff are concerned, few reliable statistics are available, except in respect of the local authority museums in England and Wales. An analysis of the 1981/82 CIPFA Leisure Statistics showed that the 214 local authorities then reporting on museum and archive activities employed between them less than 4000 staff of all kinds in these areas (including, for example, security and cleaning personnel). This is an average of only eighteen staff per local authority, or less than ten per museum. In fact, 112 of these local authorities employ less than ten staff; only twenty have more than fifty museum and archive staff of all kinds; and only eight have more than 100.

Regional co-operation: the area museum services

In the 1950s serious discussions began on the possibility of establishing co-operative, specialised regional services between local museums of all kinds (local authority, regimental, private etc) on a voluntary basis. As a result of these discussions, the Calouste Gulbenkian Foundation agreed to finance a three-year experimental project, serving the six counties of the south-west peninsula of England. This area was a particularly good one from the point of view of the experiment, in that it had a wide range of different types if museum, including a major regional museum and art gallery complex in the City of Bristol, and with smaller, but very important, local authority museums elsewhere, notably in Plymouth, Exeter and Gloucester, together with a very large number of independent museums of many types, mostly very small and established and run entirely by volunteers.

Consequently, the Area Museum Council for the South-West came into existence in 1959 as a completely 'open' organisation, managed by a quarterly meeting of the Area Council, to which representatives of all participating museums, whether public or private, were invited. No membership subscription was levied, although local authorities participating in the scheme were encouraged to make a voluntary annual donation towards the (extremely modest) administrative overheads, and the major museums and galleries of the region (particularly Bristol and Plymouth) gave generously of their professional staff time and facilities. This pilot scheme concentrated on the improvement of museum standards in the areas of conservation and restoration, display and temporary exhibitions. By the end of the initial trial period funded by the Gulbenkian Foundation, it had proved so successful that central government recommended the scheme to all other regions of the country, and offered some financial assistance, extremely limited at first, to encourage the development and improvement of local museums and galleries.

From an initial Treasury grant of £10,000 in 1963/64 (shared between the existing South-West pilot scheme and newly-established Area Services elsewhere), the central government's grant has increased to £1.75 million shared amongst seven English Services in the current financial year. (In addition, the Scottish and Welsh Services receive their grants direct from their respective Ministries).

Over the past twenty years, the Area Museum Services have each developed in different and quite distinct ways, reflecting local needs and wishes in terms of both their organisation and the kind of services that they provide. Some, notably the North-West and Yorkshire and Humberside Services have established substantial headquarters operations, with specialised conservation laboratories, display and exhibition facilities, etc, providing specialised services to the museums of their regions, and are, themselves, major employers of museum personnel. Others have seen their role as being primarily a financial one, providing grants to their member museums to enable them to purchase or employ specialised services from other museums or from the private sector, and, in such cases, the Area Service may only employ a Director and a small administrative support unit.

All the Area Museum Services operate ultimately within central government financial and policy guidelines. The division of the national grant between the seven English Area Services is delegated to the government's own advisory body – The Museums and Galleries Commission, but the level of government grant to a particular Area Museum Service is restricted to 50 per cent of its gross expenditure, and, in addition, there is an overall limit on the total grant allocated to the Museums and Galleries Commission for this area of Commission funding, set each year by Parliament in the Expenditure Plans and Supply Estimates.

The Area Services are restricted in terms of the kinds of museum activities which they can grant-aid. Most important, grants cannot be paid towards the cost of the permanent staff of the museum, towards any of its routine running costs, such as building maintenance or fuel costs, nor towards the purchase of specimens. In general, the Area Services can only assist (whether by means of grant or by the provision of specialised services) in areas relating to the care of the collections or to improvements in the public presentation of the museum, (see the current list of approved activities in Appendix I of this paper).

For many years, it has been recognised that one of the greatest needs of provincial museums is financial assistance in relation to capital building works, such as museum extensions, major improvements, etc, and a succession of official reports have urged the central government to make grants to provincial museums for such purposes. Although the Area Museum Services are not permitted to grant-aid such schemes (and, indeed, certainly do not have sufficient money in their budgets to enable them to do so), a modest start has been made over the past three years in the provision of small-scale central government assistance with such projects by means of direct capital grants through the Museums and Galleries Commission, which selects the projects from schemes recommended by the Area Services.

Although the total sum available is extremely small in relation to the needs of museums (only £200,000 in the current year), a most important precedent has been set by the establishment of this special fund. For the first time ever, central government has acknowledged that the nation as a whole has a responsibility for the development of local and regional museums. Although the provision of grant-aid and direct conservation, design and technical services are the most important activities of the Area Museum Services, they can exercise a much wider role developing the co-ordination of facilities and services amongst the museums of their region, and also for promoting co-operation between different regions, and between the national museums in the capital cities and the local museums.

In particular, the Area Services have played an important role in the development of national standards of collections documentation, and are key constituents of the national Museum Document Association, and they are also actively involved in the promotion of national schemes for the training of museum personnel.

It should be emphasised that in policy and management terms all local museums are completely independent of the Area Service, and neither the government nor the area service has any power to control individual museums which accept any form of grant-aid. (The only exception is that the Articles of Association of the West Midlands Area Museum Service requires member authorities or other governing bodies to accept and adhere to the *Code of Practice for Museum Authorities* prepared by the Museums and Galleries Commission as a condition of membership of the service, and hence eligibility for grant-aid).

On the other hand, the area services have had some considerable success in terms of persuading member museums to co-operate amongst themselves in areas such as collecting policies, and they can, if necessary, refuse grant-aid for a project if the museum concerned rejects the professional advice offered through the area service.

Although the total government grant to local public plus 'independent' museums combined made available through the area museums services appears to be very small in percentage terms (approximately £3m including the Scottish and Welsh grants, compared with the total local museum expenditure of around £70m), the Area Service grants have, over the past twenty years, had an influence on the development and improvement of museums and galleries in the provinces out of all proportion to the money involved, for at least two reasons.

First, as in most parts of the world, UK local museums find that almost all of their annual budgets are commited in advance – to meet the fixed costs of the museum, such as the salaries of permanent staff at all levels, the cost of maintaining and running buildings (many of which are important historic monuments in their own right with consequent, very high maintenance and restoration costs), and in administrative overheads, etc. It is by no means unusual to find a museum in which less than 5 per cent of its annual budget is available for museological improvements, such as major conservation projects, new storage schemes, improved documentation or security, or new and attractive displays and exhibitions. It is, of course, in these very areas that the Area Museum Services offer financial assistance, and where a grant of 40 per cent or 50 per cent of the cost of a new scheme can be of the greatest assistance to museums. Second, the fact that, in order to attract an Area Service grant, the museum must raise at least half of the cost from local sources, encourages local fund-raising by the museum, whether from its own governing authority or from private sources such as Friends of the Museum societies or local industry.

There is no doubt at all that the area museum services have, overall, proved a great success in terms of their central objective: the improvement of museums in the provinces. Their organisations may well be described as characteristically British. There is no overall national pattern so far as their organisation and structures are concerned, and absolutely no ministerial direction, control, inspection or political interference. Successive central governments of both parties have insisted that government funding throughout the cultural field must be handled in accordance with what is nowadays well established as the 'arm's-length principle', i.e. via an independent intermediary body, in order to ensure that ministers and central government officials are not in a position to control or direct policy at the local or professional level.

Local government museum and art gallery provision in England and Wales

From the mid nineteenth century until the reform of English and Welsh local government in 1975, the bulk of provincial museum and art gallery provision came from the old municipal corporations – the large industrial cities and towns of the Midlands and North, and the commercial and professional centres (mainly the traditional county market towns) of eastern, southern and south-western England . The old Rural District Councils responsible for most of England and Wales in terms of geographical area had no legal power to establish or run a local museum, and few of the Urban District Councils chose to do so.

This position was reinforced by the Public Libraries and Museums Act 1964, which restricted museum powers in England and Wales to those local authorities which were given the designation of 'library authority' – that is County Councils, County Borough Councils (ie the Cities), and one major change here was the inclusion of county councils amongst the local authorities given the power to operate museums, and embryo County Museum Services began to emerge in, for example, Hampshire, Somerset and Oxfordshire (the latter, initially, in partnership with Oxford City Council).

When the impending reform of local government was under discussion in the late 1960s, professional opinion within museums was overwhelmingly in support of the united view of the Museums Association and the Standing Commission on Museums and Galleries that, if any 'two-tier' (as opposed to 'unitary') form of local government was eventually chosen by the government of the day, local authority museums and galleries should become the mandatory responsibility of the 'top' tier. This was on two principal grounds: first, that the existing local government museums patently needed a much more substantial financial base than was currently available, which only the 'top' tier could provide and, second, that museum and art gallery users of all kinds (students, enquirers, and general visitors) were clearly being drawn from a far wider geographical area than that of the city or borough council that was currently meeting the whole cost of the service, so fairness demanded a much broader tax base in geographical terms.

However, despite strong endorsement of this view by the then Minister for the Arts, Lord Eccles (who intervened personally in an attempt to press this view in several counties, such as Leicester and Norfolk), the legislation finally passed by Parliament in 1972 made museums and galleries a 'concurrent' function which could be exercised by either the new county councils or the new district councils (without even any requirement for consultation or co-operation between the two tiers) after the 1974 reorganisation. Furthermore, under the legislation, in the absence of a voluntary agreement to the contrary, the museums and galleries of the former cities and major boroughs (much the most important providers of local museums before reorganisation) passed automatically to the successor district council for the area under the Property Transfer Orders, not to the new county council (with its far greater financial and professional resources).

Despite the dissapointing line (in professional terms) taken by the government in the new legislation, many of the county councils of England and Wales have become very actively involved in the museum field since 1974. In a number of areas, the county and district councils entered into voluntary agreements under which the museum function is exercised by the county council alone, and, under these agreements, a number of major, regional-level institutions (such as the museums and galleries of Liverpool, Newcastle, Leicester and Norwich) each became the core of a new County Museum Service, and many smaller museums similarly passed to the county councils, rather than the district councils.

The development of county museum services has been particularly marked outside the major conurbations, ie in the non-metropolitan counties of England and Wales, where the County Councils are now responsible for approximately 40 per cent of total authority museum expenditure, compared with less than 2 per cent in 1973–74.

In a few places, such as Leicestershire and Norfolk among the shire counties and Merseyside and Tyne & Wear among the metropolitan counties, new county museum services assumed responsibility in 1974 for all existing local government museum provision and related services (including, for example archaeological research and excavation), and now operate on a federated structure over a network of perhaps a dozen or more museums in various parts of the county, including in each case important new facilities established since because of the much greater resources now available. As a result the individual museums can therefore share specialised professional services, such as conservation laboratories, design and display teams, educational facilities etc. of a high standard which no single museum of its size could have provided on its own.

In other counties, county museum services exist in parallel with district council museums and galleries. For example, in Hampshire, the County Service provides a range of central facilities, and is responsible for museums in some of the smaller towns, whilst the city museums and galleries of Southampton, Portsmouth and Winchester have continued as independent institutions under their respective district councils.

In the metropolitan areas, including London, the greater part of the local authority museum and gallery provision has remained at district or borough level, and, in Merseyside and Tyne and Wear comprehensive county museum services have also been established as noted above.

It is extremely unfortunate, in my view, that the considerable number of important new county museum services established under the 1974 local government reorganisation were only just beginning to come into operation as Britain began to go into the present deep economic recession, following the 1973 oil crisis, and consequently, many plans to develop new county museum services to support the smaller district museums, and to establish completely new branch museums in places lacking adequate museum provision, have been abandoned completely or postponed indefinitely, and, in the 36 counties (out of a total of 50) in which some form of county museum provision is established, there has been far less progress than had been hoped because of severe restrictions on all areas of public expenditure.

Between them thirty three shire counties are responsible for about 150 museums and galleries of various kinds and sizes. The other two-thirds of the museums and galleries provided directly by local government in England and Wales are the responsibility of the various district councils (including the London Boroughs), and these include some of the largest and most important museums and galleries in the country, for example the City Museums and Art Galleries in Birmingham, Bristol and Sheffield, and the City Art Gallery Service in Manchester.

In the case of the majority of significant museums and art galleries that transferred to the district councils at local government reorganisation in 1974, the much sought-after broadening of the funding base did not occur, although there were a few exceptions. For example, in West Yorkshire the pattern of district boundaries adopted extended considerably both the geographical area served by, and the supporting rate poundage of, the important former County Borough museums and galleries in Leeds, Bradford and Huddersfield (Kirklees), whilst at the other end of the population range a number of small boroughs with important museum responsibilities had their boundaries and rateable values greatly extended in 1974 through the incorporation of their rural hinterland, as for example at Shrewsbury and Scarborough.

The Public Libraries and Museums Act, 1964, gave museum authorities extensive powers to co-operate in the joint provision of museum and art gallery facilities and services, and to give financial assistance to any other authority or organisation in relation to museum, etc provision. These powers were used very sparingly at first – mainly in order to make small maintenance and development grants to local charitable trusts and other private museums, but one early use of the powers was the agreement between Oxfordshire and the then Oxford County Borough which led to the Oxfordshire Museums Service (although this became the exclusive responsibility of the new County Council in 1974), followed by the establishment of a regionally-based Joint Committee under the leadership of Durham County Council in order to develop the North of England Open Air Museum at Beamish, Co. Durham.

Since local government reorganisation in 1974 there has been far greater use of these 'partnership' powers as, for example, in the constitution of the Norfolk Museum Committee which is responsible for the Norfolk Museums Service and which gives the constituent districts the ownership of the museum buildings and a say in the overall policy, although from a funding point of view this is entirely a County Council Service, and in a number of other individual cases, such as the new Harborough Museum which is a partnership between Leicestershire, the Harborough District Council and a Trust established by a local historical society. All the signs suggest that partnerships of this kind amongst local authorities, perhaps of different 'tiers', are likely to become more and more common over the next few years as a sensible response to the scarcity of funds for both specialised professional expertise and routine running costs in relation to desirable new developments, particularly in relation to (a) the desire to conserve and make available to the public historic buildings and sites that would otherwise be 'at risk', and (b) the growing number of tourism development initiatives within the museum sector.

Local authorities and local independent museums

The powers of the Public Libraries and Museums Act, 1964, in relation to the co-operative development of services or the making of financial contributions to the museums and related facilities are not restricted to those in the local government sector: local authorities are equally empowered to assist with the development and running of museums and galleries completely outside of local government. Initially this power was used mainly in facilitating the making of straightforward cash grants on either a regular or occasional basis to existing voluntary sector local museums, such as long-established Society museums ranging from those that have in effect a county museums service role such as the Salisbury and South Wiltshire Museum through to small, purely local or specialist museums.

Also, soon after the passing of the 1964 Act, a number of local authorities began to assist with regimental and other armed forces local museums, as for example in the case of an MoD decision to dispose of the former Regimental Headquarters building that has traditionally housed the Regimental Museum, in some cases since the early 1920s. At the present time a number of important military museums have been, or are in the process of being transferred to an existing local authority museum service, and there is every sign that this trend will accelerate rather than decrease over the next few years. Ministry of Defence funding of the major national-level service museums, such as the naval museums in Portsmouth, seems assured, at least for the time being, and a small number of other Service museums, particularly those in important tourist areas, may be able to generate from their admission fees a sufficiently high proportion of their costs to be able to survive at least for some time to come, but there seems every likelihood that the great majority of more locally-based Service museums, such as the now-traditional county regimental museums, will survive only if local government takes over most, if not, all the staffing and other running costs.

In addition to what may be termed the traditional independent local museum, a new 'breed' of independent museums has emerged in recent years, particularly the past 10–15 years. Most are located in buildings and/or environments of historic interest in their own right and many, probably a clear majority of these, have an industrial history theme. Typically, these are located outside the city or town centre sites that have been the traditionally preferred locations for museums, and they are very much the product of the growing demand of the motoring public for some kind of 'theme' experience for half-day or whole day excursions in place of the traditional drive to the seaside or other less-structured tourist experience of earlier decades. (There has been a parallel explosion in visitor numbers at major National Trust country houses and some of the countryside-based Department of the Environment (now English Heritage) properties).

In the museums field, one of the earliest to be established was the Ironbridge Gorge Museum – which is certainly much the most distinguished in the UK (perhaps in Europe) in terms of its historic importance, although the Museum was instituted from the beginning as a charitable trust company rather than as a conventional local government department (or as a joint local government committee or board under the Public Libraries and Museums Act 1964 – the chosen vehicle for establishing and developing the North of England Open Air Museum at Beamish, formally constituted in 1970).

Few issues have caused greater controversy within the UK provincial museum movement over the past decade or so as the claims and counter-claims in relation to the contemporary 'independent museum' movement, as advocated both eloquently and aggressively by the Association of Independent Museums, established in 1977. Looking specifically at the remarkable success of private, non-profit,museums in the USA, the UK advocates of the 'independent museum' approach argued that museums would flourish in a way that had never been seen before in Britain if only they could be entrepreneurial in terms of external fund-raising and trading activities, and be freed from the alleged dead hand of local government political and bureaucratic control.

Over the past two decades a considerable number of new 'independent museums' have been established with these basic aims, and perhaps 40 or 50 have become an important part of the national museum provision, at least at a regional standard of service, with a few (eg Ironbridge and the National Motor Museum, Beaulieu), clearly being of national or indeed international importance. However, despite genuine successes in terms of fund-raising and sponsorship, the expectation or at least hope of paralleling the United States situation was always quite unrealistic. Amongst the major countries of the world the United States system of tax deductions, under which a taxpayer can in effect choose to pay a proportion of his or her taxes either to the government or to a favourite charity, is unique and is unlikely to be paralleled elsewhere: certainly there is no sign of moves in this direction in Britain or any other EEC country. The most that is possible here is that businesses (although not private taxpayers) may be able to claim as a legitimate cost the advertising value of any duly acknowledged sponsorship of a museum or other charitable project.

Certainly a number of the major new-style 'independent museums' have raised from external sources very considerable sums, particularly for the development of their museums and facilities. However, there is little real evidence of genuinely private sources playing a major role in such fund-raising, in comparison with monies provided from various public sources, including in particular central government historic building and ancient monument grants, subventions from local authorities and New Town Development Corporations, substantial financial assistance from nationalised industries in a number of cases, together with increasingly – large-scale funding from the Training Commission. (At the peak of the Community Enterprise Programme and Youth Opportunities Programme at least one major 'independent museum' had in excess of 300 full-time employees, together with appropriate supporting funds, from the MSC, now the Training Commission, outnumbering the museum's regular staff by a ratio of more than six to one).

So far as external sources of funding are concerned, there seems to be little or no evidence so far that either public or private funding bodies, potential sponsors, etc distinguish between 'traditional' public museum constitutions and management structures and the new 'independent trust' approach. Indeed the North of England Open Air Museum at Beamish, run by a Joint Committee of four County Councils, has been conspicuously more successful in terms of both external fund-raising and the development of visitor numbers than the great majority of the new generation of 'independent museums'.

All the evidence to date suggests that in both the national and local public museum sectors private benefactors and commercial sponsors alike have been only too willing to support worthwhile projects canvassed by the leading museums and galleries. At least on the basis of the evidence to date there seems no sign of any bias on the part of potential benefactors or sponsors either in favour of the 'independent museum' or against either established or new conventional public sector museums and galleries: the overriding factor appears to be the quality and interest of the 'product' and the presentation of the case.

One of the important objectives of the Museum Data-Base Project is to ascertain for the first time both the level and sources of all kinds of external fund-raising, such as donations and sponsorship, for all categories of museums, public and private, national and local, but on the basis of information currently available it seems likely that in terms of external fund-raising the two most successful provincial museums and art galleries in the 1984–85 financial year were both conventional local authority ones, led by the Manchester City Art Gallery which raised well over £1 million from genuinely private (as opposed to 'Quango') sources towards the cost of buying the Crawford Duccio School 'Crucifixion'.

Despite any clear evidence of long-term financial or managerial advantage of the 'independent museum' option, a small number of local authorities have over the past decade or so turned either existing museum development projects into some form of charitable trust or company, although usually, as in the parallel case of many civic theatres, local government control has effectively been retained if only on an 'arms-length' basis through the membership of the governing body, resulting in what could reasonably be described as a 'Qualgo' (Quasi-Automous Local Government Organisation).

Perhaps the most successful museum established on this model is the Black Country Museum, which has expanded greatly in terms of facilities and visitor numbers since it was reconstituted as a charitable company by Dudley Metropolitan District in 1975, whilst on a smaller scale the Torfaen Museum Trust, Pontypool, took over a single small museum in 1978 and now has four branches open or under development in addition.

Such transfers of responsibility have, however, been rare, and even if there is a massive increase of privatisation of local government services in general will probably remain so. However, it is only too clear in almost every part of the country that with the funding for 'official' museum initiatives at the best static overall, and possibly in decline in many areas, many more local enthusiasts are going to try to solve perceived gaps in public museum provision by establishing a further generation of voluntary sector facilities, probably in every case seriously under-resourced (especially in terms of long-term funding and professional staffing).

In many cases these initiatives will not survive the enthusiasm of the founding members; in most they will suffer from chronic under-

funding. Certainly if the cycle proceeds along the lines of the previous ones in the second half of the nineteenth century and in the
inter-war years (both of which saw a parallel spate of voluntary
museum developments), some will eventually fail completely with
the loss of their collections and facilities, and most of the remainder
will eventually survive through some kind of local government
support – either continuing maintenance subsidies or, more likely if
the history of the two previous cycles repeat themselves, by being
absorbed into the local government museum system. This may seem
a depressing analysis, but it should be viewed against the fact that
less than a dozen of the many significant pre–1939 'independent'
museums now survive outside the public sector.

Local museums and the environment

A museum should never be introspective, concerned only with itself
and its direct services, and this is especially true of a community
museum or gallery serving a local authority area. It is widely recognised today that it should look outwards to its community and to the
landscape of the region that it serves, and develop for itself a role that
is truly relevant to that community and to its own region.

The distinguished French philosopher and practician of
museology, Georges-Henri Riviere, former Director-General of
ICOM (the International Council of Museums) developed over the
past quarter of a century both the concept and the word 'ecomesée'
(ecomuseum) to describe a museum in which both the overall policy
and the public displays and educational programme are directed
particularly to the interpretation of the local environment of the
museum. Over the past ten years or more there has been a rapidly
growing involvement with both the natural and historic environment
amongst British local authority museums, and while none have yet
adopted the French or Canadian terminology, many have developed
what is basically the 'ecomuseum' concept, more usually termed
'regional interpretation' or 'historical ecology' amongst UK
museums, but basically representing a new approach to the study of
the landscape of the museum's own region.

Ecology is primarily concerned with research into the environmental systems of the present day. Historical ecology seeks the
scientific evidence of the evolution of the landscape and of environmental systems over many centuries, and in particular looks at
the human dimension in the evolution of the landscape. This human
dimension is, of course, of great importance throughout all of
Western Europe except in the highest and most remote mountain
regions. This approach has formed the basis of both a major part of

the scientific research and publications programme of a number of museum services over recent years, as for example, in Leicestershire, where much of the new display work for the various museums of the Museums, Art Galleries and Records Service – for example, the new branch museums in Melton Mowbray (opening in 1977) and Market Harborough (1983), have been much influenced by this kind of approach.

One of the most valuable resources of the museums service to a local authority is the specialised knowledge and expertise of its professional staff. In most of the academic specialisations that local museums cover, the museum may well have the only expert employed in that particular field by any department of the council. For example, quoting Leicestershire again, the museums Service currently has thirteen staff qualified at University level in archaeology, seven in biology and ecology, four in geology, nine in fine art and decorative arts, etc. Consequently, the County Council has decided that these museum experts should be available to advise all services and committees of the County Council – but with their independent professional status being fully recognised.

It is not the job of the museum personnel to take sides in matters of public or political controversy or debate, but to put forward – as they try to do in the exhibition galleries and the museum's publications – the evidence on which the appropriate authorities can make a balanced decision. Moreover, they should be free to make such evidence available to all sides in a matter of public controversy. For example, between 1977 and 1980, the Leicestershire Service carried out one of the largest environmental survey and research programmes ever attempted in Britain in advance of the public inquiry into the National Coal Board's application for permission to develop three 'super mines' in north-east Leicestershire in recently discovered reserves totalling almost a billion tonnes. This involved an investigation of an area of almost 10 per cent of the county from the point of view of its geological, ecological, archaelogical and historic interest, together with any other relevant conservation issues. However, all of the surveys, etc of the Museums Service were published or deposited for public consultation in advance, and could be studied by all parties to the inquiry and were not reserved to the County Council in a partisan way. It is entirely right that the expertise of the museums should be at the disposal of the employing authority in this way, and, incidentally, demonstrates the value and effectiveness of a good museum service to its community and its region.

More traditionally, many museums have been actively involved in field survey, systematic local collecting, and associated recording within 'museum' fields (especially geology, biology, archaeology and folk life studies) for a century or more. However, in recent years this work has greatly expanded with the establishment of formal networks of Geological Site, Biological and Archaeological Databanks with a national coverage, and the great majority of these are housed in and managed by local museums (usually on a countrywide basis, although not necessarily by County Museum Services as such).

Local museums have been involved in local archaeological work, including small-scale excavations, for many decades, but this field too has seen a massive expansion over the past two decades. In London, the Guildhall Museum helped to sponsor archaeological work in advance of re-building on bombed sites throughout the City immediately after the Second World War, and in 1960 the City of Leicester reached a formal agreement with the then Ministry of Public Buildings and Works, (responsible for Ancient Monuments and archaeology), under which the first permanent local authority museum archaeological unit was established in the Leicester Museums.

For the next ten years there was little further development on these lines, but from 1970 the newly established Department of Ancient Monuments and Archaeology Branch began promoting the establishment of what was seen at the time as a nation-wide 'rescue' archaeology service, based on local county or regional archaeological units, and most of these had strong links with local authority museums, and a number were established as part of an expanded museums department, on the lines of the Leicester experiment.

There was a massive expansion of 'rescue' archaeology through most of the 1970s, and county or regional archaeological units were established as the result of DoE funding in most parts of England, but under a variety of management structures: county or district council, university, local society or specially established charitable trust companies.

However, with changes in policy and reductions in funding within the DoE, by the late 1970s a positive policy of disengagement from any sort of developing national archaeological service or of continuous financial commitment emerged, and the greater part of the recently estalished provision was either cut back severely, closed down completely, or thrown largely or wholly on to local government, including in particular the already hard-pressed museum services and budgets, and there is no sign of any change in central policy following the transfer of direct DoE involvement to the new Historic Building and Ancient Monuments Commissions ('English Heritage' in England and 'Cadw' in Wales).

The current policy is to concentrate on archaeological survey work, in order to identify and evaluate sites of archaeological importance.

Where it appears that these might be affected by development, the first preference is preservation and excavation is always regarded as the last resort. No matter how carefully it is done, excavation destroys archaeological sites and both official policy and professional opinion is that a site should only be excavated where it is going to be destroyed anyway, either through some form of development, or by less obvious causes, such as modern farming practices, particularly deep ploughing. The 'research excavation' of the past is a luxury that, sadly, can no longer be afforded in terms of either money or manpower.

A number of museums also have an important role in the organisation and promotion of volunteer programmes in the environmental research field. Archaeology is a good example of this, and over the country there are many thousands of volunteers working on archaeological surveys and in particular carrying out 'fieldwalking' over freshly ploughed ground during the autumn and winter. These may well be trained and supervised by museum staff, but frequently work in self-motivated local groups, usually in their own locality of perhaps three to five parishes. The members of these groups usually know the local farmers personally, and also hear what is going on in the village: the local pub is a marvellous institution in which to do archaeological survey and recording work!

Many museum services are today deeply interested in the changing patterns of their local landscape, whether natural geological features, areas of ecological interest, or man-made such as an intensively developed urban area. Typically, however, they are more likely to be dealing with a combination of both natural and human processes, for example, in studying flooded former quarry workings which are now being re-colonised by natural vegetation while, at the same time, it is being used for recreational purposes by a local sailing club or by trout fishermen.

Whilst museums and individual museum professionals, must never neglect their traditional museum values and responsibilities towards their collections of specimens, their development, conservation and interpretation, many are now finding a new and exciting role for the museums service in the study of the landscape itself, and of the relevance of that landscape to present-day society, and indeed to future generations.

There seems little doubt that local authority museums of all sizes and levels will become more and more involved with their environment in these sorts of ways in the coming years.

There is every likelihood that providing there are no really severe cutbacks in staff and other resources, local public museum involvement with environmental issues is likely to continue to increase further in the next few years.

Organisation and management structures

Within many of the major English cities and towns a Museums Department, at least in an embryo form, was one of the first departmental units to be established within the management and administrative structure of the new local authorities set up in the wake of the 1836 municipal reforms, often emerging long before education, library or welfare services.

The new municipal museum (to which was probably added a public art gallery during the fourth quarter of the 19th century), was seen by council members and the general public alike as both a mark of a civilised society, very much like the spate of sanitary and street 'Improvements' (always with a capital 'I'), and as an essential part of the parallel 'improvement' of the population at large in terms of public education and enlightenment.

The curator of the museum was an honoured chief officer of the Council, a focus for wider educational and cultural activity in the town, such as the development of local scientific societies (many of which were physically based on local museums), and probably serving as a key local administrator if and when the nineteenth century 'Parliament of Science' – the British Association for the Advancement of Science – could be persuaded to honour the locality with one of its celebrated Annual Meetings.

Some of the achievements of the earlier local authority museums in areas that would today be regarded as totally outside their field of responsibility or activity were truly remarkable. In many large towns the first municipal public libraries were offshoots of the already established museums, and some remained part of the museums service until at least the Second World War, as in Leicester where the museums remained the 'senior' service in terms of committee title, professional staffing and even locally perceived status through to the 1974 reorganisation. The story at Exeter was even more remarkable: the Royal Albert Memorial Museum is the parent institution not only of the public libraries and College of Art (as at Leicester and several other places), but also the Technical College and the University of Exeter.

As in most other fields in local government, the preparation for the 1974 reorganisation was a major turning point in the museums, and especially in the organisation and management field. During the run up to 1974 there was no clear view within local government of the role or place of museums in any new structure.

The museum profession and the Government's own advisory bodies – the Standing Commission on Museums and Galleries and the DES's Wright Committee on Provincial Museums and Galleries, all perceived that the best local government museum services in terms of both quality and efficiency were generally those that had independent department status with their own chief officer-level Director, whilst it was equally clear that a number of important museums and galleries had been badly served by their authorities while forming part of a local library service headed by that bete-noir of the museum world over many decades – the derided 'Librarian-Curator'.

However, nobody seriously challenged the century-old view that museums were first and last educational and cultural organisations with a heavy responsibility to society as a whole, and both the past and to generations and centuries to come, not merely to today's visitors to see the public displays or other facilities on offer in the museum buildings.

Indeed, this view seemed to be fully accepted and endorsed in the first large-scale management consultants' study to impinge on an important UK museum or art gallery – that of McKinsey's in Liverpool during the run-up to local government reorganisation. Although the basic approach was one that was soon to become very familiar throughout English local government, in seeking a 'managerial' rather than 'service' orientation of Liverpool's local government, the consultants regarded the City Museums and the Walker Art Gallery as outstanding and prestigious *academic* institutions, despite their obvious and very popular public role, and although they were considered too small to stand alone within the proposed new management structure, they were neither merged with each other, nor with any other department. Instead, they retained their distinct and separate identities with their own Directors of quasi-chief officer status reporting both to a separate service committee and to the Town Clerk and Chief Executive as the nominal 'full' chief officer.

However, the Liverpool solution was soon overshadowed and forgotten in the political and managerial struggles of 1972–74. The nature and scope of the reorganisation legislation was disputed up to the Royal Assent (and indeed through to the end of the 1970s in some areas with efforts to achieve 'organic change'). In this atmosphere, the museum arguments were about even more fundamental issues than management and organisation structures – which tier of local government was going to take over major museums under the unhelpful and imprecise 'concurrent powers' provisions, for example. (The last *provisional* agreement on this issue was not reached until several months after 1 April 1974 in several places, and some of the formal transfer agreements were still being worked out into the 1980s).

Although some preliminary work was done by the members and officers of the outgoing authorities following the Royal Assent, in most places the new councils elected in the summer of 1973 had effectively two or three months at the most in which to decide on their departmental and chief officer structures before they had to get senior staff recruitment under way. In the circumstances, there is little wonder that in many places the recently published Bains Report (*The New Local Authorities: management and structure*, HMSO, 1972), was seen as the answer to a Constitution Committee's prayers, and that both committee and departmental structures were simply photocopied from one or other of the various examples in the Bains Report and implemented with little or no discussion of their implications in relation to any special circumstances of that particular authority.

As a result of decision making (or perhaps more accurately decision abdication) of this kind, a significant number of great and distinguished local authority museums and galleries, together with a perhaps a majority of their lesser brethen, lost their identity and were merged into some kind of 'Leisure' conglomerate on or soon after 1 April 1974. There can be no denying the fact that in many cases the actual changes were implemented with little or no consultation with, or even common courtesy towards, either the staff or hard-working 'Friends' or other voluntary support groups, and that in some places the consequent legacy of destructive bitterness and mistrust still exists a decade later, and continues to flare up from time to time.

In a wide-ranging and hard-hitting keynote address to the 1985 Museums Association Annual Conference, the senior Professional Vice-President, Ian Robertson, had dealt at length with some of these issues:

> However, notwithstanding the efforts of a number of local authorities that have tried to maintain, despite all the pressures, economic or otherwise, upon them, properly staffed professional (museum) services with appropriate standing within local authorities, there has been a significant move since the passing of the Local Government Act of 1972 to downgrade the status of local authority museums; this has been particularly true in the case of District Council Services reorganised or set up since the 1st April 1974, for in case after case brought to the attention of the Museums Association once proud museums, often previously maintained by County Boroughs with their own chief officers, have been converted into divisions, or even smaller parts, of leisure, recreation, amenities or some other departments.
>
> While it may well be true that the actual number of people employed in local authority museums has indeed increased over the last decade, nevertheless it is quite clear that the number of chief officer posts has declined in dramatic terms. Although an attempt to justify this amalgamation of museum services into large departments may be made on the grounds of cost-cutting or cost effectiveness, in fact it has been a very expensive exercise, has caused considerable damage to the museums service and the loss of professional advice at the highest level directly to elected members. . . .
>
> It is not clear why tens of millions of pounds have been spent since 1974

trying to merge existing museum services into totally different departments; it is not clear that any savings have been made anywhere by this process and the value of this kind of corporatism to the community is not clear either.

After referring to specific, named, instances, Ian Robertson continued:

> Although this kind of situation has arisen in various parts of the United Kingdom, especially in the years immediately after Reorganisation in 1974, never before has it been stated bluntly and publicly that this erosion of local government museum services by local government is not acceptable to this profession; there are many members of the Association who have been concerned over the years with the damage done to the museums service and about the costs involved in doing that damage, concern shared by an increasing number of elected members who have doubts as to the wisdom of the course that local government management has taken since Reorganisation. All credit to those Councillors who have resisted policies that struck at the independence of this profession. Why cannot it be accepted that museum services have their own identities, and that their staffs can *loyally* serve their employers and their communities simply by being good museum professionals?
>
> It is important to emphasis that the words used above have been chosen carefully; there is no criticism here at all of the political programmes of the majority parties in any of our towns, cities, or counties, many of which have promoted the establishment of leisure services *committees.* What is being criticised are the management policies, relating to the creation of new *departments,* adopted to implement these programmes; no political party has ever been elected on a platform or with a mandate to damage our profession and the Association is quite in order to draw attention to the harm which has been done at considerable expense by the imposition of unacceptable management practices. (I D Robertson, 1985. Financing Museums: The View of a Professional. *Museums J.* Dec. 1985).

Perhaps the most remarkable thing about this address was that in the discussion session that followed, not a single person challenged this devastating criticism, even though those present included a significant number of 'generic' Leisure or Recreation Service chief officers, and approximately 150 local authority councillors, the majority of them serving authorities with some kind of 'leisure' department.

There are, however, even wider issues, in my view. For a start, what actually happened in 1972–74 was frequently a considerable distortion of the intention of the Bains Study Group which, as members of the Group have made very clear, was never to put forward rigid frameworks for automatic adoption by the new authorities regardless of local circumstances.

More specifically in relation to museums and art galleries, the Bains Working Group quite clearly and explicitly (and quite correctly, in my view), regarded museums and art galleries (and, for that matter, libraries) as part of their 'Education and Related Services' group of major functions, and *not* part of a 'Leisure' or 'Amenity' function. Moreover, nowhere does the Bains Report suggest anything along the lines of the widespread downgrading of museum (and library) services that has actually occurred in many places, and while museums are not specifically shown in the Bains examples of organisation charts libraries are, and always as an independent service, with either a 'full' or 'minor' chief officer at its head.

Although for more than a decade it has been fashionable to explain (within the professions that have lost out, 'blame' would be a more accurate term) the emergence of the new 'generic' Leisure Services at the expense of the museum and library services that regarded themselves as essentially educational on the Bains Report, this seems unfair on the members of the Bains Working Group. If these developments were prompted by Bains, they were based on a misreading and basic misunderstanding of the study (and indeed its terms of reference):

> To set out the considerations which, in the Group's opinion, should be borne in mind by local authorities in determining their structures of management at elected member and officer levels. . .
> (*Bains Report,*1972: 1)

There is a great difference between considering advice that 'should be borne in mind' and mindlessly copying sample organisation charts and claiming that an authority was 'forced' into particular perhaps unpalatable decisions 'by Bains'. Quite clearly there was a very strong conformist pressure, especially on the Shire Districts, to opt for the Leisure Service model, and the origins of this are in themselves probably worthy of detailed research, particularly into the relative effectiveness of the then embryo leisure service profession compared with the long-established museum and library professions.

Whatever the internal organisational arrangements in any particular local authority, the current 'leisure services' model of the nature, purpose and objectives of museums (see above) is an extremely inadequate one. Certainly, nearly all adult museum and gallery visitors experience museums in their leisure time, but it is quite illogical to claim that this is a sufficient reason to classify most if not all of what museums do as 'leisure' as such.

Looking at a closely related field, the National Trust's properties are visited by members of the public during their leisure time, but this cannot be used to argue that the purpose of the National Trust is to provide a leisure experience to its members and others. Its overriding legal and policy purpose and objective is the preservation, conservation and (where appropriate) enhancement of the 'heritage' buildings and land in the care of the Trust and, as policy, facilities for visitors are only provided where this is compatible with the basic conservation and related requirements.

If a 'conservation' rather than 'leisure' fundamental objective or priority is acceptable in relation to the work of the National Trust, why is it not equally acceptable in the case of the far greater number of important historic buildings and sites in the care of the nation's museum services? And if this point is conceded, why should short-term 'leisure' considerations and objectives take precedence over the duty of the museum to ensure that the material evidence of the past and present are adequately collected and conserved, not necessarily for the benefit of present generations, but for future centuries, in exactly the same way as is freely accepted in relation to buildings or sites of historic interest? Precisely the same points about the patent inadequacy of the currently fashionable 'leisure' model of museums could be made in relation to other vital functions, such as the museum's educational role.

In most respectable museums and galleries, the cost of services to the casual public visitors forms only a minority of the total cost of the museum service as a whole, and is far outweighed by the cost of the care and improvement of the basic resources of the museum's collections and its building stock, which in very many cases are in themselves of great historic interest and importance. (For example, in the case of the Leicestershire Service the average age of the buildings cared for and used in many different ways by the Service is about 270 years, and the list includes eight Scheduled Ancient Monuments and 26 Listed Buildings, including seven listed as Grade 1.)

Direct educational work, from the traditional school visits through to servicing higher education and research students, together with less obvious museum education work such as the important new developments in the community and race relations fields, all make heavy demands on staff and other resources. Museums are also taking a far more active role these days in the area of environmental research, recording and publication (see above), to the considerable benefit of local government as planning authorities.

Indeed, although there have been few detailed functional analyses of local authority museum budgets, the sample studies that have been undertaken indicate that the direct cost of services to the general public, (the area that might possibly be described as a 'leisure service'), is unlikely to amount to much more than 40 per cent of the annual revenue expenditure of a medium- to large-sized local authority museum service. (In the case of the British Museum (Natural History) which is actually funded through the Advisory Board on the Research Councils as a research institution rather than a museum as such, the figure appears to be nearer 15 per cent despite its large-scale new display programme).

No doubt much more information will be available by the end of 1988 from the current Museum Data Base project of the Museums Association (and by the Office of Arts and Libraries), which amongst other things seeks specifically to identify the relative and absolute levels of expenditure on almost two dozen different museum activities, including public opening, educational work, care of collections, care of premises, research, publication etc.

Outside the public sector, those fundamentally hostile to local government control of museums, especially the more vociferous members of the Association of Independent Museums, have exploited the massive damage and disarray of the past decade in many places to justify their claim that museums cannot hope to survive and prosper within local government, and even that the policies and practices of democratic local government are fundamentally inimicable to the successful management of museums. The positive success and development of both old and new museums, particularly many of the new County Museum Services, within local government since Reorganisation shows that the basic argument is nonsense, but there are far too many examples of wanton damage to once excellent museums and galleries for this argument to go away of its own accord.

If local government is to retain responsibility in the long term for the massive 'heritage' resources currently in the care of its museums, it will have to prove itself once again competent and worthy of this heavy responsibility.

If it does not do so then there will be increasingly strong, perhaps irresistible, pressure for the removal of many major museums to either central government as some kind of 'national museum in the provinces' (the post-abolition solution already enacted in the case of the Merseyside Museums and Walker Art Gallery, Liverpool), or (more likely) to the 'independent museum' sector, where the key management decisions are taken in the light of direct advice to the governing body from a qualified and competent professional Director.

Finance and local government museums

It is probably fair to say that there are only three things that are certain about local government's financial involvement with museums. First, that museums form an insignificant part of total UK public expenditure, and that this is mirrored in the proportion of local authority spending on museums. Second, that there are, at least in percentage terms, enormous variations between the levels of museum expenditure by different, often very similar, authorities. Third, that largely as a consequence of the very low level of expenditure, coupled with the inequalities in provision, there are virtually no accurate or meaningful comparative financial statistics in this area.

The current Office of Arts and Libraries estimate is that total UK public expenditure on libraries, museums and the whole of the arts combined amounts to just under 2 per cent of total public expenditure; museums represent rather less than a quarter of this proportion, and the two dozen or so major national museums and galleries (largely in the four capital cities) account for about 65 per cent of the total public museum expenditure.

In terms of the nation's GDP, total public museum and art gallery spending is nearer to 0.5 per cent, and from leading the world in museum provision in the eighteenth and nineteenth centuries, the UK must now be near the bottom of the league table amongst the countries of the developed world, and indeed has fallen far behind many very poor developing countries, where the establishment of high quality museum services at national, regional and municipal levels is usually regarded as one of the proofs of the establishment of a civilised society.

The UK position appears to be even worse when looked at in terms of current levels of capital expenditure. The opening of only three significant new provincial art galleries in the whole of the UK in the forty years since the last war should be compared with the opening of four in 1984 alone in West Germany. Looking even nearer to England, and to a country whose economic fortunes since the war have certainly been no better than ours, two of the current capital schemes in Paris – the new Science Museum complex at the Parc de la Villette, and the new museum of the arts of the nineteenth century in the former Gare d'Orsay have between them at the present time an annual budget equivalent to about 80 per cent of total UK annual museum expenditue, capital plus revenue, national plus local. These two projects represent 'new' money, and the equivalent of the 'main programme' continues unabated, indeed expanding, as well, so that there are many other albeit less spectacular, capital projects elsewhere in Paris (the substantial extension of The Louvre, for instance), and throughout provincial France.

To some extent, English local government at least is, very tentatively, taking the law into its own hands in relation to the massive backlog of capital expenditure in the museum field. Against a Standing Commission on Museums and Galleries 1978 estimate of a UK provincial museum capital expenditure in the museum capital expenditure backlog of at least £100m (largely based on a project by project assessment and excluding the funding of any new developments), successive Government Expenditure Plans allocations have been massively overspent in percentage terms. For example, in 1981/82 the 'planned' allocation was £5.0m, but the outturn was £7.9m, and by 1983/84 the gap had widened to over 100 per cent with £5.6 million 'planned' and an outturn of £12.6m. The current indications are that despite the pressure on the 'Other Services' capital allocations, this trend will conform to the 'planned' 1985/86 level of only £5.2m – around a quarter of the cost of the new Burrell building in Glasgow or the new gallery in Stuttgart, (or nine and a half working days' capital budget for the La Villette project in Paris!)

There is clearly great variation in the level of museum provision or other support (if any) between different, often otherwise very similar, local authorities. For example, out of twenty largest county councils in population terms, eight have no recognisable museum service at all, only three of these make any significant financial contribution to non-county council museums of some kind, and in only four are there comprehensive county services with insignificant provision at district council level. On the other hand, except in the four counties with an exclusively county council museum service almost all districts with a population of more than 200,000 have some form of museum provision as do perhaps 40 per cent of the smaller districts.

To some extent local authority provision is a reflection of tradition or the scale of involvement with museums of a particular city or town in the nineteenth or earlier part of the twentieth century, or other accidents of history. For example, a considerable proportion of the newly established museums of the past two decades have begun with attempts to find an appropriate use for an important historic building under threat in some way.

However, an even greater factor in the wide variations between different authorities is the extent and nature of other museum provision in the area. Not unexpectedly, local government expenditure on museums is relatively low in the four capital cities (virtually nil in Cardiff and Belfast) because of the large and comprehensive scale of the national museum and gallery provision in these areas. Similar, although less obvious considerations apply in Cambridge and (especially) Oxford, where the major university museums and galleries funded centrally through the University Grants Committee, take the place of the traditional municipal museums and galleries to a considerable extent, and there is substantial public museum provision by the universities in some other places.

Less obviously, where there is large-scale Ministry of Defence museum involvement, as in southern Hampshire, the pressure on local authorities for museum development may be reduced to some extent, and of course the existence of concurrent powers leads to overlapping provision, and obscures the total level of public funding of museums in any particular geographical county or other area.

Again, everyone is hoping that the new Museum Data-Base will give a much clearer picture of total levels of museum provision of all kinds, including the private and 'qualgo' sectors, not least in financial terms. However, less comprehensive studies, such as my own attempted analysis of total museum expenditure in 1981/82 on a county by county basis, adding available local government data to the published estimates or accounts of the main national, MoD, university etc museums, showed a picture very different indeed from the crude RER or CIPFA statistics.

To begin with the number and kind of local authority museum services in a particular county or other unit has a significant effect. Although the principal county and district museum services in Hampshire are all in the middle range in terms of expenditure, the total local government museum provision is in fact far higher than in apparently high spending shire counties, such as Leicestershire or Norfolk, which have little or nothing apart from the County Museum Service in each case. The differences are even more marked, and if funding from various kinds of central government sources are taken into account, the spending per head of population in London (where local authority spending is generally well below average) is around nine times that of Leicester, Norfolk or Avon, or six times that of Merseyside, the most generous metropolitan county. Also, both Oxfordshire and Hampshire move well up the 'league table' because of their large and important University and Ministry of Defence museums respectively.

Available local government financial statistics are a very poor guide to what is really happening in detail within the museum field. The Rate Expenditure Returns (RERs) depend very much on departmental organisation and on the mode and scale of central support and administrative expenses to particular services, although the latest attempts to standardise accounting practices may produce greater uniformity and hence comparability. The treatment of assistance to the voluntary sector museums also varies greatly, and may well be charged to expenditure heads under section 14 of the Public Libraries and Museums Act, 1964, such as tourism, historic building grants, or even miscellaneous charitable donations, etc – especially if the local authority has no worries about the spending limit under section 137 of the Local Government Act, 1972.

The same is true of other areas of public spending on museums: there is no uniformity of either accounting or Parliamentary Vote practices even between the major national museums. In some cases premises costs are budgeted separately, in others they are included in the annual grant, and the same is true of purchase fund contributions, and the position becomes even more confusing as you descend the 'league table' of nationally financed institutions. . Again, everyone is currently playing a waiting game in the hope that the Museum Data- Base Project will produce the answers.

Two things are, however, abundantly clear. First, that the national institutions, like most if not all central government services, have been treated far more favourably that local government museums by successive governments over the past two decades, and the already wide gap betwen the two areas in terms of standards of provision, staffing levels, capital or revenue funding. Few if any local government museums have matched the 120 per cent increase in the staff (already generous by local government standards) of the National Maritime Museum during the 1970s. All too often the only justification (?) for significant reductions in assumed or planned local authority museum funding during the annual Public Expenditure round has been that the local sector figures represents, in effect, what is left over in the total Arts 'pool' after meeting 'known ministerially approved commitments of the national institutions'.

Second, that local government as a whole has simply refused to make the sorts of cuts in either existing services or perceived additional needs that successive Rate Support Grant settlements have implied , especially when these have in part been demanded to pay for growth in the central government Arts sector. Consequently, despite one fairly substantial revaluation of the local government museums RSG provision, the gap between 'planned' expenditure in central government terminology and actual local government expenditure on museums has widened very greatly, so that by 1985/86 the forecast English local authority outturn for museums is £60.1m against and RSG settlement figure of only £43m, representing a shortfall of 33 per cent on the current account (on top of the even larger forecast 'overspend' on capital).

It is equally clear that there is a continuing upwards pressure on total local authority museum expenditure for a number of reasons. For example, each year a significant number of local authorities are entering the museum field for the first time, mainly in response to general local demand, or more specifically in relation to the preservation of an historic building or the perceived economic benefits of a museum service in terms of tourism.

Also, overall there appears to be a very significant shift of expenditure from central government to local government in the museums and related areas, such as the very substantial transfers of archaeological responsibilities and of Regimental Museums previously funded by the MoD. Improved security standards and systems also add to running costs, as does the very necessary pressure for improved documentation and inventory control standards as the value of collections escalate rapidly in both intrinsic and financial terms.

Finance, or more accurately the lack of it, is and will probably remain the key issue facing the local government museum service, which has been chronically underfunded and undervalued for so many years. I often wonder how this small and dedicated profession has continued to develop and improve the public facilities so that the museum service makes an economic contribution to the nation from tourism alone (let alone to formal and informal education) that is out of all proportion to the nation's miserable investment in this key area of its heritage.

APPENDIX

Area Schemes and Services Eligible for Grant Aid

(Annex A to appendix D of the Tenth report of the Standing Commission on Museums and Galleries, 1979)

1 Preparation of publications sponsored by Area Museum Services.
2 Conservation Schemes and Services (including restoration and repair and the equipping and staffing of related laboratories and workshops) covering:

  a easel paintings;
  b paper including prints, watercolours and drawings and archives relating to artefacts lodged in a museum or gallery;
  c decorative arts including furniture finishes, decorative paintings, gilding, laquer, metal work and frames;
  d ceramics;
  e architectural decoration including frescoes, murals, stained and painted glass lodged as bona fide artefacts in a museum;
  f natural history including preservation and modelling of birds, animals and plants;
  g geology;
  h archaeology;
  i ethnology;
  j textiles;
  k science and technology.

3 Professional advice generally including surveys of existing museums and galleries, advice on the creation of new and the reorganisation of existing museums, advice on display, storage and environmental control, procurement, conservation and restoration.
4 Photography and the provision of photographic equipment.
5 Short term storage (note 1).

6 Display schemes and exhibitions including refurbishment, permanent and temporary accomodation, procurement and installation of display cases, environmental control equipment related to display and storage (ie to control humidity, temperature and lighting), sound equipment and other specialised gallery display equipment. Related essential printing and publicity material (note 2). Security systems.

7 Advice and assistance to local education and other schools authorities as regards the role of the museums and galleries in education generally (note 3).

8 Documentation in museums and galleries including cataloguing and recording, information storage and retrieval systems.

9 Training of museum curatorial, technical and warding staff.

Note 1: Expenditure on the provision of new buildings or on major structural alterations for storage or any other purpose is not eligible for grant aid but rental of accommodation to provide storage as a temporary measure and the refurbishing of permanent storage accommodation including installation of services and environmental control features and equipment are admissable.

Note 2: The provision of air conditioning is eligible for grant aid as part of environmental control equipment whether this is required for display or laboratory and workshop facilities.

Note 3: The provision of facilities intended exclusively for the use of schools in connection with museums and galleries contribution to education should be funded by local education and other schools authorities.

Note 4: The cost attributable to staff, transport and administration generally (including share of overheads) generated by eligible schemes and services are eligible for grant and should be included in the cost of each scheme.

6 Sport — shifting sands in turning tides

Mike Fitzjohn*

Introduction

As the surface of a beach is constantly recast the resulting shape is in part due to the nature of the sand itself, but is far more influenced by the relentless action of the tides. So it is with sport: whilst the inherent characteristics of the activity and its organisations are important, its future will in large part be determined by the demographic, economic, social and political tides which wash over it. This chapter seeks to examine the nature of some of these tides and, in particular, their likely effect on local authority provision for sport.

The Rationales for Public Sector Involvement

The reasons for the intervention of the state in leisure provision in general, and sport in particular, have been addressed either directly or tangentially by numerous authors[1] from a variety of perspectives — historical, political, sociological, organisational. It is not the intention of this chapter to dwell unduly on theoretical perspectives, but rather, briefly to summarise some of the more commonly advanced rationales in order to provide a background to the subsequent discussion. It is important to appreciate that the significance of such rationales varies over time and across the political spectrum, and that even at one point in time several rationales will be influential, often being in opposition to one another.

'Sport for its own sake', the classic 'end in itself' argument, suggests that sport is enjoyable fun and requires no external justification. Whilst this is the principal rationale for the voluntary sector in sport, and indeed the casual sports participant, it is patently not a tenable position for public sector involvement.

'Catering for demand' was the predominant ethic of the public sector in the late 1960s. Its principal emphasis is on meeting articulated demands and it is therefore essentially a reactive posture. Whilst in the late 1970s and early 1980s it largely gave way to public sector strategies based on a more interventionist approach, in practice it remained of considerable importance, and in the late 1980s is enjoying something of a rejuvenation.

'Recreational welfare' as a rationale deems sport to be a 'public good' in its own right, to which all members of society should have access. It leads to notions of recreational disadvantage, giving policy emphasis to those who do not take part in sport, and is, for example, the rationale which has led to the Sports Council identifying 'women' as a priority group[2,3].

'Recreation as welfare' sees the provision of opportunities for sport as a contributor to other social policy goals. Those most commonly cited include:

- personal health goals — physical, mental and social.
- public health goals — savings to the National Health Service, reduction in lost production time, etc.
- social, deprivation goals — ranging across the political spectrum from 'quality of life' arguments at one extreme to 'sport as social control' at the other.

What distinguishes such goals is that, with the exception of some of the personal health goals[4], the perceived benefits are largely unsubstantiated. Nevertheless the arguments have been strongly supported by governments of all political persuasions in the past ten years, albeit deriving from very different political philosophies.

The 'economic rationale' recognises sport as a major contributor to the national economy, generating nearly 400,000 jobs and £4.4 billion consumer expenditure annually[5]. Its pursuit has rarely been of overt significance in the direct provision of sports facilities and opportunities by the public sector, but is more often manifest through the use of other local authority powers designed to stimulate and encourage the private sector. Likewise central government sees such investment as a stimulant to international trade.

Finally, 'local and national pride and prestige' is never far below the surface as a justification for public sector involvement. This is manifest both at local level, as shown subsequently in this chapter, and at national level in calls for more public money at the inevitable inquest after each Olympic Games[6].

Local authority provision for sport

The last twenty years have witnessed a burgeoning of sports provision by local authorities, of which only the briefest synopsis can be given here. Such provision, of course, is not new, and for 150 years or so authorities have provided public baths and parks, driven at least initially by the public health rationale. What distinguishes the last 20 years is the range and volume of provision.

The 1960s witnessed a growing national interest in 'leisure' and rising public expectations. The response of central government was the establishment of agencies such as the Sports Council and the Countryside Commission, and the response of a few local authorities was the provision of relevant facilities, particularly for sport. In 1970, however, there were still only about 20 indoor sports centres; today, depending on precise definitions, there are certainly over 1,000 in England, and perhaps nearer 1,500. Similarly some 600 public indoor swimming pools have been built since 1970, 60 per cent of those currently available. Such provision was fuelled by local government reorganisation in 1974: over 200 swimming pools, for example, were opened in the three years 1973–75. The same period has witnessed public provision for many newer types of facility — roller rinks, ice rinks, artifical grass pitches, country parks — as well as the improvement and refurbishment of more traditional amenities such as playing fields and swimming pools.

By the mid 1970s there was too a growing recognition among local authorities that 'provision' meant more than the traditional custodianship of facilities. This led some authorities into a number of relatively new policy areas, including:

- forging closer relationships with the voluntary sector in sport by giving grants to clubs, organising local sports councils, etc.
- developing better links with Education Authorities (again aided by local government reorganisation) by developing joint provision and dual use centres, increasing the range of facilities available to schoolchildren, etc.
- encouraging the development of the private sector in leisure by, for example, the use of planning powers and 'partnerships'.
- encouraging high level achievement in sport by providing top class facilities, promoting events, promoting summer schools, supporting local authority elite squads, giving training grants to teams and individuals, employing coaches, and giving facility hire concessions. It has been estimated[7] that the current value of grants, coaching, and facility hire alone is some £4.3m annually.

By 1980 there was a growing awareness among local authorities that their sports and other leisure provision was not being used by the whole community. Whilst broader government initiatives had stimulated a growing concern for the 'inner city', numerous studies of sports facilities showed that, in very general terms, the archetypal user was young, white, male and middle class — women, older people, ethnic minority groups and the poor, in contrast, were under-represented. Many of these issues were crystallised in the Sports Council's 10 Year Strategy, published in 1982[2]. The response of local authorities, in many instances supported financially by the Sports Council, has been the appointment of staff able to take sport out to specified groups in the community on a peripatetic basis.

By 1987, therefore, local authorities in England were estimated to be spending about £400m a year on capital investment[8] and nearly £700m a year on revenue expenditure[9]. They had a workforce in 'recreation, parks and baths' of about 80,000[10].

What has public investment achieved?

It is of course extremely difficult to prove 'cause and effect' in matters of this kind and, as the introduction makes clear, sport is but sand in tides of broader change. Nevertheless, it is possible to indicate a number of achievements in which, at minimum, public sector investment has been strongly instrumental.

Between 1977 and 1986 the proportion of adults participating in indoor sport rose from 21 per cent to 28 per cent[11], an increase of one-third. Whilst a number of activities contributed to this increase, by far and away the largest was indoor swimming, rising from participation by 5 per cent of the population in 1977 to 9 per cent in 1986. The overwhelming majority of opportunities to swim are provided by the local authorities, notwithstanding the rapid growth in private provision in recent years. In this one activity alone therefore there has been a significant return on the authorities' investment.

Local authorities must also take some credit for increases in participation in other sports. At the broad level, only 25 per cent of sports participation now takes place in voluntary sports clubs and, whilst there was about a 5 per cent growth in clubs between 1975 and 1985, there was little perceptible change in their total membership. The growth in participation in the recent past has largely been via local authority facilities, via commercial facilities and in casual activities, such as jogging. At the more specific level a survey of a major sports centre in Greater Manchester[12] showed that over a third of participants had never played their particular activity prior to the centre opening — about 30 per cent of swimmers and about 50 per cent of players in the 'dry' sports.

The second major achievement of the public sector in general, and local authorities in particular, has been in extending the sporting franchise to those who have traditionally found it difficult to take part. Whilst local authorities are not uniquely equipped to meet the needs of such people — housewives, the unemployed, ethnic minorities, etc — they have nevertheless shown themselves more willing and able to do so than the private or voluntary sectors in sport. Thus York et al[13] concluded that public facilities were tending to draw higher proportions of participants from economically disadvantaged groups.

The third achievement of local authorities is that they have created a market in which the commercial sector, and to a lesser extent the voluntary sector, can thrive. Whilst central government has continued to treat sport as peripheral, local government has brought it 'centre stage'; by providing facilities and opportunities for participation in particular, local authorities have helped to stimulate a culture and public demand for leisure goods and services which has a considerable impact on the national economy. Total expenditure by the commercial sector in the UK is estimated at almost £2 billion, of which just over half comprises the manufacturing and retailing of equipment, clothing and footwear. The sector is estimated to employ 120,000 people[5]

It would be easy to conclude thus far that sport in the public domain is buoyant and healthy — little could be further from the truth. Before examining the current position, however, it is necessary to examine some of the tides which form the subject of this paper.

The demographic tide

Despite the best efforts and considerable successes of the Sports Council and local authorities in seeking to extend participation among older people, sport remains an activity dominated by the young — whilst 67 per cent of 16–24 year olds take part, the figure drops to less than 25 per cent among those over the age of 60[11]. But the demographics are 'against' sport, with a projected decline of one million (15 per cent) in the 16–24 age group in the next five years. In contrast, the 25–59 age group is set to expand by over one million. For some voluntary clubs, especially those catering for the traditional team spsorts, the former could have disastrous consequences, and it could provoke a lessening in demand for local authority pitches. More generally, all providers, incuding local authorities, will need to turn their attention to a more mature market in future.

The distribution of the population will change too. The South East of England, particularly the Thames Valley, will continue to witness major growth and in such areas there will be both increased demand for existing sports facilities and increased pressure for new facilities. The private sector will have a major role to play. In contrast, declining urban areas will face the twin problems of inadequate facilities and an over-representation of disadvantaged people who are unaccustomed to taking advantage of sporting opportunities. In these areas the role of the public sector, especially its peripatetic workers, will be more important than ever. The needs of rural areas will change as well. Little is known about the likely demands of the more affluent immigrants; will they demand facilities of an 'urban' nature in their locality, or will they eschew such things in their rural idyll, preferring to commute to leisure as well as to work? At the other extreme, some 25 per cent of all rural households live in or on the margins of poverty; they will not have such choices and will depend on the public sector.

The employment tide

In the past five years the decline of manufacturing has continued whilst service industries have gone from strength to strength, and this is likely to continue into the foreseeable future. If theories of leisure being a counterpoint to work are accepted then it seems likely that as fewer people are engaged in heavy manual work they may seek more physically demanding leisure. Indeed it is this shift in the employment structure, inter alia, which has led public policy, particularly that of Health Authorities, to encourage people to take more exercise in their daily lives.

The growth of the labour market in the past five years has been almost exclusively accounted for by an increasing number of women in service occupations, about half of them part-timers. For the future, therefore, working women are likely to have more disposable income but less free time. Sports providers will need to offer a better product to maintain or increase their market share of leisure, and will need to be more flexible in their timetabling.

The general trend downwards in unemployment is likely to continue, although the unemployed as a whole will continue to form a significant market for providers. Youth unemployment, however, will fall dramatically in the next five years because of demographic trends and labour shortages in some areas and a growing concern in industry about the reduction in the potential labour pool. The leisure industries in general and local authority leisure services in particular have traditionally relied on this pool to fill a lot of low-paid manual jobs and may find themselves in severe difficulties in recruiting and retaining staff in the future. Conversely, with more young people in work there will be scope to attract more of them as consumers, and thereby to off-set demographic decline.

The social tide

There has been a growing interest in health issues in recent years and it is probably no coincidence that many of the sports which have shown most rapid growth — walking, swimming, athletics (including jogging)and cycling — have been widely associated with the promotion of healthy lifestyles. This has given considerable impetus to the commercial sector and will continue to do so. However, the interest is largely middle class and wider market penetration is likely to take time. It does, though, provide both a challenge and an opportunity to public providers to assist the Government in achieving broader policy objectives.

Shopping is increasingly being viewed as a leisure activity in its own right and designs for major centres are often incorporating sports facilities together with other forms of leisure provision. It is important for planning authorities and local authority Leisure Departments to have a clear view of the kinds of sports facilities they believe to be appropriate for such development and the management structures suitable for them. Such developments, however, provide authorities with the opportunity to achieve a level and type of sports provision in their area which they could not possibly contemplate from their own resources.

Although for the population as a whole the amount of 'non-work' time continues to increase, this does not necessarily imply more 'disposable leisure time' for sport. In the past five years, for example, greater leisure time has largely resulted from an increase in annual paid holidays rather than any reduction in the working week — prima facie this is likely to benefit the tourist market more than the local sports market. Likewise technological developments, eg home computers and other newer leisure opportunities, are also competing for this additional time. Some groups, such as women moving into the labour market, in fact now have less leisure time, as shown previously.

Leisure expenditure has grown since 1982 and is predicted to have an annual growth rate of between 3 per cent and 8 per cent over the next five years. However, there are likely to be shifts within individual market sectors; expenditure on holidays and sports participation is growing whilst spending on cinemas and sports spectating is falling[14].

The environmental tide

Most countries of the European Community can now produce more than they can eat or sell at market prices and accordingly it is likely that substantial areas of marginal land will go out of agricultural production in the next ten years. The resulting opportunities for sport include both better provision for rural residents, eg playing fields, and better access to the countryside for urban dwellers for a wide variety of activities, eg walking, orienteering, air and water sports, etc.

The political tide

Although the above trends are of considerable significance for the future of sport, it is the political tides which are having, and will continue to have, the most profound effect. In the specific case of local authorities it is these tides which tend to dominate the planning and management of leisure services to the virtual exclusion of all others.

First, and predominant among these, are the whole range of measures which the Goverment has taken in the past eight years to control and restrict local authority capital and revenue budgets. Among the more significant consequences of these controls have been:

- the replacement of long term capital planning with pragmatic year-to-year budgeting.
- the increasing need to put together complex financial packages through trusts, joint boards and the like to ensure that capital schemes proceed.
- an increasing dependence on external sources of funding such as grants from the Sports Council, Urban Programme grants, private sponsorship, etc.
- an inability to maintain and upgrade the fabric of existing facilities.
- a difficulty in providing the necessary revenue funding to run the large number of facilities built in the last 20 years.
- pressures to reduce revenue deficits by reducing staff and/or raising prices and other forms of income.

Whilst such pressures have had the beneficial effect of stimulating managers to be more self critical, flexible and imaginative, at the same time they have brought to a halt the previous period of expansion and indeed, in some areas, have led to retrenchment. Perhaps the most unfortunate consequence of all has been the impact which such measures have had on the ability of local authorities to cater for the needs of disadvantaged groups at a time when many such groups were beginning to respond to initiatives.

A second, and more recent, political tide has been the decision of the Government to require local authorities to put the management of the majority of their sports facilities out to competitive tender. This process is as yet in its early days, but a number of facts are already clear:

- a few local authorities, anticipating the legislation, have already put their facilities out to tender on a voluntary basis.
- the majority of local authorities are planning to split their existing leisure services operation into two parts, one to perform the 'client' role and the other 'the contractor'. This will enable a clear division of responsibilities to be developed, and will facilitate the production of tenders by the existing labour force.
- the major commercial leisure companies do not appear interested in tendering for such contracts, and the smaller ones are ill-equipped to do so.
- the key to the medium and long term impacts on sport will be the precise terms and conditions, eg re-user groups, pricing, standards of maintenance, etc, which are embodied in contracts, and the Sports Council is currently offering advice to local authorities in this regard.

However, the current Secretary of State for the Environment wishes the role of local authorities to be curtailed even further. He wants a halt to conventional investment programmes by local authorities in sports and leisure facilities and believes that in future authorities should be allowed to use public money to stimulate such investment by the private sector, but should no longer own facilities[15]. Any such development would not only reduce the opportunities available to the community at large, but would disproportionately affect those least able to avail themselves of opportunities provided by the commercial and voluntary sectors. The Sports Council, in its recent strategy review[3], commented, 'any diminution in the role of local authorities as providers of sporting facilities and opportunities will substantially undermine the achievements of the past and the Council's strategy for the future'.

In education too there are profound changes afoot which will have an impact on sport. The Education (No.2) Act, 1986 and the Education Reform Act, 1988, in particular have raised a number of fears for the sporting community:

- the quantity and quality of physical education likely to be developed within the national curriculum.
- the possibility of charges being introduced for participation in some sports activities.
- the future community use of school sports facilities as the control of premises is passed from Education Authorities to school governors and headteachers.

It is worth noting in passing that there are other trends in education, not wholly related to the activities of the Government, which will influence sport. In particular is the current debate on the nature of physical education and the provision of sporting opportunities for young people, recently reported on by the School Sport Forum[16]. This calls, inter alia, for local authorities and Education Authorities to develop a more co-ordinated approach locally to meeting the needs of young people.

Reverting to the actions of the Government, the effects of transport deregulation on the sporting community are difficult to judge as yet. In many suburban areas, where minibus services have latched on to profitable routes, initial impressions are that services have improved; in contrast, in some rural areas and at off-peak times services continue to be inadequate and this has served to compound the problems of many of those who already find it difficult to take part in sport.

There are two further issues deriving from the political tide which are of rather more concern to the voluntary sector in sport than to local authorities, although they also have an interest — the privatisation of water resources and the proposed rating revaluation associated with the introduction of the community charge. In the former case the large number of sports groups which depend on the unique resources of inland water bodies and rivers or the large tracts of land owned by Water Authorities are concerned that privatisation of the industry will result in reduced opportunities for sport. Many sports clubs are also fearful that the proposed rating revaluation will be to their detriment, although the Government has sought to reassure them that the actual amount which they pay in rates is unlikely to change significantly for the majority of clubs.

The future of local authority provision for sport

As the previous analysis indicates, some tides, such as the demographic, have turned and their likely impact on sport is fairly clear; others, such as competitive tendering, are on the turn and their impact is uncertain; yet more, such as the political complexion of future governments, have still to turn and their impact is unknown. A view of the future, therefore, inevitably ranges from what might appear blindingly obvious to the purely speculative.

Future provision and policy inevitably depend on the nature of future governments. Any move further to the right might see the sale of local authority facilities to the private sector, the levying of admission charges to parks and open spaces (or those which remain), provision based entirely on the ability to pay and perhaps even the total demise of local authorities. A move to the far left could witness substantial increases in taxation and public expenditure, a massive increase in the number of public leisure facilities, the free use of such facilities, and the taking of private assets into public ownership. Neither of these scenarios is likely in its entirety, but individual elements may be possible. Public leisure services in general, and sports provision in particular, are more likely to continue to be driven by a mixture of economic and social rationales and political control will influence the balance achieved between them.

What is clear, however, is that the financial pressure which local authorities have experienced in recent years will continue in the foreseeable future and that their activities will be geared to the economic use of resources above all else. In the case of sports provision this will manifest itself in a variety of ways.

The role of local authorities is likely to move away from direct provision by themselves and more towards facilitating/enabling provision by others. Whilst Nicholas Ridley would like them to 'go the whole hog', the view of the sporting community itself, including the large majority of local authorities, is that whilst an increase in the enabling role is to be welcomed, this should not be at the expense of the direct provision role.

The development of such an enabling role will bring local authorities into a much closer relationship with the commercial sector in sport. In particular this is likely to be effected by use of the statutory planning processes, by capital and revenue partnerships, by sponsorship and by local authorities providing sites, technical advice and help with administrative hurdles. In scale it might vary from the development of a local commercial squash club to a quasi-regional bid for the Olympic Games.

Such an enabling role is also likely to bring local authorities into a much closer relationship with voluntary sports clubs and other voluntary groups than has been the case in many instances. This again may apply to the provision of facilities and/or their subsequent management and can serve to meet both the 'economic use of resources' and 'community development' goals of authorities. It would certainly accord with the policies of the current Government for encouraging the voluntary sector to take a greater role in social welfare, although the ability of the voluntary sector in sport to cope with this role must be questioned.

The development of the enabling role and the pressure on resources are also likely to result in the growth of more co-operative, partnership and joint ventures within the public sector. Whilst some of these may be pragmatic 'marriages of convenience', and majority will be in the pursuit of carefully articulated goals and policies. Thus local authorities and Education Authorities are likely to come together better to meet the needs of young people, as recommended by the School Sport Forum[16]; the pioneering work in some areas between local authorities and Health Authorities in promoting exercise and sport are likely to be extended; Leisure Departments and Social Services Departments may well work more closely in seeking to meet the needs of various disadvantaged groups.

The future of the direct provision role of local authorities must inevitably be more speculative and depends to a large extent on the outcome of competitive tendering. At one extreme it is argued that if all public facilities are managed by private companies, then for many local authorities there will be little incentive to provide new facilities and in time the direct provision role will vanish altogether. At the other extreme it is possible to envisage the majority of facilities still being managed, perhaps marginally more efficiently, by the existing staff, but wearing a slightly different hat. Again a mixture somewhere between the two extremes seems the more likely scenario.

What again is certain, however, is that the need for economy will be paramount. In capital provision there is likely to be an emphasis on facilities with high revenue earning potential such as tourism related projects and leisure pools. At the other end of the spectrum there is also likely to be an emphasis on upgrading existing provision to keep abreast of consumer requirements and this will focus mainly on relatively new facilities, ie built since 1965, rather than pre-war pools and similar amenities. What is likely to be 'squeezed' in these two trends is what might be termed the 'run of the mill' local sports centre or swimming pool, high on debt charges and running costs.

In the management of sports provision there is likely to be a more overt emphasis on marketing, with all its ramifications, to ensure in particular that opportunities are more accurately targeted to clearly identified markets. Whether such targeting is essentially directed to high revenue earning groups and activities or to groups deemed to be in 'social need' will depend on both national and local politics.

The ability of local authorities to pursue the early 1980s trend of developing more community based sports opportunities, both through employing sports development officers and peripatetic workers, and through work with community based groups, must be questioned, since such work is very staff intensive. Much of it has in any case been funded by Training Commission programmes and is unlikely to continue, at least in its current form, under the aegis of the Training Commission.

There seems little prospect, therefore, of any expansion of local authority staff and in many areas there may well be contraction. It has been postulated that the introduction of modern technology into Leisure Services may free existing staff for more 'people based' work, but there is little tangible evidence of this actually happening. What is clear, however, is that the kind of trends outlined in this Chapter have major implications for staff training, especially management training. There will be a greater need to develop staff who have a wider range of planning, financial and general business skills than has been the case in the past.

Conclusions

A broad market analysis suggests that sports consumption continues to reflect the increasing polarisation in society between the 'haves' and the 'have nots'. The private sector will continue to serve the needs of the 'haves' and it may well be that the public sector will shift in that direction too. The fate of the 'have nots' remains in the balance: the Sports Council, in its strategy review[3], argues in pursuit of its broad goal of 'Sport for All' that only a continuing strong public sector can meet the needs of the disadvantaged; the turning tides, especially the political tides, may dictate a different scenario.

References

1 See for example:
  Travis A, Veal A, Duesbury K & White J, (1978) *The Role of Central Government in Relation to the Provision of Leisure Services in England and Wales* Centre for Urban and Regional Studies, University of Birmingham.
  Travis A, (1979) *The State and Leisure Provision* Joint Panel on Leisure and Recreation Research, The Sports Council/Social Science Research Council.
  Coalter F, Long J & Duffield B, (1986) *Rationale for Public Sector Investment in Leisure* Joint Panel on Leisure and Recreation Research, The Sports Council/Economic and Social Research Council.
  Roberts K, Lamb K & Minten J (1987) *Explaining Leisure Provision* Departments of Sociology and Physical Education, University of Liverpool (mimeo).
  Whitsun D, (1987) *Leisure, the State and Collective Consumption* in Horne J, Jary D and Tomlinson A (eds.) 1987 *Sport, Leisure and Social Relations.*
2 The Sports Council (1982) *Sport in the Community – The Next Ten Years.*
3 The Sports Council (1988) *Sport in the Community – Into the 90's.*
4 Fentem P, Bassey J & Turnbull N (1988) *The New Case for Exercise* The Sports Council/Health Education Authority.
5 Henley Centre for Forecasting (1986) *The Economic Impact and Importance of Sport in the UK*, Sports Council Study 30.
6 The Sports Council (1985) *Olympic Review – Preparing for 1988.*
7 Taylor P, (1988) (forthcoming) *Local Authority Support for Excellence in Sport*, The Sports Council.
8 The Sports Council (1987) *Local Authority Investment Intentions Survey, Summary Report.*
9 Chartered Institure of Public Finance and Accountancy (1987) *Leisure and Recreation Statistics, 1987–88 Estimates.*
10 Central Statistical Office (1987) *Monthly Digest of Statistics, No.502, October 1987.*

11 Office of Population Censuses and Surveys (1979) *General Household Survey, 1977.*
    Early computer tabulations from the General Household Survey (1986).
12 North West Council for Sport and Recreation (1982) *The Impact of a New Sports Centre on Sports Participation and Sports Facilities.*
13 York C, Dench S, Minten J & Roberts K, (1987) *Indoor Sport Provisions and Participants,* Departments of Sociology and Physical Education, University of Liverpool (mimeo).
14 Gratton C & Taylor P, (1987) *Leisure in Britain.*
15 Ridley N, (1988) *Enabling Not Providing.*
16 School Sport Forum (1988) *Sport and Young People – Partnership and Action.*

---

* The author is a Senior Research Officer with the Sports Council, and gratefully acknowledges the use of material gained while working in that capacity. However, the views expressed in this Chapter are personal, and do not necessarily reflect the views of the Council

7 Tourism and entertainment services in local government

Ian Gill

Introduction

Historically, local government has had a heavy involvement in tourism, in part legitimised by the recent acceptance of its economic significance and its ability to cheaply create permanent employment.

Like many other areas of its activity, the role, and indeed the very involvement of local government in tourism, is being challenged and capital revenue and staffing restrictions put in doubt the extent to which it can properly meet changing demands and needs, even in those areas where its involvement is accepted. It is also clear that in those areas of tourism where local government itself is going to play a continuing role, it will need to review procedures both at member and officer level. Opportunities in the highly competitive field of tourism, cannot wait the outcome of a cycle of members' meetings, and loath as members may be to do so, they must give the officers involved maximum freedom and flexibility in terms of pricing, operation and staff; reserving to themselves the right to judge and take action on the results. At officer level, there needs to be a single contact, who can see both the accommodation and facility providers through the mass of consents, licences, controls and hopefully, the help being offered and exercised by a wide range of departments in the local authority. Above all, entrepreneurial marketing presentation and selling skills which are essential to the effective operation and promotion of tourism services, must be recognised as of equal importance alongside the more established professional skills in local government. Work done by the Local Government Training Board divides tourism into three areas: (a) Infrastructure; (b) Promotion/ Marketing; (c) Provision of Tourism services (entertainment, catering, etc). I would like to look at the possible roles which may involve local government in these three areas:

(a) Infrastructure

It is clear that the provision of infrastructure will continue to fall to be dealt with by local government. The difficulty facing local government relates to the need for substantial additional infrastructure to meet the needs of tourism, which may well be seasonal in nature. It may well need a public relations exercise for the value of tourism to be spelled out in order to find a ready acceptance of this apparent additonal burden at member and ratepayer level. The same argument applies in relation to higher standards of parks, gardens, the larger areas of open space, beaches, etc which form the very basis of the product being sold particularly by resort areas. The difficulty is at a time of financial restraint, which is already reducing services, to maintain, and indeed arguably increase, the monies being put into these areas, though again it may well be worth the benefits which are enjoyed as a result of the enhanced environmental standards which are part of the resort product. It is interesting that in many cases those who have retired will have been attracted by those standards which are now at risk and indeed there is clear evidence that those enhanced standards are of assistance to resort areas in attracting light industrial and commercial developments.

(b) Promotion and Marketing

It is clear that the most effective way forward will be by the creation of partnerships between the private sector and local authorities. We are likely to see the growth of the Marketing Bureaux concept, or alternatively it may well be that the success of the Area Tourist Boards in Scotland may be worthy of consideration in England and Wales.

The more difficult area is likely to be in the development of direct booking systems and the packaging of holidays. It may well be that partnerships formed for promotion and marketing can create a body to deal with this aspect also, but it seems more likely that the initiative, at least in the early stages will need to be taken by the local authority. It may well be that this can be substituted for the work traditionally done on guides and will fit easily into the tourist information role currently carried out by local government. It needs to be stressed, however, that if local government is to be involved, it will need to move from its neutral role of helping all equally to an acceptance that it must work with those who are prepared to contribute and help themselves. This will not be an easy task for local government, either at political or officer level.

(c) Provision of Tourism Services

These services, clearly fall into the category which would be covered by the proposed legislation on contracting out and indeed like other local authority trading activities, are prime targets for privatisation. The difficulty in relation to privatisation is that, as I develop in the entertainments section of this Chapter, far from being profit centres, they are loss makers. Nonetheless, there may be economies to be achieved by contracting out to private management contractors, particularly if local government is not able, within its structure, to provide the flexibility and human resources which these services will require if they are to survive by continuing to adapt and change to meet changing public tastes.

Key issues and future of tourism

In any assessment of tourism within the UK one must fully appreciate the benefit that tourism brings. The disbenefits are obvious to everyone; the lack of parking spaces, the wear and tear on ancient structures, such as our cathedrals, castles and stately homes, the traffic jams and the crowded shopping centres. The benefits, however, far exceed any inconvenience suffered by the resident population; in fact I believe it to be vital to the country's economy. Over one million people are directly employed by the hotel and catering industry and many more are employed in the provision of entertainment, attractions and amusements.

In 1983 British residents on holiday within the UK were estimated to have spent £5,350m whilst income gained from overseas tourism was estimated to amount to a further £3,651m. This income does not just benefit those directly connected with tourism. It is, for example, used by hotels to pay staff, purchase food, clean and replace linen, refurbish rooms, acquire equipment, employ entertainers and maintain and improve facilities. These services though not directly connected with the tourism industry are therefore nevertheless to some extent dependent on it and they in turn pay staff, purchase equipment, etc and so from the first receipt of the money it has a spreading effect amongst the community. This is known as the multiplier effect.

Tourism also has a benefit which is not frequently appreciated by local residents and that is, that tourists are only attracted to pleasant areas which are clean and well maintained, thus by providing an environment which is attractive to the holidaymaker, the environment of the residents is also enhanced.

The British Home Tourism Survey defines a tourist trip as a stay of one or more nights away from home for holidays, visits to friends or relatives, business, conferences or any other purposes, except such things as boarding education or semi permanent employment. In local authority terms it is, however, traditional to include within tourism, day trippers.

Tourism was originally based on the desire for a change of air and surroundings and the health giving aspects this evoked. For this reason, tourism developed in the UK around inland spas and seaside villages, the latter rapidly giving up their dependence on fishing and developing as tourism resorts. Holidaymakers are naturally attracted to areas which are a complete break from the industrial or city environment in which they normally live. Most resorts are surrounded by agricultural land and this adds to the attraction of the seaside situation. For this reason also, there has been little development in industrial terms. Most resorts have some form of light industry but this is kept to the periphery of the town so as not to detract from the town's visual attraction to visitors. Tourism has therefore developed as not only the major industry in seside resorts but also in many cases, the only possible major industry within those resorts.

The original function of local authorities was to provide the infrastructure for a town based community. However, it was rapidly appreciated that with increased traffic to the town, additional provision would be necessary for visitors. Resort towns therefore of necessity carry an additonal burden in terms of the provision of services for visitors. Local authorities are concerned with maintaining a standard of life which is acceptable to the community at large. Appreciating that resorts were dependent on the visitor traffic, local authorities have extended this role to the provision of services which would improve the facilities available to both residents and visitors, such as swimming pools, sports facilities, theatres, beach activities, etc.

Further, most resorts, both seaside and inland, have used public financing to improve parks, to introduce flower beds to main promenade areas and otherwise enhance the visual impact of the town. With the boom in the '50s and '60s there was also a need to develop accommodation finding services as well as to advise visitors of the amenities and attractions available in the resorts and the surrounding hinterland. Many authorities developed a service of this type which from 1970 onwards was gradually absorbed by the National Tourist Boards' Tourist Information Centre network. Local authorities have, for the most part, also taken on the role of producing a guide for the town which would encourage visitors to select a particular resort for their holiday. Whilst mainly an accommodation finding vehicle, this too developed by the introduction of editorial on the attractions of the resort in question. As time has gone on, the service provided by local authorities has of necessity increased, the stronger challenge from overseas holidays has had to be met by a greater marketing effort by local authorities, who now carry out a number of promotional functions in addition to the production of the traditional annual guide. This role will be further developed later.

Over the past ten years heavy industry has continued to decline and inevitably the steps taken to combat this down trend have involved an increase in the use of automation with the subsequent loss of jobs. Gradually the potential of tourism as a major employer, with its labour intensive, automation immune, character, has gained respectability and the scathing stigma of 'Mickey Mouse jobs' has been removed. With over three million people now in the dole queue, there is only 'work' or 'unemployment' and tourism offers jobs, possibly not at the highest level of pay, but at least in pleasant and attractive surroundings.

The National Tourist Boards, in recognition of this new found respectability, have pressed for all areas to consider tourism as an alternative industry. One town, which previously would not have been considered to have any tourism potential, the City of Bradford, is one of the new generation which has taken up the challenge and has developed services to such an extent that package holidays now list Bradford as a venue. Bradford cannot, of course, offer the attractions offered by the traditional resorts and so a new form of tourism has sprung up, that of themeing, in Bradford's case, industrial heritage. However sophisticated we become in the world of modern technology, there is still in most people an interest in the working conditions of their forbears, especially as they no longer have to experience it! Bradford has taken this nostalgia, has improved its broken down obsolete woollen mills and is now able to offer visitors an insight into the work of the cotton and woollen industries at the turn of the century.

This, of course, has presented a challenge to what would hitherto have been termed traditional resorts. In addition, inland towns have developed the services offered to their residents. As earnings have increased and people's expectations of life have likewise risen, more and more industrial towns have invested in more elaborate sports facilities, entertainment centres and even position as hitherto of offering the holiday maker something which is very different from the services available in his home town. In previous decades this challenge would have been responded to by a greater effort from resort authorities to offer new attractions but, due to the current restraint in terms of both capital and revenue expenditure and staff numbers, this response has been slow and piecemeal throughout the country.

The investment that has taken place has fallen into two categories;

those resorts fortunate enough to be included in the Development Zones entitled to Section IV grants and those that have achieved without this aid. One of the resorts which has benefitted to a great extent through the use of Section IV money has been Scarborough who have found that the public acknowledgement by the English Tourist Board of the work envisaged, together with the actual receipt of Englist Tourist Board funds, has resulted in the attraction of funds from the private sector as well as local authority input. As a result, considerable refurbishment has taken place in the town which is now far better equipped as a conference venue. Rhyl, has produced an indoor weather facility known as the 'Sun Centre' which has introduced the concept of a controlled weather environment in which swimming, surfing and other 'fun' activities can be enjoyed. This development, which is run on far more commercial lines than has usually been the case with local authority activities, is the forerunner of similar facilities run in a variety of management styles, at Great Yarmouth, Felixstowe, Bridlington and Blackpool. Undoubtedly, many more such resort based all weather complexes will follow.

In addition to the challenge by the new breed of tourism orientated industrial towns and the general increase in leisure facilities in large towns with big catchment areas, traditional resorts have also faced an acceleration in the amount of holiday taking at overseas destinations. Countries such as Spain, who a mere twenty years ago were not geared up to any great extent to the holiday market, have with help from the Spanish Government, indulged in a building programme of immense proportions and have traded on their ability to offer the one feature which cannot be guaranteed in the UK and that is 'sun'. It is known and accepted that the Mediterranean is a lot less healthy than the Atlantic, but it cannot be denied that the water is warmer. The beaches may not be as clean and not offer as many amenities but the sun shines for a good proportion of the day. Accommodation in the new glass palaces which have sprung up within the last ten years is generally of a far higher standard than that offered by establishments in the UK and is also relatively cheap.

British resorts have, of course, seen this threat and have endeavoured to respond to it, but accommodation in the traditional resorts, whilst comprising around 50 per cent of the total bed stock in the whole country, is concentrating mainly in small units. Considerable investment is needed by hotel proprietors to upgrade their establishments to that point where all bedrooms have private facilities whilst at the same time any high increase in the cost of hiring the room may result in a currently low bed occupancy rate being further reduced. Many of these establishments find themselves in a 'Catch 22' situation, in which the cost to improve is very finely balanced against the necessary increase in revenue to pay for the cost incurred.

Whilst not wishing to present an entirely gloomy picture of the problems facing resorts, I do not feel these should be underestimated. One further and possibly inevitable development within resorts has been the increase of city dwellers who have retired to resort areas. Unable to fill hotel accommodation on a regular basis throughout the year, many proprietors have sold out to the owners of retirement homes and nursing homes for the elderly. The accommodation does, of course lend itself to this purpose, and ironically the greater the improvements already installed, such as the provision of en suite bathrooms, the easier their adaptability into homes of this type. Inevitably, the more the elderly population increases within a resort the greater the demand for the social services associated with a population of this type, thus creating a further strain on local authority resources and increasing the need for specialised homes. The elderly sector is not, however, the only demand on hotel accommodation. A recent move by the DHSS has encouraged the dissemination of the residents of institutions for the mentally and physically handicapped into a role of integration within the community. Only in part does this involve an integration into the community in which the original institution was situated; naturally there has been a demand for small units and where better than holiday accommodation or boarding house accommodation, which is not paying its way by traditional use!

This trend has been further developed by a demand for accommodation for the unemployed. Whereas only a few years ago proprietors were loath to consider the taking up of tenancies by persons not employed, the realisation that a regular and often enhanced rent could be gained because of a person's demand on the DHSS, has resulted in some resort proprietors even advertising in large cities to attract the unemployed to their area. The problem became so bad that the law was changed to prevent massive numbers of unemployed taking up residence in resorts for what could by the sceptics be considered a permanent holiday. This in its turn has presented other problems, but it is not the remit of this chapter to develop this argument further. The fact remains that there has been a considerable change of use of tourist accommodation and that the greater the number of unemployed, handicapped and elderly in an area, the less likelihood for an innovative approach to lead the town forward into the current demands of tourism.

How are local authorities responding to these problems and trends?   On the one hand an apathy from government and some parts of the resorts' own resident population towards increased expenditure on tourism services and on the other hand a need to update amenities and marketing techniques if the economy of the resort is to continue to be sustained by the tourism industry. That the resorts are committed to finding a solution to this dilemma is a clear acknowledgement that, for many resorts, there is no feasible employment alternative.

In acknowledgement of the desire by government to see more services operated by, or to a greater extent financed by, the private rather than the public sector more and more authorities have devoted considerable staff time and expertise to attracting private sector development to their resort. There is no doubt however, that the current government is not satisfied by this increase in the partnership approach by local authorities and privatisation of traditionally local government provided services is now a distinct possibility.

I do not propose within this Chapter to consider the political aspects of this likelihood nor to debate the pros and cons of the privatisation or contracting out issue, but in any assessment of future trends, the possibility of privatised or contracted out services must be taken into account. The concern expressed by many colleagues within local authorities is that the private sector will only be interested in taking over activities that have real profit potential. This means that profit making functions now used to bolster up 'loss leaders', thereby adding to the overall services to the community, will be sold off leaving a multiplicity of uneconomic (and therefore non-maintainable) services. Alternatively by careful packaging the private sector may be forced to provide an uneconomic service in order to gain a profit making one, but will respond by cutting down the uneconomic function to an unacceptable limit.

Sometimes it is necessary in any forecast of the future to step back and reconsider what services are currently provided, what the benefits of these are and how they will need to be developed for the future. What attracts a holidaymaker to a resort? Let's examine the sequence of events which result in a successful holiday.

Firstly, the poster, media advertisement or TV advertisement which attracts the holidaymaker's interest — designed and booked usually by a local authority employed 'tourism' officer. Why? Because he is a professional with expertise in this type of work? *No*, because a similarly trained employee with the private sector would be just as capable but because a local government officer can be assumed to be unbiased. Having been attracted by the advertisement the prospective holidaymaker sends for the guide which has also been prepared by local authority staff, for the same impartiality reasons. From the guide, the holidaymaker selects his establishment and the booking confirmation and any additional advance information has been traditionally an exchange between the client and the establishment proprietor. Assuming for the purposes of this exercise, the chosen resort is coastal, what does the holidaymaker expect on arrival? He expects to have access to information on the resort, on any special events occurring within the period of his stay, suggestions for outings, etc. He expects clean beaches, waters free of sewage, pleasant surroundings, places to park the car at reasonable prices, parks to walk through, entertainment for the evenings and sporting facilities for daytime activities.

I would like to briefly consider these functions.

The initial advertising scheme may well originally have been suggested by an agency and, it could be argued, could equally well be placed directly by that agency, but on the instructions of whom? No commercial operator would be willing to take his orders from a hundred or more establishment proprietors. How likely is it with vested interests involved that the advertising campaigns could be left to one or two of the proprietors to produce an unbiased scheme on behalf of them all? At present no on-cost is added to the costings of the brochure to cover officer time, a commercial operator would obviously require to do so, is this a possible additive that local authorities could consider for the future and if so, is this a function which should be taken over by the private sector? Again I would argue that the question of neutrality is overriding.

The guide is already an outmoded advertising vehicle. Overseas holidays are, in the main, sold through travel agents with communications achieved through a computer linked Prestel Gateway. The first resorts to adopt this system — Bournemouth, Brighton, Hastings, Scarborough and Torbay — launched a combined brochure and introduced a UK resort product bookable through travel agents. More resorts will undoubtedly follow this lead.

At present the bedstock, from which sales are made, is held in a central computer owned by a private computer agency but maintained and controlled by the five resort local authorities. Eventually some of the larger hotels and self-catering establishments will input information directly, but for the vast majority of smaller establishments some inputting agent would be required to operate on their behalf. If this agent comes from the private sector additional charges will fall on the establishment and ultimately on the client. The system for UK resorts will continue to be developed and other features which go to make up a holiday — theatre tickets, car hire, coach trips, boat trips, 'attraction' entry tickets etc will be added. In the not too distant future the network will be able to be accessed from overseas, thus making is possible for the European visitor and even the North American visitor to arrange and pre-book an independent itinerary, including accommodation, before ever leaving his home shores.

Ultimately entry to the system will be accessed within the UK directly by the public through the medium of their own television sets, with payments of all or part of the booking made by punching in their credit card number.

I foresee that the guide itself will materially change in its purpose. At present it is very much an advertising media for accommodation. In future, it will, I believe, develop very much as its name suggests and become a guide to the attractions and amenities of the area to which the holidaymaker is going and one which he will carry with him and use during the course of his stay. As I have previously suggested, there is no professional reason why this work and the accommodation finding services could not be carried out by the private sector, but the difficulty will arise if such a programme is ever implemented, due to the natural desire by the private sector to make a profit, which may make the necessary on-costs prohibitive to the smaller establishments and the risk that the private sector, influenced by a greater contribution from some establishments than from others, might adopt a natural bias in favour of those who pay more. There is also the inevitable concern that the town or area will no longer be in control of its own image and it is therefore inevitable that some form of local authority participation will be necessary.

Over the last ten years we have seen a great development in the field of marketing bureaux, with the lead given by Plymouth. These bureaux differ in size and composition according to requirements of the resort which they service, but basically they are semi-independent organisations set up under the auspices of the local authority, with both funding and membership from both the public and private sector. Whether the bureau system in some form or other is the answer for every resort is perhaps questionable. A lot depends on the total co-operation of the commercial sector and this involves the bringing together of a great number of interested parties and establishing a common objective — not an easy thing to achieve!

For the first two elements of the holidaymaker's proposed visit, the presentation of the advertising and guide and the selection and booking of the hotel, will undoubtedly in future, through the greater introduction of computerised systems, be more and more a service which will be undertaken by either the local authority or marketing bureaux. We then need to consider what the holidaymaker expects to find on arrival.

To start, I believe that we underestimate precisely what we have to offer. The UK holiday should be an enjoyable experience in pleasant and friendly surroundings where there is no problem over 'plane delays, passports, inocculations, currency, foreign food and an indecipherable language. Perhaps what is necessary is very much a PR job amongst our hotels and boarding house proprietors, to encourage them, regardless of the standard of accomodation, to offer a warm and friendly welcome, which cannot be equalled by our overseas rivals. There is no doubt however, that standards of accommodation do need to improve. Some resorts, having been previously defined as within a development area, have benefitted from Section IV grants and have used this to install en suite bathrooms and generally improve the facilities offered by the establishment. In resorts which were not hitherto designated in this way, such development has been regrettably minimal. That Section IV money is now available countrywide is an advance, but whilst grants are running at about 15 per cent, I do not believe that the incentive is sufficient for the progress that is necessary.

A national grading system has now been set up by the four National Tourist Boards although this has not met with universal approval or acceptance by the whole of the hotel industry. The scheme in Scotland has been improved by an additional 'qualitative' assessment, which has been monitored by the English and Welsh Boards who are now considering a similar addition. Although this is likely to improve the situation and give the prospective client a clearer assessment of what can be expected, there is still likely to be confusion between the Boards' schemes and those of the National Motoring Organisations, Egon Ronay, etc.

As to the resort itself, cleanliness is perhaps the greatest requirement of the holidaymaker and there is no doubt that cleansing could be carried out by a private contractor. What needs to be established is how great is the control necessary to ensure that the work carried out is sufficiently frequent and sufficiently thorough to produce the effect required; for one thing is certain, once local authorities disband their own cleansing departments in favour of contracting out to the private sector, there is little likelihood that this trend could be reversed. Much the same can be said for most of the functions of local authorities.

Perhaps two of the services which would appear to lend themselves to privatisation are the entertainment and catering departments. The problems affecting entertainment are propounded in a following paragraph because, I believe entertainment can be and perhaps should be considered in its own right, but entertainment does fall very much within the overall experience offered to the tourist.

Catering also is a service of local authorities which is used for a number of purposes but in this exercise I wish purely to examine its tourism aspect and in this connection it is difficult to separate the two services. Most resort local authorities run one or more theatre complexes, and the majority of these were built in the early part of this century. As a result, they were designed for a far more elegant age, requiring a considerable amount of upkeep and are not structurally designed for the needs of today. The buildings, however, are there, are a feature of our landscape and hard as it is, they should be maintained. Ironically, the very sector of the community who are most vociferous in their demands for public entertainment, the accommodation providers, are the very people who have a vested interest in ensuring that holidaymakers stay in their establishments rather than go to the theatre. This attitude will need to change if theatres are again to prosper. Already, many resorts have at least moved with the times to the extent that they accept credit card payments and with the increased introduction of computerised booking facilities, booking by remote agencies such as travel agents are becoming more common. Hopefully, the theatre visit will, in the not too distant future, be inbuilt into the holiday package offered to the prospective holidaymaker and this might well be the salvation of resort theatres.

The catering department has in the interim, and will undoubtedly continue in the future, to provide a vital role in not only adding to the facilities offered to theatre patrons, but also subsidising the loss on theatre bookings.

Entertainment is a generic word and covers far more than the show provided within the theatre environment. Punch and Judy shows on the beach have, for example, been a feature of the seaside holiday for well over 100 years and are still attracting good audiences of children. Amusement arcades also continue to do a thriving business in prime spots through virtually every seaside resort in Britain. It has, however, been noticeable in this connection that the current trend in videos and computer games has made its mark on these centres. There is hardly one which now concentrates on penny slot machines and bingo, to the exclusion of fully automated, sound emitting, visually programmed wizardry. It is, perhaps, surprising that bingo has lasted as well as it has. Possibly because of the move to high prize money, it clearly continues to attract an excellent following, especially amongst the senior citizen section of the community, despite its proximity to the space age machines of today.

Fun fairs continue to do well, but have vastly changed in the rides they offer from the Merry-go-Round of a few years back to the 'White Knuckle Rides' of today. Thrill upon thrill is now a basic requirement of the younger generation, with rides which defy gravity, plunge the occupant at high speed into total darkness or suspend them high above the ground. Everything is bigger, faster and more exciting than before. Many fun fairs now operate a single price entrance fee, which allows entrance to the fun fair and to all the rides, without further payment.

Carnivals, of course, are another attraction but over the years their popularity has, except in a few exceptional cases, declined. Jersey, of course, still has a thriving Battle of the Flowers and Spalding's annual flower decked carnival floats are still a highlight of the year in that area, but only those resorts who are able to provide something different in this line can still realistically promote Carnival Week as a feature. It is, perhaps, sad that we have not adopted the far more carnival orientated approach which is such a feature of European Catholic countries nor the impressive South American *Mardi Gras* style carnivals which last several days.

There has, however, been a great interest in the development of theme weeks based on the literary associations or the historic period of the town, such as the 'Dickens Weeks' staged at Rochester and Broadstairs. There has also been an increase in the re-enactment of historic events connected with a town, such as the Civil War battles re-enacted by the Sealed Knot. These features, which are popular with residents, UK tourists and overseas tourists alike are likely to grow in audience appeal in the future.

However much we accept that there is a vital need to improve the product we are selling, by upgrading hotels, by adding new features such as wet weather facilities, we must accept that capital expenditure of this type is likely to be slow in coming. Promotion must therefore be based on the product as it is and within the last few years there have been great moves in the field of marketing. Themed promotions are the current mode and indeed have proved very successful in making both the UK resident and the overseas visitor aware of different aspects of the British holiday scene. The English Tourist Board's 'England Entertains' promotion is a classic example of this and drew attention to the existence and excitement of the live theatre and its place in the perfect resort holiday. The English Tourist Board are also pushing the idea of bringing entertainment to the people rather than people to the entertainment, but street entertainments are not new and indeed many places have made a feature of such entertainment in the past, such as the Helston Floral Dance. Perhaps, however, we need a national promotional theme of this type to remind us of just such activities.

Also on the theme of activities, there has been an upsurge in the interest in taking a holiday which either incorporates some learning process such as the acquiring of a skill, the development of a hobby or participation in a sport. There are many instances of resorts and indeed commercial holiday operators who have responded to this surge of interest in activity holidays and have produced products built round the chosen subject. The big advantage of catering for enthusiasts in any particular field is that they are unlikely to be concerned about the time of year in which the activity takes place nor except in a few cases the weather conditions prevailing at the time. Seaside resorts in particular are able to offer a wide range of activities which cannot easily be provided by inland towns and this inevitably adds a special element to the holidays of the participants.

Special interest holidays involving visits to archeological sites, stately homes, industrial heritage, nature reserves and other similar venues, have also very much come to the fore and this is something which should continue to be developed in future years.

More and more resorts are turning to the marketing of the holiday product and without the involvement of capital expenditure are producing a number of festivals and special events which now form a major part of the programme of activities offered by these resorts. Some features have been around for a long time, for example, the illuminations at Blackpool which annually attract a million visitors, but other, perhaps more lighthearted events such as Southport's camel race are appearing all over the country. This is undoubtedly a trend that will continue and should attract vast quantities of onlookers to the resort.

The main forces of my argument so far has been based on the problems and likely future development of the traditional resorts, mainly because, as I have explained, for these areas there is very little in the way of alternatives. Ultimately, nothing will be gained and much will be lost to the country as a whole if resort areas are allowed to further run down and eventually to die. Nevertheless, there is no doubt that tourism as an industry is available to everyone and is a relatively cheap way of setting up jobs. Towns naturally spring up where there is trade or agriculture, a stately home or area of other special interest. These elements are capable of interpretation and development and there is rarely any subject under the sun which does not have a special interest to a particular sector of the world's population.

Inland towns in particular need to look at the image they already portray. If they are currently thriving with a strong industrial base in the boom industries, it may be that tourism, as an alternative or as an addition, is merely a possibility for the future. If, however, the industrial base of the town is declining, now is probably the time to examine the potential of using tourism to create interest in the industrial heritage the town contains. At the turn of the century, no one would have been interested in seeing a miner's cottage for example, as these were commonplace, and therefore had no relevance. Today, an insight into the living conditions of our recent ancestors, especially in view of the rapid advances of the twentieth century, is of fascination to all ages and classes. As I have previously quoted, Bradford have developed this angle to such an extent that they look set to become one of the resorts of the future.

Even London, with its enormous input of tourists annually, is beginning to re-look at its buildings and develop tourist attractions from broken down warehouses. The development at St Katherine's Dock by the Tower of London is a classic example of this and is an area in which it is now more pleasant to live, more attractive to the tourist and quite unique in its setting. York too, already a 'honeypot' for attracting tourists, now houses the successful Jorvik Viking Centre, which by skilful presentation, gives the visitor an insight into what life was like in the period when Viking raids on England were commonplace.

These are developments which could, to some extent, be emulated by virtually every town in the UK, but it requires insight, the ability to look at the town's features with new eyes and the will to create a product which can be interpreted and enjoyed by the visitor.

What must be remembered by towns newly considering tourism is that tourism does not just happen. It has to be planned for, it has to be controlled and it has to be developed, if it is to have any real future and any real meaning in terms of jobs and visitor appreciation. Right now we are at a point of change and our response to it will establish the future prosperity or decline of UK tourism. Tourism is a product which can be sold by every country in the world and we must never forget the strength of that competition nor cease to fight for our own, very considerable, share of that market. We are a unique land and we should seek to exploit that very quality but, at the same time, there is much we can learn from other countries.

When we think of the United States of America for instance, what images leap to mind? Is it the Niagara Falls, the Grand Canyon and the Empire State Building or Disneyland, Sea World and Universal Studios? The latter, gimicky perhaps, but all firm favourites among the American population as well as with foreign visitors. We have of course started on the development of theme parks in this country with Thorpe Park, Alton Towers, the miniature theme park 'Gulliver's Kingdom', and, due to open in 1991 — 'Wonderworld' at Corby. It is significant that only two theme parks are seaside based, the thriving Pleasurewood Hills on the Suffolk coast and the theme park based on Alice in Wonderland proposed for Llandudno.

From Europe perhaps the most significant feature has been the continued popularity and development of spas, helped by the recognition of their value by the medical profession. Regrettably, the British Medical Association has been loath to endorse the value of British spas in the same way. Having started the holiday phenomenon, spas have for some years been in a decline, but within the last ten years there have been strong moves to re-emphasise the health giving aspects of these towns and spas are making a comeback. It is significant that health farms, without the natural features of mineral springs, have been quick to take advantage of the increasing emphasis on health and fitness, a trend which is now resulting in the addition of a range of facilities from gymnasia to jacuzzi to sun beds in many hotels: again following a trend established in the USA.

The reassuring aspect of the current state of overseas tourism is the buoyancy and expansion of tourism in cold climate countries. In this respect it is particularly interesting to notice the development of centres such as those constructed and operated by Sporthuis Centrum in Holland, which by the development of extensive indoor leisure facilities linked to good quality accommodation units have turned seasonal centres into all year round centres, achieving a year round occupancy of level of over 80 per cent, as at their Nottinghamshire based Center Parc.

The new found respectability of tourism in the UK has been an established fact in Europe for many years and money has therefore been available for investment in European developments for a very long time. The UK has only recently had access to general funding and as a result, having been the leaders in the holiday field, have fallen behind in the development of facilities. The structure of tourism in local and central government terms varies from country to country, and the higher recognition by central government in France and other countries as shown itself in terms of higher investment being achieved resulting in the development of purpose built summer and winter resorts.

It is extremely worrying, that in as much as tourism is a highly competitive market, to find that even within the EEC the varying attitudes of governments are such, that the UK may yet find itself in competition with products which result from substantial government subsidies. It seems to be in stark contrast with the attitude of the EEC in relation to the regulations such as that relating to the quality of bathing water, where the UK is now having to implement standards which, while relevant to the warmer and non-tidal situation in the Meditteranean, have little relevance to the colder waters surrounding the UK.

On promotions and marketing of tourism, the continental systems place heavy reliance on joint working between local authorities and the more professional and compulsory Chambers of Commerce which exist elsewhere in Europe.

On the question of standards, the voluntary approach of the UK contrasts starkly with the compulsory and often governmental systems adopted by our EEC partners. Nevertheless, in spite of these differences, the UK tourism product, based as it is with its strength in history, constitution and tradition, remains the envy of Europe and if central and local government support continues will remain highly competitive.

The next ten years

The renewal or provision of new infrastructure will depend to a great extent on whether the restrictions on local government spending are lifted and how many of the services provided by local authorities are contracted to the private sector. As far as marketing is concerned, local authorities will almost certainly develop a marketing bureaux system, but whether this could ever become truly independent of the local authority is unlikely. The marketing bureaux concept will vary from resort to resort as will the balance of control, and of revenue, between the public and private sectors.

Local government itself is on the verge of a radical change, the extent of which can at present only be surmised. One thing is certain, the hybrid that will emerge will be fundamentally different to that which currently exists and will probably continue to be subjected to tight government expenditure controls. The role such an authority will be able to play must therefore be a matter of conjecture and I have thus set forth my views with this in mind.

I believe what is needed for the future development of British tourism is clear, whether it can be achieved and whether local authorities will have a role within the effort to achieve, is less clear.

The work by the National Boards to encourage the upgrading of hotel accommodation must continue. As the century draws to a close, the holidaymaker is becoming more and more sophisticated and his demands for a better standard of accommodation more apparent. Undoubtedly the larger hotel groups have already implemented the changes necessary to bring their standards up to an internationally accepted level and within the smaller hotel groups a definite move is being made in this direction. However, it must not be forgotten that the majority of bedroom units are contained within establishments of 15 bedrooms or less and these proprietors are unlikely to readily find the money to put in the necessary improvements, especially as by including en suite facilities, they will probably need to reduce the number of bedrooms already in the establishment. There will always be a need for lower priced accommodation, but there will nevertheless reach a level when this is balanced by the standard of accommodation on offer.

The days when holidaymakers were expected to leave the establishment by 9.30 am and not return before 4.30 pm are very fortunately for the main part long gone, but there is still a great deal of PR work to be done to encourage hoteliers and boarding-house keepers to trade on the welcome and the homely atmosphere which they can offer. It does seem amazing that in 1988 there are still establishments whose adverts, as a sole promotional tool, mention spring interior mattresses and hot and cold water. For those that have improved standards and for those that intend to do so, it is important that the National Tourist Boards and the motoring organisations come together to produce a single set of standards which can be applied throughout the UK. These standards must, if they are to have real meaning, include the quality as well as the standards of the establishment.

The conference market is in financial terms of tremendous value to a resort area, but it must be appreciated that 5000 delegate conferences do not happen every day of the week. By far the greater market is in the small meeting of between 10–200 delegates and this should be borne in mind when a resort is planning a new conference centre. The British Tourist Authority/English Tourist Board Conference Databank, which is operated on behalf of the Boards by the Middlesex Polytechnic, allows resort officers, chain operated hotels and individual establishments keen to increase their conference trade, to purchase contact names and addresses from a computerised and constantly updated data base. This excellent scheme also enables users to specify the size of conference/meeting which they are interested in attracting, the month they wish to fill and various other relevant criteria and the charge is calculated according to the number of contact names supplied and the number of refinements in terms of stated criteria used. This must be seen as a tremendous step forward in cutting out much of the vital research which has had to be carried out by resort officers wishing to attract conferences in the past. Tele-conferencing is currently possible but even with the likely advance in technology over the next ten years, I do not think it is likely to become common in this country. Coastal resorts therefore, competing as they are with a strong inland challenge, need to establish precisely what the conference organiser is seeking and ensure that these facilities are provided. Brighton, Harrogate and many of the other big centres may well need to provide facilities for instant translation of a number of languages and for the requirements of television and radio coverage, but these requirements are not at all necessary for the smaller conference market, unless it is hoped in the future to attract small overseas conferences to our shores.

The resort guide, as we now know it, will undoubtedly start to phase out and will be replaced by a computerised booking accommodation register. On a local level, this will probably be held and accessed by the staff of the Tourist Information Centre and will be able to assist members of the public booking accommodation either on arrival in the resort or by phoning or writing in beforehand. Establishments willing to offer commission to travel agents will also have their bed stock held on this computerised register, but will within the resort context combine in a brochure with other resorts, produced in a style similar to that adopted by overseas travel operators and available through travel agents. Some resorts will almost certainly use this system for a direct sale booking scheme following the lead of the Isle of Wight Tourist Board.

The supply of information to the incoming tourist will continue to be of great importance and will probably become more comprehensive in nature. At present the Meteorological Office are prepared to give daily forecasts five days in advance which would provide resorts with the information on such things as likely rain or sun, wind speeds, sea conditions, for which they claim an 80 per cent accuracy. This, of ocourse, will be of tremendous aid to resorts staging a festival or sporting event, which might be dependent on the weather or which might require special provision to cope with adverse weather conditions.

Information regarding the resort's history and places of interest are also likely to be more in demand and many resorts will probably offer guided walking tours on a regular basis. Visual interpretation centres such as those at Bannockburn, Stirling and the Thames Barrier will undoubtedly be further developed in many towns, as will staged re-enactments of historial events or product variations of the *son et lumière* type of show. Tourist Information Centres will no doubt become more commercial and will offer, in addition to the sale of publications, guiding services, bureau de change where appropriate, sale of souvenirs, local crafts and handicrafts, etc. No longer can local authorities sit on the fence trying to establish a reasoned balance between the demands of the commercial sector that local authorities should not compete in areas in which they consider they have no role and the need to reduce expenditure. If this is the age of competition between public and private sectors, this logic must be carried to its ultimate conclusion and local authority services allowed to take whatever commercial decisions are necessary.

In any forecast of the future, the most difficult service for which to make definite assumptions is that of entertainment. I have, of course, treated the aspect of entertainment as a separate item in this chapter and cover in detail the problems and possible solutions I see for entertainment in the future. However, entertainment does fit very much within the tourism package and it is perhaps correct that it should be referred to briefly here. Entertainment is undoubtedly the most fashion conscious service that local authorities provide. It requires a great deal of entrepreneurial skill and to some extent, almost divine guidance, to be sufficiently ahead of the trends to provide the right format at the right time and at the right price. The private sector undoubtedly has the advantage in that it is more easily able to respond to the current fashion, but against this, the theatre industry except in London and a few key areas, is not thriving to the same extent as it was. There are, therefore, relatively few promotors in the entertainment industry that are keen to actually take over theatres and risk the loss this may incur. Against a background of television in virtually every home, videos cheaply available and a failing film industry, a great deal of work will need to be done to persuade the new generation of holidaymakers that a theatre visit is an important part of their holiday.

The catering department is yet another service whose future hangs very much in the balance. It may be that the move by some authorities to introduce a complete evening out by combining a meal with a show is the answer and one which certainly should not be overlooked in attempts to contain losses. There is no doubt that local authorities are at a disadvantage by paying bar staff according to the local government terms of service, rather than the more commercial approach, which would be adopted by the private sector, but nevertheless this service too could be an integral part of the 'evening out experience'.

One of the main features of British resorts is their individuality and I would not advocate that any resort attempt to emulate the style of another. There is, no doubt, however that British weather being as unpredictable as it is, any appraisal of the amenities available to the holidaymaker must include a consideration of providing a wet weather facility. The Great Yarmouth Marina Centre, the Rhyl Sun Centre and Blackpool Flume Pools are forerunners of a far more urgent and countrywide need to provide something that visitors can do regardless of the weather. I would expect however, the next ten years to see the type of facility offered expanded and a considerable degree of innovation will be necessary to make it feature as an attraction.

There is undoubtedly a market for virtually every tourism product and a great deal of research is necessary to establish precisely where that market is and how it can best be approached to obtain the maximum response from it. There is no longer a future for the Tourism Officer who repeats the activities of the previous year on an annual basis. There are, of course, traditionally successful markets and these will continue to be of value, but we must constantly seek both to attract the young to the idea that a British holiday is an extremely enjoyable experience, as well as to review the sectors both at home and overseas, who may not have considered a British holiday.

Finally, tourism has proved itself a winner in every sort of community, from seaside resorts to historic towns to inner cities to rural areas. Let me look at those in turn, and ouitline the opportunities for each.

Historic towns

Historic towns are magnets and always will be. So the question is not how to create the tourist tide (and certainly not how to stem it) but how to manage it and channel it. That entails making provision for the weight of numbers and, by means of tourist information, steering visitors towards local shops, places to eat, places to stay, car parks, and so on. Historic towns are part of our heritage: by showing you care, visitors will respond sensitively, and ratepayers will learn to see tourists as an asset and not a nuisance.

Rural areas

The country is another magnet, and again the question is how to manage the numbers and help visitors spend their time (and money) enjoyably. There are plenty of ways that work and don't spoil the landscape: pick your own fruit/vegetables, model farms, cottage industries, farmhouse teas and accommodation, self-catering cottages. Provide picnic areas, mark paths and bridleways, keep teaching people how and why — and they will use the countryside and not abuse it.

Inner cities

Tourism can rejuvenate the inner city. Old or redundant buildings can be put to new and attractive uses for the tourist: disused warehouses and industrial buildings can be refurbished and begin life anew as exhibition halls, museums, craft workshops, art centres, restaurants. Local hotels which cater for businessmen on weekdays now become weekend hotels for the holidaymaker. And the end product is not just money in the citizens' coffers, but a boost to civic pride as well.

Seaside resorts

The annual migration will continue as long as people yearn for sea and sand, fresh air and freedom. But today's tourists have highly diverse needs, and resorts must learn to identify and satisfy them. For many resorts tourism is the only job creator, and whole families have to live all year on what they earn in the season. Hence the importance of off-peak breakaway holidays and money-spinning conference business in spreading the season and broadening the market. The better the resort plans its activities the better for visitors — and residents.

Entertainment

The provision of live entertainmemt is a major factor in attracting
visitors to a resort and an important part of the holiday experience
once they are there. In as much as local authorities own and operate
the majority of theatres at the seaside, they have a major interest in
their success, both in local economic and financial terms. The difficulties being currently experienced are substantial, ranging from obsolete
and outdated buildings to a major decline in customers. An English
Tourist Board Report 'Curtain up on the Resorts' states 'for too long it
has been taken for granted that there will always be good live
entertainment at the theatre, but the decline in visitors and visitor
spending has combined with the economic recession and unemployment to put this assumption to the test.'[1]

The main causes of decline which they identified, in addition to
those already mentioned were:

1 Competition factors such as entertainment and hotels and alternative
entertainment provided by TV and video, changes in public taste and a
decline in theatre going.

2 Product Factors, such as a lack of artists of popular appeal, the high cost
of big name artists, high ticket prices and reduced standards of production.

It is against this difficult background that entertainment must make
its case for the increasingly scarce Local Authority capital and revenue resources. Capital is needed to modernise buildings to meet the
increasingly sophisticated needs of today's public. The need for high
standards does not stop with the public areas however, as artists will
not perform in theatres which do not compare in terms of backstage
facilities with the inland theatres and top cabaret spots where they
perform for the rest of the year. Additionally, in order to meet the
competitive situation in which they find themselves, entertainment is
demanding the use of new and exciting changes of style and presentation, incorporating the latest sound and lighting techniques, all
demanding further capital investment. The commercial sector also
seeks a need for continuing change, with complete refurbishment
and re-styling occuring at increasingly shorter periods to meet the
needs of what is becoming very much a 'fashion' business.

Revenue expenditure is needed to meet the staffing and maintenance costs of buildings designed in a period when these were not
such a significant factor as they are now. Increasingly fire and other
safety regulations have also imposed additional burdens, both in
equipment and staffing terms. An essential element in promoting
shows is advertising, another expensive area, particularly if one
makes use of TV. One could go on listing areas of expense, but the
net result is, in the majority of cases, a substantial deficit, bringing
with it increasing criticism from Members and ratepayers alike. The

result is a plea from those involved, to treat live entertainment in the same way as the provision of amenities such as libraries, parks and gardens, sports and leisure centres. The difficulty is that the same scepticism is being shown by Members and ratepayers to continued increases in expenditure in those areas of activities. It is clear that over the next ten years, there is likely to be a further reduction for a demand in live entertainment, with an increasing tendency for the main stars to concentrate on a series of shows at a limited number of large well equipped theatres, chosen on a regional basis.

Seaside resorts, with sea for 50 per cent of their catchment area, are unlikely, with one or two exceptions, to feature in the list.

The future is likely to lie in a contracted seasonal programme, with the survival of the theatres dependent on an acceptance of their usefulness as a resident based centre for activity year round. It is clear that the private sector is not sitting in the wings intent on taking theatres over, but an alternative method of buying in the private sector on a Management Contract basis may well achieve economies, and marketing presentation and selling skills, for which Local Government is, only now, recognising the need. The major economy is likely to be achieved by involving the private sector in this way; in a more flexible system of staffing in terms of pay enhancements and hours worked, together with a flexibility in pricing control and operation, which still seems to be difficult to establish within the Local Government system, even for trading activities such as theatres.

Reference

1 English Tourist Board (1984) *Curtain up on the resorts*, London : ETB Report No. PE/836/2M/6/84 : ETB/366/84.

8 Community leisure

James Munn, Chris Field and David Liddle

Introduction

Community leisure is not a new concept, but it is one which is still not certain of universal acceptance, especially in terms of its practical application. There is a growing awareness that local authorities will not have sufficient resources to tackle the changing needs of their populations. They will have to act as catalysts for a whole range of new initiatives using the resources of many agencies, and harness their energies within new public/private/community coalitions. There is an increasing recognition that this will mean much closer co-ordination, joint working and joint use between different local authority departments and especially a new facilitating and enabling role in the community.

This chapter brings together three contributions from practitioners, who, in different ways, have tried to extend the boundaries of local government into the realms of community leisure and community development. James Munn, Director of Recreation and Community Services for the City of Birmingham, looks at *Leisure and Community in the Post Industrial Era*. He considers that 'the most important single resource of the post industrial society will be its human capital, and the skills and knowledge it can harness'. There is a major challenge for local authorities to support their populations in the development of socially useful roles and more active participation. He argues for the opportunities which exist in a co-ordinated approach to leisure and other related needs, crossing 'traditional' service divisions and embracing the widest range of agencies in the community.

Chris Field, previously Director of Leisure for the London Borough of Greenwich, and now Chief Executive of The International Shakespeare Globe Centre in Southwark, develops James Munn's theme in *Community Leisure: the Fifth Wave*. The importance of integrated facilities for the whole community is emphasised — youth facilities; toddlers' play groups; community halls for social functions, and so on. Chris Field also airs a number of practical issues, for example the perennial problems of managing licenced bars. He argues that the advent of multi-purpose structures and the expansion of joint provision leads naturally to an emphasis on local provision for the community.

The final part of the chapter is by David Liddle, and concerns *Youth and Community Services as part of local authority leisure provision.* David Liddle is Director of Community Leisure Services for the County of Avon. In 1985 Avon County Council created a new Department of Community Leisure which includes the county library service and the youth and community service. He looks at the compatibility of the youth services and education and discusses what leisure and youth services have in common. He concludes that the most important issue is not so much the departmental base as the commitment to an outgoing community development approach.

PART 1 – LEISURE AND COMMUNITY IN THE POST-INDUSTRIAL ERA
James Munn
Director of Recreation and Community Services,
City of Birmingham

Introduction

It is now clear that many communities within the UK are part of a post-industrial society, and whatever the upturn in the economy, the level of job sharing in the future, and the degree of rationalisation of the taxation and social costs of unemployment, there will be a problem of unscheduled free time for a substantial number of people. Labour requirements are now shrinking in manufacturing as they did in agriculture, several decades ago, within an industrial society.

If we accept that shortly the thousand hour working year will be the norm within a high technology and communications-based society, then the primary input will be knowledge, and the most important single resource of the post-industrial society will be its human capital and the skills and knowledge it can harness. At the base of all technological skills and back up is a history of education, research and development. This trend will accelerate such that in the next century community development and community education will become the leading service industries and employ a large percentage of the working population.

The great debate now and through the next decade, will be about changing attitudes – social, political and bureaucratic – towards the concept that each individual not only has a set of leisure rights but more importantly (within a matrix of involvement) has the right to find a socially useful role within his or her community; and one which will allow them to apply management, technical, and promotional skills – as well as enthusiasm and commitment – in the planning and management of their own neighbourhood. However the realisation of these objectives will require local authorities to develop directly and indirectly a wide range of initiatives involving all public, voluntary and private sector agencies.

The progressive local authorities in the 1990s therefore will be those which not only generate efficient practices enabling them to compete in the market place, but also, establish enabling non bureaucratic political structures, which will harness the vast resources and skills of the community sector at local level, while creating opportunities for the private and commercial sectors to play their role to its fullest potential; a strategy indeed which is about the needs of people and their identifiable communities, not those of the public sector bureaucracies.

A new challenge

The challenge is indeed a severe one for the public sector, as there will be demands on resource management skills of a high order, together with new bureaucratic initiatives; – probably, the weakest areas of local authority performance over the last two decades. The problem is compounded by changes in the economic and social structure over the last twenty years. Today we have a society where demographic changes have created a Britain now facing the major problem of reconciling the increased demand for health and social service provision of an ageing population, while being apparently unable to redirect the surplus capacity of staff and buildings in the education system. Worse, total social security expenditure is now at the highest level in real terms, since the second world war. The increase in recent years has been due, however, not to improved benefits and economic growth, but to a very considerable increase in the number of welfare dependents in the population; a vast resource of community-development labour which is untapped within most local authorities.

These are not temporary features, but long-term demographic

trends generally ignored within strategies for recreation and leisure. Britain like many early industralised societies has an ageing population. The number of pensioners (men aged over 65 years and women aged over 60 years) now approaches one fifth óf the population, and it is predicted that by the year 2001· nearly half of the 59m Britons will be over 40.

The other major demographic change is, of course, the increase in long term unemployment. This has been especially severe in its impact upon young people. No previous generation since the 19th century has experienced lower living standards than those of its parents. Both political and economic life had assumed ceaseless growth since the second world war. The adjustment of aspirations to the new realities is not easy for society at large. For the young with no resources – either material or psychological – to fall back upon it will be especially difficult. This pattern of youth disadvantage is overlaid with a further pattern of ethnic minority discrimination. Thus (holding educational attainment constant) black young people have double the unemployment rate of their white counterparts.

The emerging scene is therefore one of a public sector which has been unable to harness its existing and programmed resources effectively; and bound by a host of separate bureaucracies, and agencies, who see the development of any inter-departmental strategy as an area of identity erosion, not an opportunity to improve the quality of the living environment in a host of 'village communities' – rural and urban.

Regrettably, too, the various professions associated with the different services for many years were not performance orientated and so 'specialist', they frequently lost sight of the management objectives. Perhaps more relevant, the various specialisms within leisure services had little or no corporate awareness, seeing conflict as an alternative to specialism. Over the years there is ample evidence of the development of a strong separatist role, however professional, which created an unco-ordinated approach; one which was more concerned with the technical servicing of the different committees' policies, than with what the service was actually achieving – and at what cost?

The progressive authorities through the 1970s were indeed those who manipulated the bureaucracies and cut across the traditional divisions between departments. They were also effective in their ability to articulate problems, be innovative, develop initiatives, find new angles to old systems and above all, they appointed managers in key positions who could influence the environment in which they operated.

Lord Scarman perhaps put his finger on the problem when he said in his report, 'That the failure of many attempts over the last three decades, to tackle inner city decline successfully is striking. One of the reasons is a lack of an effective co-ordinated approach to tackling inner city problems. To achieve it local communities should be fully involved in planning, in the provision of local services and in the management and financing of specific projects. The voluntary and private sectors must be more effectively involved in the attempts to tackle inner city decay'.

In these circumstances therefore it is a sobering thought that some thirty years have gone since we were first warned that the three major problems of civilisation in the 1980s would be over-population, over-pollution, and leisure, in that order. Perhaps more tragic, in the early 1960s the monitoring of response to new leisure facilities and related demand indicators crystallised need towards neighbourhood oriented facilities where a multi-interest programme theme could be generated; one which could cut across the artificial boundaries of the arts, sport, etc, and be supported by a sound social theme. Significantly, studies also indicated that well over 60 per cent of all recreation demand related to indoor facilities. For many local authorities, therefore, there has been a premature arrival of the future, as the attitude of society towards living environment priorities has bypassed the approach of the separatist system, and many communities are paying dearly in social structure terms. Why?

There are four major reasons. In many urban and rural areas we have failed to plan for people. We have not developed a system in Britain which would effectively harness resources across the tiers of local government or indeed across the traditional roles of separate departments. We have failed to create planning and management structures which would allow the community to be involved in the development process. Above all, perhaps, we have not recognised the demands and disciplines of successful community management, and its relationship with the political structure. Where, then, have we gone wrong?

Until the last decade, valid leisure opportunity for most communi-ties was treated very much as a quasi-welfare programme and a concept bound up with ideas concerned with the health and physical well-being, allied to periodic injections of culture and heritage. The attitude of society which had conditioned that outlook changed increasingly with the rapid improvement in living standards. The crucial need in social terms to have access to leisure compensations is now seen as an area of provision with a major part to play at all stages in a person's life; certainly one which is considered essential within any total approach to the living environment and the develop-ment of stable community structures, involving not only the com-munity and public sectors, but also the private.

Planning, until very recently, was largely a land-use exercise based on standards for facilities in isolation. There was no overall approach which recognised total community need and, therefore, the 'recreation opportunity' component was never central to the planning process – hence the host of facility-starved, socially-deprived neighbourhoods in many areas of the UK. A glance at the CIPFA *Leisure Service Statistics* or various research papers will leave no-one in any doubt that the density of development in the conurbations particularly has been totally inadequate to meet community need.

Co-ordinated services for, and with the community

History will, therefore, determine that in the community development field, poor resource management, particularly at senior level, was the greatest weakness of the public sector during the 1960s and 1970s. The absence of a strong cost-effective policy statement on the living environment, followed by a well co-ordinated community services policy from central to local government, can now be seen as a key omission in the system which had serious implications for many communities in respect of the social structure today.

What has been tragic, and certainly inexcusable, is that almost twenty years have passed since the progressive authorities in the field first began to implement the recommendations of the joint Ministry of Housing and Local Government/Department of Education and Science (1964) circular, and harness the economic advantages of fully integrated community development – never mind the dramatic social gains possible, given sound community management. The implications for under-fives, families and pensioners were as obvious as were opportunities in Sport for All. Resistance to the concept has been a vital factor in accelerating the decay in many of our urban conurbations where bureaucratic blockages to opportunity, on a massive scale, have been a major component in the decline of the social structure.

In many urban neighhbourhoods, therefore, it is quite clear that the rigid application of the traditional planning formula, concerned principally with homes, jobs and schools, has created circumstances where facilities indeed exist but tragically, the absence of any inter-agency management policy, perhaps within the same local authority, prevents any access to vacant facilities for community groups trying to meet their leisure needs. Schools today are, in embryo form, the community cenîres so badly required in many neighbourhoods.

The problem is compounded by a host of superb, prestigious facilities, many of regional specification, with totally inadequate social provision. The application of a weak management philosophy, perhaps in the town centre and certainly at a radius of several miles from people's homes, then creates the first element in the boredom formula – an issue developed in the Government sponsored reports *Fair Play for All, Recreation and Deprivation in Inner Urban Areas* and *Why Lock Up Our Schools?*

If the various neighbourhoods with populations of 20,000 to 30,000 possess only a pub or two, with community use of nearby schools limited to traditional youth and further education age groups for only 200 days in the year, then there exists a sure recipe for boredom and social decay. Across the UK it is now recognised that all the recreation resources within an authority cannot be invested in the provision and management of one or two major facilities, many of which illustrate a design brief where the requirements of the community, or indeed management, were not the key elements. The result of such a policy over the country as a whole is a host of severely under-privileged neighbourhoods which have been totally overlooked in terms of recreational need.

We need a 'total systems' view which sees planning and policy-making as a central human activity; rational, but also creative and intuitive; political, yet dynamic and evolving; and at the same time concerned with important choices between human values.

Management

The progressive authorities recognise that their objectives would only be achieved if management in the departments and various facilities was soundly structured, community, not specialist oriented, cost effective not bureaucratic, and above all professional and innovative. Education and training for management in local government leisure services will, therefore, be an important development in the future. The motivation, marketing and promotion disciplines required for successful management allied to a total empathy with individual leisure needs are qualities not found every day.

Of course, in some ways local government only has itself to blame. For years we have commissioned new facilities of capital cost in seven figures, and yet have seen fit to implement management structures which were no more than 'man and dog' operations, or remotely controlled club programmes. Little wonder, therefore, that in some areas of leisure provision we are not achieving our policy goals, with adjacent communities failing to gain access to new facilities, in any way commensurate with the local authority investment – so inhibiting the development of any political momentum for the service.

Management training schemes to degree level within a defined professional career structure were important recommendations by the Government's Committee on Recreation Management Training. The implications for other departments in the local authority structure must be clear, particularly when it is considered how difficult it can be for one to assess management performance within certain traditional departments, never mind in isolating the frequently elusive accountability element within the decision-making process of the bureaucracy.

Progressive local authorities also recognise that however well they utilise resources in housing, education and recreation, and however well they reverse the social and economic effects of declining traditional industries, sound community management in the future will have to be paid for and quantified in respect of rateable expenditure against the social planning goals within the overall philosophy – to a level where there will be an opportunity to equate investment in community development services with the stability of social structures in most neighbourhoods.

Many aspects of the total leisure programme, particularly at neighbourhood level, with their substantial debt and servicing costs will seldom approach viability and cannot, therefore, be left to the commercial sector. How long do we stand and watch younger generations, often frustrated and bored, being media-bombarded with sex and violence, with an urban system in many areas apparently bent on destroying its youth?

In terms of achieving stable community structures at local level, councils therefore have a straight choice. On the one hand, they can treat community development services as a low priority frill on the budget, within an environment where boredom dominates the scene beyond the home, surrounded by a crumbling social structure; or, on the other hand, they can develop a positive commitment to co-ordinating resources at all levels of government in a manner geared to the creation of valid opportunities within a full recognition of the disciplines and qualities required for sound community management. A glance at the many and various 'Inner Cities' reports surely must make the case stronger than ever. But time is running out!

Community development

Whatever administration we have at Westminster, the key to the future development of the social fabric will be an acceptance that the greatest untapped resource of all now exists within the community sector, and the local authorities which can establish effective professional and political structures to harness the available skills and commitment, will play an important role in stabilising and invigorating the living environment. In short, 'volunteering' is fast ceasing to be an activity practised by a small minority for the benefit of the majority, but is becoming the natural means whereby the majority of citizens may become involved in their own community, whether in the form of pressure groups, whether by physical work in their immediate environment or in other ways. The distinction between 'voluntary work' as a minority service function and 'voluntary work' as the natural expression of individuals' desire to be involved in the development of their living environment, is the direct result of the growing awareness that the voluntary sector has a vital role to play in the management and community development process; the latter through the recreation and community arts programme which can make such a substantial contribution to the stability of the social fabric. The report *50 Million Volunteers* identifies the major problem for voluntary groups as one concerning their relationships with local authorities.

A host of initiatives will be required to gain stability, continuity and a sense of purpose in the community sector. It will be vital for local authorities to build partnership structures which will allow voluntary groups to be involved in a wide range of public sector services to a level where all concerned, planners, architects and managers – as well as the community – can appreciate the local authorities' planning goals and community objectives and, above all, by what means they will be realised.

In that context there will be considerable scope in the future for local authorities to involve well structured voluntary groups and associations in the management of a wide range of neighbourhood services which have, until recently, been the traditional responsibility of the local authority. These community and environmental development programmes, perhaps in association with future MSC type schemes, perhaps under the umbrella of a national social wage, will aim to co-ordinate effectively the considerable management, technical and motivating skills now available within the unemployed, and in the long term, those who will be 'sharing' their professional roles.

Vandalism and delinquency have their grass roots within the instability of the neighbourhood environment and a sense of 'community' which it creates. Clearly, there will be little improvement in incidence levels until the community as a whole feels that it has a stake in the facilities around them; that they belong to the people and exist for their benefit. Regrettably all too often it is the worst areas of urban deprivation where we find the voluntary/public sector relationship to be at its weakest.

More formal authorities/voluntary sector links have attracted

attention, certainly following the Scarman report. These represent
the fuller political partnership by the formation of joint liaison and
management committees to co-ordinate programmes and services at
neighbourhood level. Within these structures the fullest,
non-bureaucratic but positive and subtle supporting role of the local
authority is essential. In some areas the joint committtees are composed of equal representation of the local authority, in the shape of
its ward members, and the voluntary sector; a partnership approach
to community development and a detailed local authority involvement in the social fabric.

The evidence suggests that a marked advantage of these structures
is that they generate considerable involvement and participation for
the community in planning and management concepts locally, while
creating a very accountable role for elected members. In addition,
there can be an interesting 'coal face' involvement for local authority
officers of several disciplines, during evenings and weekends. Accordingly, considerable political momentum can be generated for
neighbourhood projects and services; the elected member and appropriate officers becoming closely identified with the cost effectiveness and efficiency of a totally community-oriented operation, one
which not only identifies the community objectives of a neighbourhood but, more importantly, details how they will be realised in the
future.

Furthermore, most of the problems associated with the extended
use of school sites are managerial and, therefore, can be overcome.
If, given sound management, loss of autonomy is the main disadvantage for the education service, then in the future we must have a
system which can integrate resources at all levels of government
within a comprehensive plan geared to community need.

If local authorities are to meet the needs of people in the future at
neighbourhood level, the next decade will require not only the
promotion of joint schemes on new and extended schools but a
range of initiatives which will allow community use of existing schools
in their standard form. Clearly, enlightened management policies
and structures will be required between participating authorities and
departments but it will be vital for the recreation agency, where
appropriate, to make a capital contribution, if only to provide the
necessary but modest management, control and social facilities.

It will also be important to appreciate, within any resource management approach, that a Shire district council or metropolitan district Leisure Services Committee, instead of constructing a large
centre of regional specifiction could make best use of the available

capital in terms of community opportunity, by injecting facilities in to perhaps two or three neighbourhood schools in partnership with the appropriate LEA. Both school and community gain considerably within such an approach which is extremely cost-effective in both capital and revenue terms.

Conclusion

Within a post-industrial society, it is accepted that all social groups have a set of leisure rights, which the public sector must directly and indirectly attempt to realise. Consequently, the enabling role of the local authority in establishing local community management and political structures will be very important in creating webs of opportunity and a matrix of neighbourhood involvement. At the same time, performing as the site owner in joint community/private sector projects, or as the catalyst for a wide range of agencies, the local authority can generate projects of commercial potential, so contributing to the renewal of the regional economic base. In short a job creation role – both in community and private sectors.

Critical, will be an acceptance that whatever one's discipline within the leisure services field, the promotion and marketing of leisure opportunity in association with intense community sector involvement, will be much more important than simply the provision of facilities. The quality and validity of the leisure experience will, therefore, be a much more significant concept than simply the provision of services – or perhaps it is not as important that people use our recreation resources as that they have a positive and fulfilling experience.

The fabric of urban society is the point at issue. Quite clearly, in resource management terms, in many areas we have been muddling through and that is a euphemism for failing to plan forward. Unless we can grasp the nettle we will find ourselves part of a divided society. The future role of the senior local authority corporate managers must be about the successful development of the post-industrial village, urban and rural, within which people will be able to generate socially useful roles and relationships, while meeting their personal leisure needs within a comprehensive community-oriented approach; one involving several government, local authority and voluntary agencies. If we fail, violence will certainly become the tool for social change. The issue is not about which department delivers the services, it is about a partnership with and for people.

PART 2 – COMMUNITY LEISURE: THE FIFTH WAVE
Chris Field
Formerly Director of Leisure,
London Borough of Greenwich

The significance of leisure activity is now more widely understood. The term no longer conjures up Victorian images of the rich or the workshy but it is seen as the essence of man's life experience and a relief of stress as well as support of health.

Many factors, including increased longevity, new technology, unemployment, the emancipation of women, increased affluence and faster childhood development have created conditions whereby a substantial proportion of the community are seeking leisure activity.

The most popular national pastime would appear to be watching television and the benefits of that facility are very substantial. It is probable that our society is much more aware of world events and trends than hitherto and probably more perceptive. Moreover, it provides many happy and satisfying hours of entertainment which is a boon to many and a mercy for the immobile.

Nonetheless, a diet of even good television is debilitating as it is a passive experience and suppresses community and creative skills.

Every citizen needs a good opportunity to recreate in exercise of mind and muscle so as to retain or develop agility and intellect.

Educationists of the nineteenth century recognised this need for children and built up an infrastructure of school workshops and playing fields which have consistently been enhanced to the standard of today.

However, these were traditionally restricted to daytime education. The best of them are in the private sector restricted to a comparative few and there are many geographical areas of serious under-provision, mostly in the inner city. Even the post war phenomenon of adult education has only reached a comparative few and the real achievement of leisure provision in the public sector was the coincidence of the Wolfenden Report (showing the need for post school provision) and the comparative affluence of the 1960s.

Provision

With the recognition of the economies of scale and shared services, came the co-location of large municipal facilities, the development of management structures and the emergence of the professional leisure manager.

Although central government itself did comparatively little, its agencies were active and strategic provision plans were drawn up by national and regional bodies. Under these overviews, emphasis understandably was on good quality facilities serving large catchments and many excellent provisions appeared.

Structures

Local authorities established leisure committees during the 1970s in order to develop and manage centres for sport and the arts which have provided much fulfilment for many. These committees usually embraced the traditional services of libraries, entertainments, parks and swimming pools and two main forces, one of recreation and the other of arts have been fashioned. They have worked reasonably well.

However, the most central requirements of every community have been in some danger of being subsumed within these structures.

Play

Philosophy
One of these is the child's basic need for play and in many ways, this must be the fundamental responsibility of every local authority. Services for young people have been at the origin of all our leisure provision and, as with so many important developments, they were innovated by the voluntary sector with the YMCA and NPTA making notable contributions.

Facilities
The village playground (even if an urban village) is the most important early leisure experience for most of us. Contemporary parents still seek the safe, stimulating, fun-creating, nearby playground. Children need the physical stretch and the social contact to enable them to develop character and confidence.

The evolution of the working mother led to a need for out-of-school and weekend supervised activities and the play centre emerged. Some of these were provided on school sites but the majority were dovetailed into village halls, redundant buildings or surplus space. A few have been purpose built. The adventure playground was developed to create conditions for robust play and a chance for children to demolish and build interesting structures.

The play scheme
Coincidentally, harassed parents during the longer school holidays formed play schemes on local sites with the help of local councils and the specialist play worker developed.

Inner city children who had never had a holiday were taken by a range of transport devices to tented or hutted camps in the countryside or near the sea. These holidays away may prove to be the most significant leisure experience of many youngsters. A few days of fun, discipline, music, comradeship and control have enriched many.

Younger children
One O'Clock clubs for parents of toddlers and Pre-School Play Groups for nursery ages have focussed on special group needs and enabled early development.

Other important developments included city farms, pet competitions, involvement in professional football clubs, junior clubs, special provision for the handicapped, drama sessions, play buses and play days.

Nonetheless, the most radical development of all has probably been the enlivenment of the traditional fixed equipment playgrounds in parks. The introduction of safer equipment and surfaces has eradicated the need for permanent playground supervision which, in any event, had been of limited benefit. Instead, these playgrounds now have leadership only during high summer and holiday peak periods providing stimulation and control. The playground attendant is a vanishing species.

With all these burgeoning enterprises, a comprehensive play service has now developed to complement the more formal youth service and to ensure every child has fulfilling leisure time.

Voluntary involvement
Neighbourhood groups have formed around local facilities and many authorities have created district play associations to enable co-ordination and advice. These are usually composed of a large majority of parents with a leavening of councillors, play workers, police, social workers, fund raisers and youth workers.

Play workers
Professional play leadership is now a fully recognised discipline with a professional institute and an expanding body of knowledge. In addition, the army of part-time and voluntary playworkers is becoming increasingly better trained and informed.

Management

All of this needs management and many district councils now have a Play Manager (with at least one Assistant) and these are crucial appointments for the development of the service.

A number of authorities have still not yet reached this stage of development and persist with a service from the recreation department with a sports bias. Physical recreation has much to contribute to youngsters' leisure but the modern play service is substantially broader and more subtle.

One crucial component is access to cultural activities and especially drawing, painting, drama, music and dance. Books and story readings are also important. Most programmes at play centres will be far more orientated to arts and entertainment than sport.

Character

Play Work is more concerned with the development of character and adjustment to society than any specific activity. This is a very different function than sports leadership.

Young people need to not only express themselves but to let off steam. This can occasionally lead to tension with other more adult groups and neighbours so that play management requires a sensitive balance of conflicting needs. Play managers operate in highly volatile situations where normal management science has to be replaced by management art.

Recent progress

In recent years, communities have come to fully recognise the need for play facilities and insist on their provision within their neighbourhood. However, opinion as to precise location and style are widely different.

The House of Commons itself took up the issue in 1983 and responded vigorously to an Early Day Motion which caused the Prime Minister to state her support for Play, appoint a Minister for the functions and establish the Play Board. Improvements in information provision, training and technical knowledge are now helping the local initiatives to develop whilst Play Board has now become the National Children's Play and Recreation Unit within the Sports Council.

Youth service

The importance of close relationships between the Youth and Play Services is apparent. Although play facilities are less structured and less formal than youth facilities, there is much complementary work to be done.

There is a good case for the amalgamation of the district Youth Committee and the Play Association but there are also some arguments for keeping them separate. A compromise of occasional joint meetings of both bodies may be appropriate.

There are increasing considerations of transferring the Youth Service from the historic educational committee to that of leisure services. This has been successful at shire county level and Birmingham has now taken the initiative. This is really a natural process which gives the Youth Service (like the Library Service) a senior status rather than scrag-end of agenda attention. This movement appears likely to accelerate during the next decade.

Adult community leisure

Multi-purpose
Adult community leisure has simultaneously come to full consciousness within many local authorities. In the original reach for a broad range of specific leisure facilities, the essence of the multi-purpose village hall was occasionally overlooked. Strikingly, it is in the inner city that this need is most expressed with pressure of demand for meeting rooms, community halls and centres.

Meeting rooms
Perhaps the small scale tenants' meeting room is, in practice, the essence of all our leisure services. These communal spaces provide individual opportunity for enjoying a community rather than existing in isolation. Social, cultural and recreational activities are arranged for children, pensioners, wives and other special groups. Football teams and music groups can be created, political parties and anti-quarian societies can meet and bingo and other indoor games can be played.

If the use of the room is restricted to tenants, there is a case for management by the estate office but it is probably better to use the marketing and programming skills of contemporary leisure departments. In any event, it would be better for the estate if outside open membership groups are allowed occasional use as these will provide extra opportunities for participation by residents.

The room can also be used for small scale functions from children's tea parties to a small wedding celebration. Charges for hiring by groups and non-residents will raise a useful income.

There will be plenty of management problems from competing uses to noise complaints but clear policies and sensitive handling will minimise the effect.

This simple amenity has come to be the most prized by communities and may be the most cost effective leisure unit.

Community halls
Nonetheless, it is desirable to have a larger facility in the style of the village hall available for catchments of more than five thousand residents in the town or a large country village. This will need a large room of about $1000m^2$ together with toilets, storage and ideally a kitchen.

The hall will be popular for larger social functions, public meetings and entertainments.

The management style will be light and not distant. One London Borough has the halls operating in a network under the wing of large community centres with the group serving districts of twenty thousand people.

Community centres
These centres should desirably have a hall of at least 1500^2 but, as importantly, need a cluster of smaller rooms. The use of sliding partitions can be effective (as with single halls) but sundry rooms will usually be intensively used by the population. A kitchen cafe is essential and a licensed bar almost so.

Licensed bars
The latter is a management headache as controls of alcohol, tobacco and cash need to be stringent. Even the best controlled bars experience occasional irreconciliations but if these are not identified immediately and adjusted, a pattern can easily develop into a crises.

There is also a hazard of the bar becoming dominated by non-participants to the detriment of the range of activities of the centre. A sensitive control is preferable here but it must, nonetheless, be fully capable of sensing the emergence of a problem and nipping it in the bud. Notwithstanding, the tensions are worthwhile as this service can lubricate the work of the centre and link separate groups effectively.

Mere booking of rooms to clubs and societies without fostering inter-relationships and a sense of community will fall short of the fundamental opportunity of proactive community leisure development.

Properly managed, the bar can also generate a useful income to assist in the funding of the centre. Many managers have been able to find volunteer bar staff for at least limited periods and that is the secret of the financial success of many bars in single activity buildings such as rowing and hockey clubs.

However, it is more difficult in the multi-activity complex to create the loyalty that will sustain the scrupulous punctuality, honesty.

hygiene and courtesies that are vital. There are successful examples of a compromise where members of the centre are given a small (£5) sessional fee. At some large centres, skilled bar staff are employed which solves many of the management problems but obviously reduces net income.

It is perfectly possible to have a mix of volunteers, sessional and full-time assistants together with occasional involvement of management personnel. However, it is best to have a simple arrangement.

Public halls
Most local authorities run at least one large municipal hall. Many have more than one and provide specialist banqueting suites and entertainment auditoriums. These amenities should be part of the structure of opportunities for community leisure and managed and marketed as such. The traditional arrangement of a booking junior in the Town Clerk's department merely accepting requests is no longer appropriate.

Publicity
Indeed, the marketing mechanisms of the leisure department should embrace all the halls in the district. As one objective will be to facilitate access by the community to all leisure opportunities, it is useful to include all the buildings in one 'Halls for Hire' leaflet.

These should cover the local authority halls, church premises, school facilities, defence establishments and commercial buildings. One central new technology system can operate bookings with appropriate redistribution of costs.

Management by the community
With the exception of the large public halls, for which the best community representative is probably the local authority Member, the community facilities should have elected house committees. These can represent the user groups, local tenants and residents associations and other special interests.

If a meeting room or community hall with a small house committee is a satellite of a large community centre, it should have at least one representative on that centre's house committee.

District community council
The local authority should create a district-wide grouping of representatives of all the community centres into a local community council on the lines of the suggested Play Association.

The voluntary establishments need to be fully involved in this Council. Initial approaches may meet with a hesitant response due to

anxieties about bureaucratic intentions and it could be best to provide assistance for the independent bodies to meet separately at first
under the chairmanship of one of their members. However, it is
desirable that they become equal partners in the large umbrella
organisation.

The Community Council should also provide a structure for
membership by the user groups in some form of affiliation.

A management committee will be needed to represent all the
house committees, the specialist user interests and the local authority
in a group small enough to be executive.

It will be important for the local authority elected Members to be
seen to be involved in these management processes.

Community development

Whilst the primary concern of these services will be the provision of
fulfilling opportunities for self expression and personal development
from leisure pursuits, there will be other potential roles for these
amenities and their managers.

The dissemination of information will be one of these. Although
fully authoritative advice will rarely be available at a community
leisure facility, the staff will have usually been trained in referral
techniques and will be required to guide individuals to the
appropriate agency.

Apart from concern for the individual, these leisure facilities will
have the opportunity to contribute to the development of the whole
community. Ginger groups can be assisted to pursue complaints or
enthusiasms and programmes can be geared to develop a sense of
village or town identity.

CLAT's

These amenities should be exploited by sports and arts action teams
which can be bettered by the creation of community leisure action
teams based on the community centre and operating across the
network of satellites and recreation and arts specialist facilities including the parks and libraries.

These small (2–3 person) groups can galvanise more effective use
by non-joiners through imaginative and subtle innovation and
cheerful cajoling.

Adult education

The objectives of self expression and development are common to
leisure and non-vocational education services. Moreover, the
specialist education courses for adults have a close link with the adult
community leisure activities and frequently take place in the same or
similar buildings.

Close relationships have been building up and this process should be encouraged.

Summary

The traditional emphasis of leisure (and educational) services has been on specialist facilities. The arrival of multi-purpose structures in the 60s and the expansion of joint provision in the 70s has now led naturally to the emphasis on local provision for the community. Youngsters' needs, those of other individual groups and the wider opportunities for community development are causing authorities to establish support mechanisms for the basic needs of community leisure.

This third force may not have massive staffing or financial resources of the cultural and recreational services but, if measured in significance to society, it is obviously a major component. As a generality, these facilities are more volatile than libraries and pools and require more able and subtle management.

Those local authorities which are concerned about the development of community leisure are now constructing central organisations which can be schematically reflected as Fig. 8.1.

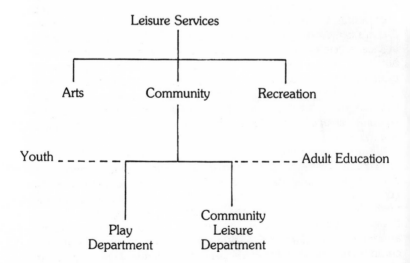

Fig 8.1 – A model for a community leisure services department.

PART 3   YOUTH AND COMMUNITY SERVICES AS PART OF LOCAL AUTHORITY LEISURE PROVISION

David Liddle
Director of Community Leisure, Avon County Council

Introduction

There is considerable and growing interest in separating local authority youth services from education departments. Although historically sections 41 and 53 of the 1944 Education Act were seen to give statutory authority for Youth Services this was never more than a convenient existing peg on which to hang the post-war development of local authority youth services. By using a very broad definition of education, many activities, including youth and community services, can be called educational, but the future may well lie in developing another context for these services. Other statutory authority for the provision of youth services has been found in the Physical Training and Recreation Act 1937 which was subsequently repealed and replaced by the Local Government (Miscellaneous Provisions) Act 1976. Whatever legislation is relied upon, however, there is no statutory duty upon a local authority to provide a youth service, a position which this service has in common with many local authority leisure services. In any case there is no statutory requirement which lays down the departmental arrangements which local authorities must adopt in the youth service and it is now urgent that the youth service nationally reassesses and revitalises its professional objectives if necessary within a different organisational structure.

It is still relatively uncommon for a local authority's youth service to form a part organisationally of its leisure services, and most commentators have inferred that the nature and emphasis of the youth service in such a context must be likely to change. In fact, the uniting of youth and leisure services poses as many questions about the nature and purpose of leisure services. This paper will, therefore, attempt to look for an understanding of 'Leisure' in which youth and community services have a complementary, valuable and necessary place.

What is 'leisure' in local government?

Leisure services in local government are still mostly collections of disparate services, largely reminiscent of local government generally prior to Bains. Baths managers manage baths, parks managers practice municipal horticulture and librarians run services based on the lending of books for home reading. Little appears to unite these separate callings and few attempts have been made to evolve a philosophy of provision even where these services have been grouped together in leisure directorates. Leisure Management is concerned primarily with the techniques of providing and operating buildings and facilities. Necessary though this is there needs to be an underlying purpose which unites these services if a comprehensive strategy is to be produced.

The publication in 1982 *Leisure Policy for the Future* began to give national recognition to the importance of providing a basis for leisure services. Local authorities were seen to have 'a leading responsibility for the quality of life of all citizens'. Recognition of this role was increasingly reflected in efforts by local authorities to 'understand the needs of their communities . . . and to serve those needs which others do not meet'. Barry Sherman went further when writing in the Local Government Chronicle of 11th January 1985 – 'Leisure is not only about providing people with things to do, it is also about helping people help themselves and others'.

Leisure management should not just concern itself with activities for their own sake. It should also ask 'Why?' and 'How?'. Both questions will become increasingly important as the significance of leisure in society generally and local government in particular increases. The answers will help clarify the purpose of leisure services and provide a basis for relationships with other providers of leisure, social and community services.

Youth services and education – how compatible are they?

It is important for any service that it should operate within a structure where its values are shared and respected. This is especially true when the people concerned feel that they have a distinctive approach to philosophy and practice.

The Youth Service is one of the few services in local government in which a more or less equal state of partnership exists with the voluntary sector. Major national bodies such as the uniformed organisations and the churches have a long and distinguished tradition of service to youth. Their aims and priorities need to be recognised by local authorities in determining their own provision. Another aspect of partnership is to be found in the fact that much youth provision, especially in smaller communities is founded upon voluntary community-based effort, and many local authority youth centres draw very heavily upon voluntary help for youth work, management and support. The need to allow for and to recognise that partnership is central to the delivery of the service. The spirit of partnership can be difficult to develop in education departments whose main concern is the provision of statutory services.

In its practice youth work emphasises the qualities of being non-directive, experimental in nature and leading towards participation with and control by its clients. These elements are, of course, to be found in formal education but their significance to the youth service tends to distance it in terms of attitude from education rather than to unit them.

There are some practical situations where the differing emphases of education and youth can lead to the values of the youth service taking second place. Dual use is an example.

Two motives usually lie behind dual use. Firstly, facilities which are needed can be made generally available more cheaply than by purpose-built provision. Secondly, more economic use can be made of buildings, facilities and equipment which have already been provided at high cost. There are other values, however, which a youth and community service will want to emphasise. To be of most value, facilities should meet community needs as fully as possible. This means that communities need to be enabled to formulate and express their wishes. These views when expressed may not always coincide exactly with those of the providers. Communities need an independent champion and this is the role youth and community services should adopt. In addition, community involvement in the management of facilities is essential if dual use schemes are to be successful in terms of design, access, promotion and operation. Youth and community services should be free to enable communities, by improving skills, resources, organisation and confidence, to maximise their effectiveness. This requires some organisational independence to be effective.

Different emphases between youth work and education are also apparent in school-based youth work. Frank Booten in *Deschooling the Youth Service* (Youth Service Special No. 8 1977) and Anthony Jeffs in *Young People and the Youth Service* (1979 cf pp 65–85) claim that the justification for school-based youth work has often been the economy of provision rather than the effectiveness of it. It cannot always be easy for school-based youth workers to pay as much attention as they would like to developing the neighbourhood role, work with the unemployed or with young people not attending that school.

The report of the Archbishop of Canterbury's Commission on Urban Priority Areas *Faith in the City* quoted a senior employee of the youth service as saying

'Being a discretionary service, the youth service is part of "education" in which the school dominates. There is a feeling that the youth service is the "Cinderella" . . .'

There does seem to be a widespread feeling in the youth service that when the resources of money, equipment, building repair and maintenance and administrative time come to be distributed, youth services do not get their fair share. It is interesting, however, that *Faith in the City* nevertheless went on to recommend that youth services remained part of education rather than leisure because of the fear that leisure would place too great an emphasis upon 'optional spare-time leisure pursuits as the purpose of youth work provision'. This fear represents a misunderstanding of the purpose of leisure provision itself.

There is no suggestion that the formal education process or the people involved in education are unable or unwilling to share youth service values or express them. There is no suggestion either that these values cannot be accommodated by or within education departments. It is rather a question of where, organisationally these values are most likely to be effective within a local government context. Where youth and community services are part of an education department the resolution of conflicts and the allocation of resources will be pursued internally and schools will tend to win. A separate department with a separate chief officer and committee may actually hasten and encourage the development of an effective community service.

The present state of the youth service

The problems of the youth service are extensively catalogued by the people within it, at meetings, in reports and in the professional press. The rehearsal of its problems is an endless subject of debate. In its relatively short local government life the service has been the subject of four major reports, from Albemarle, through Fairbairn and Milsom to Thompson. Popular topics for debate include the purpose of the youth service, youth work methodology, detached versus centre-based work, low usage rates and challenges to main stream youth work from eg Training Commission and Intermediate Treatment. There appears through this debate to be three factors which are widely held to be true within youth work.

Firstly, that the youth service has changed little since the 1960s and is badly in need of revitalisation.

Secondly, youth work lacks professional self-confidence. New regulations which will mean that teachers are no longer automatically qualified in youth work will help. Youth work, however, is still striving for the status and respect which their educational colleagues have established so successfully. In career terms youth work is still widely seen as second best.

Thirdly, a phrase recurs in debates on the youth service which indicates the continuing search for a context in which to see youth work – 'There is an insufficiently wide definition of objectives'. This reveals widespread dissatisfaction with the definition of youth work as 'the Social Education of Young People'. The problem is partly to do with the difficulty in describing or defining 'Social Education' satisfactorily. It is more connected, however, with the same issue which needs resolution in leisure services, namely that a more widely drawn framework is needed in which to express the purpose of the services and within which both services can grow and develop.

What do leisure and youth have in common?

Both services have in common that they are voluntary. That is, people use youth services and leisure services in their own way and in their own time. People use the services in ways which suit their own needs as they perceive them. Both services, therefore, are competing for people's interest against alternative uses of their time. They both, consequently, share a need and an obligation to promote and extend their use, especially among non-traditional users and to make themselves attractive.

As well as providing for the use of leisure time, however, both services in a local government context place emphasis on the quality and constructiveness of the activities concerned. Youth services have often appointed specialist officers for creative activities and for sports and recreation. There is added benefit where these activities are integrated with leisure provision.

Much unites leisure and youth services in their approach to the use of buildings which in both cases aim to be accessible and welcoming to individuals and responsive to community needs. There are ample opportunities for youth work to be carried out in libraries and sports centres – places where young people naturally congregate – just as activities of an active and passive nature can be introduced into youth centres.

The aspects of partnership which are so much a characteristic of the youth service are shared also by leisure services. Local authorities are no more the sole providers of leisure than they are of the youth service. In the case of leisure the partnership is also with the commercial sector and there is a potential benefit to the youth service of being involved in this partnership.

A wider context for leisure and youth services

To identify factors in common between leisure and youth services is not, of course, to imply that the main purpose of either is to be found in those factors. The services are united by a more fundamental purpose.

Community Development is the process of enabling individuals and groups to acquire more influence over the issues which affect their lives. It starts with helping people learn about themselves so that they can identify with others.

It continues with the process of helping communities express their identity, their needs and their wishes and is ultimately about enabling communities to acquire the skills and power to influence the way society works.

Community Development is important because it involves an improvement in the quality of life, education, self-esteem and self-confidence of individuals. This is the rationale for participation in sports and recreation and in community arts and drama. It was the motive that led to the growth of the Public Library movement and sustains it today. It was the reason our parks were created and for emphasis being given to access to the countryside.

It is also important because if communities cannot articulate their needs, or if we do not find ways of listening to them, the services that we provide can be misdirected and wasteful.

Community development is important because it involves redistributing power, skills and opportunities among communities. Where these are unequal some groups dominate others, alienation and social tension grow and the process of creating a fairer society is held back.

All this may seem a long way from the day to day concerns of the sports centre manager, branch librarian or youth worker. In fact, it is the fundamental purpose which unites their efforts and provides the context in which they can work together and with others.

Where leisure and youth services have been united into one local authority department it has too often been for reasons connected with dissatisfaction with the youth service as part of education. To some extent this stems from some of the incompatibilities between education and the youth service outlined above. For the union to be successful, however, the positive benefits need to be identified, stressed and built upon. Organisationally leisure and youth have much in common. Philosophically both need the other to help identify the context of community development which is the fundamental purpose of both and within which both can flourish. For youth and community services to be part of local authority leisure provision is good for leisure and good for youth. It has the potential also to benefit the communities they serve.

Postscript

Whatever the problems within the urban social fabric during the 70s, the principle of giving local communities a major stake in the planning and management of their own neighbourhood in the late 80s is now more important than ever. The great need for an effective matrix of public, private and community sector strategies is now absolutely clear and most relevant to current government legislation for improving the delivery of traditional public services and the management of schools within the terms of the Education Reform Act.

9 Alternative futures for the public leisure service

Ian Henry

1 Introduction

The purpose of this chapter is to identify and explore some of the alternative future scenarios for local government and to consider their consequences for the provision of leisure services. The aim here is not to produce precise and accurate prediction – such an exercise would be fraught with dangers. Rather the aim is to map out a framework which can make sense of some of the key factors that are influencing local government form and structure, and will therefore affect the nature and delivery of local authority leisure services over the next decade. To this end five models or styles of local government are described as 'ideal types', and the conditions which would give rise to each of these five types are identified, together with their consequences for leisure service provision. The structures of the discussion for each of the models is illustrated in Figure 9.1.

The preconditions for the emergence of each type of local government are discussed under three main headings:

Prevailing ideologies of central and/or local government

Five categories of ideology are employed in the analysis;
- neo-liberalism,
- traditional, 'one nation' conservatism,
- social democracy,
- utopian socialism,
- scientific socialism

Prevailing economic conditions

Factors considered under this heading include:
- rate of growth or contraction of the economy;
- the level of unemployment;
- the rate of inflation;
- the strength of sterling.

PREVAILING CONDITIONS   CONSEQUENCES FOR LEISURE SERVICES

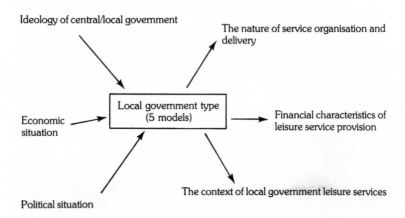

Fig 9.1 – The future of local government leisure services: a framework for discussion.

Prevailing political conditions
- party control of central and/or local government;
- the strength of such majorities or the existence of coalitions;
- central-local relations.

Similarly the consequences for leisure services of each of the five types of local government are analysed into three sets of factors in the following way:

The nature of leisure service organisation and delivery
- changing concepts of client needs and therefore of services required;
- consequences of change for the role of the professional and the skill requirements of leisure professionals;
- changing nature of organisational structures in local government.

Financial characteristics of local government leisure services
- consequences for leisure services of requiring higher/lower resource generation or of changing income-cost ratios;
- altering the pattern of resource allocation within public sector services;
- changing revenue-capital relationships;
- effects of changing the methods of resourcing local government for leisure services.

The context of local authority leisure service provision

- changes in the size and structure of public (voluntary and commercial) sector(s);
- changes in the relative influence or power of politicians, professionals and public in the local authority decision-making process;
- central government influence and the role of the leisure quangos in local authority leisure policy.

The above factors will not receive equal and comprehensive treatment in the analysis. Constraints of space and time, and overlap with other chapters in this book preclude this. Emphasis will however be placed on the more likely future scenarios and the consequences for leisure provision.

2 Alternative models of local government for England and Wales

The construction of ideal types represents only the beginnings of analysis, but can make some contribution to forward planning in the political system, in highlighting issues for debate. The discussion of the five local authority types below will identify major costs and benefits for each type, not with a view to promoting one or more models as preferred options, but rather with the aim of clarifying the terms of any such debate. The reader should nevertheless be aware that identifying certain consequences as costs rather than benefits (or vice versa) will be dependent upon the values or perspective of the commentator. Potentially contentious consequences of such models may therefore be described below as *both* costs and benefits.

2.1 The contract management model

This model sees local authorities as responsible for the provision of only those services which are considered essential, and either unlikely to be provided by the commercial or voluntary sector or unsuitable for provision within those sectors. Local authorities in such circumstances may manage the provision of certain services (eg policing) because these services cannot be devolved to private contractors. However, under this model, in the majority of service areas the role of the local authority is limited to supervision of private contractors undertaking provision of essential services (eg overseeing the operation of an education voucher system in a privatised system of schooling, monitoring the implementation of contracts for grass-cutting and landscape maintenance, etc). Indeed in such a scenario responsibility for *direct* provision of services may be transferred to central government leaving local government with responsibility for operating a system of competitive tendering for other services, and for 'quality control' in the provision of such services.

The primary arguments for this approach to local service management are firstly, that it minimises public subsidy by reducing the number of services provided and by introducing an element of competition between bidders for local authority contracts; and secondly that it reduces state intervention *per se*, which for some (in particular the 'new right') is synonymous with an increase in the freedom of the individual.

2.1.1 The ideological preconditions of contract management in local government

The ideological rationale for this approach to local government is provided by neo-liberalism. This political philosophy is associated with commentators such as Milton Friedman and Hayek whose views have been espoused by the New Right in the present Conservative Government, and more particularly in its Cabinet, though rather less evidence exists of such Tory radicalism at local authority level. (There is an interesting contrast here with radicalism in the Labour Party, which is a much more visibly potent force at local level).

In order to appreciate the conditions under which the contract management model might emerge it will be necessary to gain some understanding of the value position of those who advocate it. The values which are central to neo-liberalism (in the sense in which it is employed here) are freedom of the individual to pursue his or her own best interests unfettered by the state, and the responsibility of the individual for his or her own physical and mental well-being. Neo-liberals recognise that a society which operates according to such principles will inevitably manifest inequalities, but they argue that such inequalities are the price which has to be paid for preserving freedom. Hayek (1946)[15] for example argues that 'in a free society undeserved fluctuations of income are inevitable'. The major debate between the new right and the new left in British politics (between neo-liberals and socialists) has focussed on the issue of the primacy of 'individual freedom' or 'equality' as principles for guiding government action. While neo-liberals argue that freedom and equality are *incompatible* as goals, socialists argue that equality of opportunity is a *prerequisite* of personal freedom.

The opposition of neo-liberals to state intervention in the economy is based on the claim that it promotes inefficiency and unfairness. The root cause of unemployment and inflation, neo-liberals argue, is the tinkering with the economy for which successive post-war governments of both major parties have been responsible. Money has been pumped into the economy on two major pretexts – attempts to protect uncompetitive industries, and the disbursement of social benefits from the public purse. In both types of case this leads inevitably to inflation since industrial subsidy and social benefits are funded ultimately by the printing of money or taxation. The former devalues currency and thus induces inflation directly; the latter leads to a raising of price levels on the part of those who are taxed, fuelling inflation indirectly. Both such policies lead to increased costs for healthy industry and therefore a lack of competitiveness abroad. Industrial inefficiency, it is argued, is rewarded with subsidy, while successful industry is unjustly penalised through increased taxation. Thus the principle of individual freedom to succeed (or fail) through his/her own efforts is frustrated in either a mixed or a totally planned economy.

The objections of neo-liberals to state intervention in the economic sphere are mirrored also in their concern over social policies, and in particular the growth of the welfare state. These objections are similarly rooted in a concern for efficiency and fairness. State monopolies like the National Health Service are regarded by the new right as being inevitably inefficient, since they lack any meaningful competitors to spur them on to greater productivity. Furthermore, it is argued, publicly provided services which are free or sold at a price well below the market rate, are likely to generate very high levels of demand so that it becomes impossible to differentiate between those with a real need for the service and those whose demands are unjustifiable. In addition, by providing these services at minimal or no cost the state is seen as removing the stimulus for the individual to take responsibility for his or her own welfare, thus making 'weaklings' or 'dependents' of its own citizens.

Finally, the welfare state is also seen as contributing to the growth of social instability. The state defines a number of people's wants as 'rights', and attempts to fulfil them through the provision of a range of social services (including leisure). However, when services are provided free, or at a minimal cost, demand is extremely high, and cannot be fully met. Thus with an impossible strain placed on public services, some of the needs or wants which have been recognised by the state as rights are not being met, and those citizens whose needs are not met will feel that they have a legitimate grievance against the state. These individuals will therefore feel justified in registering a protest often in a socially disruptive manner. The welfare state is thereby seen by neo-liberals as contributing to the risk of civil disorder by raising expectations which cannot be fulfilled.

This is not to say that neo-liberal political commentators advocate that no state intervention whatsoever should take place, but rather they urge that the limits to such intervention should be tightly defined. Friedman (1962) for example identifies three types of role which the state might play in social and economic policy. The first is that of 'umpire and rule maker', identifying and administering the rules which guarantee individual freedom. Even an effective competitive economic system requires the backing of government to ensure that it runs smoothly.

The second such case is one in which public benefits are to be gained with little or no loss of individual liberty and where costs are not prohibitive. There are two general classes of such classes – the first is monopolies and other similar market imperfections; the second involves 'neighbourhood effects'. There are unlikely to be many monopolies in the leisure sector which strict monetarist arguments would support. 'National' galleries and other unique national cultural resources may be exceptions. However, Friedman does use an example drawn from the field of recreation to illustrate the types of 'neighbourhood effect' which might justify state provision of facilities or services. He cites the case of urban parks, arguing that these constitute 'public goods' for which it is impossible or impractical to charge all those who receive benefits:

> 'For the city park it is extremely difficult to identify the people who benefit from it and charge them for the benefits which they receive. If there is a park in the middle of the city, the houses on all sides get the benefit of the green space and people who walk through it or by it also benefit. To maintain toll collectors at the gates or to impose annual charges per window overlooking the park would be very expensive and difficult'.[12]

Friedman's third principle justifying public sector investment is paternalism. He considers for example that it is appropriate for the state to operate services for the mentally ill. He is less certain however of the case for regarding the education of children as beyond the realm of individual responsibility, giving some support to the notion that parents should be responsible for the welfare and education of their children rather than the state. This final case is noted in order to illustrate the rigour with which Friedman wishes to apply the criteria he has adopted for justifying public sector involvement in social and economic affairs.

Neo-liberalism, as outlined here, provides a rationale for the minimalist approach to state provision of services indicated in the contract management model of local government. However, it is also important to note the economic circumstances in which such an ideological position is likely to flourish, together with the political conditions required to put the neo-liberal prescription into practice.

2.1.2 The economic pre-conditions of contract management local government

The development of an economic theory consistent with neo-liberal ideology was one of the key features of British politics in the 1970's. The rise of the new right and of monetarist economics in the Tory Party was in large part a reaction to the failure of Keynesian macro- economic policies to sustain post-war economic growth and to maintain full employment. The 1970s and early 80s provided the economic conditions in which one might expect the political values of the right to become attractive (to politicians if not to the electorate).

The floating of major currencies in 1971/2, British membership of the EEC in 1973, and the quadrupling of oil prices in 1974 accelerated Britain's changed position in the international economy. For a variety of reasons Britain's structurally anachronistic economy could not cope with the growing crisis in world trade and currency markets. The result generated a new term in economic theory, 'stagflation' – no, or low, economic growth, alongside growing unemployment and inflation – a combination of features for which Keynesian economic theory could not provide an adequate explanation, and therefore seemed unable to generate policy solutions. It was under these conditions that the new right was able to promote the argument that a radical shift away from state welfare was required to revitalise the economy, to ease the burden of public spending and to encourage Victorian values of self help, family responsibility and advancement through hard work.

These economic features, high inflation and unemployment coupled with low growth, could be seen as necessary rather than sufficient conditions for the development of neo-liberal thought, in that this same failure of Keynesian economic policy also regenerated interest in the economic and social critique of the Left. However, any attempt to specify necessary conditions for the emergence of particular social philosophies implies a form of epistemological determinism which is theoretically unsound. The preconditions discussed here for each model of local government should only be regarded as 'sufficient' in character, and therefore likely to be consistent with, rather than to determine, the kind of changes in local government operation described.

2.1.3 The political preconditions of contract management local government

The political conditions which one would expect to be consistent with the development of the contract management type of local authority are a Conservative government with a clear majority in Parliament (so that the prospect of effective rebellion is minimal); dominated by ideologies of the right; offering fiscal incentives and legislative powers for the severe reduction or removal of direct service provision, and the development of contracting arrangements. The return of the Thatcher administration for a third term with a clear majority constituted such conditions.

The imposition of the contract management approach by central Government on unwilling partners at local level can only be achieved by legislation. The present Conservative administration's desire to minimise local autonomy in pursuit of central Government macro-economic policy has already been illustrated in the series of measures since 1980 which have reduced central government contributions to local spending, enforced tighter cash limits and provided for the setting of maximum rate levels for individual authorities by central Government. Finally the Local Government Acts of 1987 and '88 introduced compulsory competitive tendering into a number of local authority activities, including several in the field of leisure services.

Councillors of many political persuasions are concerned about possible decreases in quality of service, increases in costs, and creaming of services away from those most in need.

However the Government is firmly committed to further privatisation and competition and further legislation is likely. Legislation may be supported by further expenditure squeezes to enforce additional savings and encourage moves towards the contract management approach.

At the time of writing the main local government leisure services to be exposed to this approach are the management and marketing of sports and leisure facilities (eg sports centres, leisure centres, swimming pools etc) and a consultative paper on the financing of the public library service. However, the voluntary implementation of a contract management approach across the board of local leisure services is likely to be limited to traditional Conservative strongholds. Even here the adoption of comprehensive contract management is likely to be partial since Conservative local authority leaders have often shown themselves to be less radical than their Cabinet colleagues.

2.1.4 The nature of leisure service organisation and delivery under contract management local government

One of the cornerstones of the neo-liberal argument is the proposition that 'the public interest' cannot be specified. This is in part because of the difficulties inherent in any attempt to sum the complex interests of all individuals in a society, and in part simply because the interests of certain individuals and groups are mutually incompatible. Given the impracticability/impossibility of specifying the community's interests and needs, the individual is left to pursue his or her own interests through the market place.

The notion of 'meeting the leisure needs of the community' (which is an aim commonly expressed in policy for local authority leisure services), is regarded as serious. Indeed the interests which are served by local government leisure departments are seen as sectional, and dominated by the interests of leisure professionals themselves. The concept of leisure need promoted by the new right (if need is the right term in this context) is one of free market pluralism.

The structure of local government provision in the leisure field under the contract management approach would alter fundamentally or even disappear. Leisure provision for the most part may be seen as the luxury end of social policy and perhaps only three categories of provision are therefore likely to continue to receive subsidy under this scenario. These are:

- Where financial 'neighbourhood effects' accrue. Leisure provision which provides an essential element of the infrastructure for local capital accumulation may be retained, eg tourism promotion, the marketing of a town, city or district may be a candidate for public subsidy given the difficulties of establishing precisely who benefits from such expenditure. This is perhaps more accurately described as a merit than a public good, but it is an area of the present operation of public sector leisure services which may not be effectively undertaken in a free market;
- where social 'neighbourhood effects' accrue. Friedman's example of urban parks falls into this category;
- where externality effects, such as a reduction in anti-social behaviour, are thought to accrue, subsidy may be continued. A common (though as yet empirically untested) claim is that leisure spending on certain disadvantaged groups obviates higher law and order or anti-vandalism expenditure. Public subsidy for facilities and services in areas of high risk might well be regarded by some neo-liberal thinkers as shrewd investment.

However, in each of the cases cited above it would be possible to contract commercial or voluntary sector organisations to operate such services on behalf of the local authority. The skills required of public sector managers in such areas are therefore likely to be limited to the ability to specify and monitor standards of performance among those commercial and voluntary sector operators under contract to the authority. The skills of the operational manager which represents the major concern of current professional courses (eg those of the new Institute of Leisure and Amenity Management syllabus) would be virtually irrelevent since contract management local authorities would have few staff and a negligible amount of direct service provision.

2.1.5 The financial characteristics of local authority leisure services under contract management local government

Given the minimalist provision implied by the contract management model, leisure expenditure is likely to be severely restricted. Two types of authority seem likely to present exceptions to this rule. The first is local authorities encompassing tourist destinations where leisure expenditure on promotion and on the environment (eg maintenance of parks, beaches and other similar attractions) will be a significant factor. The second is inner city authorities with considerable social problems and a tendency towards social unrest.

2.1.6 The context of local authority leisure service provision under contract management

Both the contract management and 'financial stringency' models of local government (see para 2.2) are related to a major restructuring of the commercial leisure industries. It is not simply the case that the public sector is shrinking; the commercial leisure sector is also being restructured (see Chapter 1).

Monetarism aims to reset the balance between the public and private sectors, claiming to aid private business and in particular the small business. It is certainly the case that fiscal incentives have been offered to small businesses by the current administration. Nevertheless, cuts in the money supply in the early 1980's, coupled with other antagonistic factors led to a considerable reduction in output and the highest rate of business liquidations since the war. Furthermore, cutbacks in public spending have not significantly reduced public spending as a proportion of national income because national income has fallen in real terms, and the bill for unemployment benefit and social security payments has risen (as well as other areas of central government spending like defence and law and order).

Radical political economists (cf. Barratt-Brown, 1984) have argued that the net effect of these circumstances has been to benefit multi-national capital. The falling value of the pound has encouraged foreign investment in this country and this helps to explain the rapid growth of the 'big three' multi-nationals in the leisure field, Grand Met, Rank and Trust House Forte (cf Torkildsen, 1983). Evidence of industrial concentration in any commercial area is difficult to obtain. However, the interest of companies such as Ladbrokes and Mecca in smaller scale operations such as snooker halls and health studios, indicates that terrain, which has traditionally been regarded as that of the small scale entrepreneur, is becoming increasingly attractive to the larger companies. The selling off, closure or contracting-out of public sector leisure facilities may well reduce competition, and therefore risk, in the field of local small-scale leisure provision and open up the market to larger-scale operators.

A plethora of studies of local government in the 1970's stressed the influence of professionals in the policy-making process (cf Benington 1975; Cockburn 1977; Dearlove 1973). The contract management approach clearly reduces (or at least changes) the influence of professionals by transferring service provision to other sectors. However, it also assumes a considerable reduction in the influence of the local politician, who is likely to be constrained by central government legislation limiting local authority expenditure and activity. The restrictions on the influence of both professionals and politicians are intended to enhance the position of the individual elector and consumer who with lower public spending (and lower taxation) can exert greater influence on provision in the commercial sector through his or her spending patterns. Low income groups have lower disposable incomes and are therefore less likely to stimulate a response to their individual demands in the market place. However, it must be said that these are often the very people the public sector has failed to attract to its own facilities and services.

Reductions in service areas other than leisure may well also have consequences for the leisure opportunities of various members of the community. The attempt to reduce state involvement in the field of housing pensions, personal social services and health care, for example, which is implied by the contract management model, shifts responsibility for aspects of care back onto the family. Since housework and family care fall predominantly to women, such policy changes seem likely to reinforce inequalities in leisure for women. Reductions in childcare facilities, school meals services, and service provision for the elderly, the handicapped, etc. are consequent on policy change in other fields but potentially exert considerable influence on leisure life-styles.

The position of the leisure quangos under the contract management approach may be considerably weakened. The Sports Council's role is diminished in that it is unable to influence local authority provision (because direct provision is minimal), and the aspects of its work which relate to promoting national prestige through sporting performance might well devolve to the voluntary sector in the shape of the Central Council for Physical Recreation (which has always argued that it should perform this function anyway).

The Countryside Commission and the Arts Council might be regarded as guardians of particular forms of tourist attraction which indirectly meet their own costs by generating additional tourist revenue. However, given neo-liberal values, such functions are likely to be seen as more effectively carried out by the private market or by central government departments. Quangos are opposed in principle by the new right because not only are they insulated from the pressures of the free market, but also they are not even subject to electoral scrutiny. The result, in respect of the Arts Council is seen by commentators such as Kingsley Amis (1979), as inefficiency and the fostering of poor aesthetic judgement. Amis argues that arts administrators are encouraged to justify their position as guardians of public taste. This they do by funding avant garde, experimental art forms which are unable to obtain funding from the commercial sector or private patrons. The result is that thousands of pounds are wasted on 'works of art' (such as the Tate Gallery's bricks sculpture) which represent by definition, art forms which other experts (in the commercial sector) see as worth little. If Arts Council officers were spending their own money, Amis argues, their priorities would be very different.

Furthermore the neo-liberal argument that concepts such as the public interest or the common good are misplaced, suggests that the new right are unlikely to support the notion of a shared cultural heritage which can be defined for society as a whole. A small proportion of the leisure quangos' responsibilities might be taken up by central government on the grounds that incentives to investors, and a multiplier effect, would be generated by sustaining environmental or cultural tourist attractions which would not otherwise be supported by commercial interests. Even this role would be limited given the type of strategy promoted by the Arts Council, under its Secretary-General, Luke Ritner, who was appointed partly because of his experience in generating business sponsorship to offset the public costs of arts provision.

2.2 The financial stringency model

Many of the arguments for the contract management approach are a natural extension of those which have been made for the reduction in local government expenditure. The financial stringency model of local government is less ideologically inspired than that of contract management; that is to say there is no opposition *in principle* to local authority direct provision of services. Rather financial stringency can be seen as a pragmatic response to economic arguments which suggest that public sector spending is parasitic on wealth created in the private sector, and that high levels of public borrowing 'crowd out' private investment.

This model therefore implies an increasing squeeze on local authority spending with a consequent restructuring of local authority financing and provision of services.

2.2.1 The ideological preconditions of the financial stringency approach to local government

The contrast between the financial stringency and contract management approaches to local government may be illustrated by reference to the major ideological debate within the Conservative administration. The Tory 'wets', traditional or 'one-nation' Conservatives, tend to align themselves behind financial stringency but against the new right in their more radical measures for rolling-back the frontiers of the Welfare State.

Roger Scruton (1980) has characterised Conservatism as a political philosophy deriving from three core values:

Tradition Conservatism is anti-utopian. It eschews radical change since there is no guarantee that such change will result in improvement (and may indeed bring major, unforeseen disbenefits). It values the present set of institutional arrangements as the distillation of years of experience and these arrangements should not therefore be lightly dismissed;

Authority Hierarchies are inevitable in society but positions of advantage carry with them responsibility towards society's less fortunate members;

Allegiance If authority is exercised responsibly it will engender allegiance – eighteenth and nineteenth century Tory notions of a caring squirearchy are replaced here by policies of mild welfare reform.

Traditional Conservatives, who are represented in for example the recently formed 'centre forward' group, are now concerned more about the Rightwing radicalism which is dominant in their own party and in the Government than they are about socialist radicalism. The set of welfare arrangements at local and national level represents the post-war consensus in social policy. To radically alter the welfare structure which they now see as part of the British tradition risks eroding the allegiance of the poorer members of our society, and poses a threat to authority. Without a stake in society they have little or no reason for maintaining social stability.

While one-nation Conservatives recognise the need to respond to the current economic difficulties of the State, they wish to do so by limited incremental change (in the form of a selective squeeze on public spending) rather than by radical reforms. For this reason there has been considerable opposition within the Tory Party to the erosion of local autonomy and the disturbance of central/local relations represented by rate-capping legislation and abolition of the GLC and Metropolitan County Councils. Furthermore they maintain that the radical reform of the social security system carried through in the Social Security Act 1986 ultimately represents a threat to social order.

While traditional Conservatism (as it is characterised here) may provide the ideological preconditions for the financial stringency approach, it should not be forgotten that this approach was first implemented by the Labour administration of 1974–9. However, this was rather less a policy derived logically from political principles than the result of external pressures from the International Monetary Fund (which placed conditions on a major loan) and of the influence of anti-Keynesian economic analysis (specifically that of Bacon and Eltis, 1978[1]). Indeed debate within the Labour Party, in relation to local government issues, focused primarily on the disjunction between the political values represented by the Party and the economic policies it was attempting to implement.

The term Social Democracy has been used to denote the post-war consensus on policy issues which operated within a Keynesian framework of welfare provision funded through the surplus generated by economic growth. Social democracy is perhaps best described as a pragmatic compromise between the interests of capital and labour rather than an ideology *per se*. In the 1970s however this pragmatic compromise shifted from Keynesian approaches to economic management, to that of financial stringency. There is a sense therefore, in which, under certain economic conditions, ideological compromise is a condition of the financial stringency approach to local government.

2.2.2 *The economic precondition of the financial stringency model*

The economic conditions associated with this model are those outlined for the contract management approach, low economic growth and high levels of inflation and unemployment. The major difference in terms of preconditions for the two models is one of political values, rather than economic circumstances.

It is perhaps an obvious point that it is not economic conditions themselves but political interpretation of such conditions which generate policy responses from government. Some commentators (cf Kogan and Kogan, 1982[17]) have claimed that the publication by Bacon and Eltis of their 'crowding out' thesis in a series of articles in the *Sunday Times* in 1975 was particularly influential in determining Labour government economic policy. The Bacon and Eltis thesis (which is expounded more fully in their book, *Britain's Economic Problem: Too Few Producers*) is a species of the neo-liberal economic argument outlined in earlier sections of this chapter, but places particular emphasis on the role local government plays in soaking up greater resources (money and manpower) thereby forcing up taxes, rates and wage levels to the detriment of private industry. Although this analysis has critical weaknesses (cf. Newton and Karran 1985[19]) it appeared at the time to represent an improvement on the Keynesian paradigm, the explanatory power of which seemed exhausted. This is a case in which economic theory or perhaps political pragmatism seems to have overridden the ideological commitment of a Labour government.

2.2.3 The political preconditions of the financial stringency model

A strategy of financial stringency towards local government is compatible with 'centrist' politics or coalition governments or hung parliaments. It can often represent a social democratic compromise between more radical policies of both the left and the right.

2.2.4 The nature of leisure service organisation and delivery under the financial stringency model

The concept of leisure need incorporated within this model of local government will be dependent upon the ideological predisposition of particular proponents. Essentially two value positions were identified as preconditions of this approach, traditional one-nation Conservatism or social democratic pragmatism. The concepts of leisure need consistent with these levels must be distinguished.

If neo-liberalism is associated with 'cultural democracy', (allowing the individual freedom to choose between cultural offerings through the market place) Conservatism can be identified, in relation to arts policy, with the 'demoratisation of culture'. Emphasis on the nation's 'cultural heritage' and the education of the population to appreciate that heritage are consistent with the goal of a unified society which is central to Conservative thinking. The corollary of this Conservative notion of cultural need and commitment to traditional high cultural forms, is that community art forms with a populist or class-based rationale are likely to be dismissed as dangerously divisive.

In relation however to sport and other leisure forms some Conservatives express reservations about the role of the state. Sport in particular, it is claimed, carries with it certain benefits but ironically these benefits are lost when the state steps in to use sport or leisure for extrinsic purposes.

> The role of the state is guardian and foster parent. It cannot invade the institutions of leisure without perverting them to its own uses and losing sight in the process of what those uses are (Scruton 1980, p. 168).

The conservative approach therefore casts the state, and specifically local government, in an enabling role, rather than one of direct provision.

The pragmatism of the social democratic approach is evidenced in the White Papers of 1975 *Sport and Recreation*, and 1977 'Policy for the Inner Cities' where leisure is recognised as 'one of the community's everyday needs' but is also conceived as a means of social control. The compromise between the social goals of labour and the economic goals of capital takes the form of an argument that social expenditure is justified when failure to invest in recreation would incur greater costs than savings. During the period of financial stringency 'leisure as a means' has predominated over 'leisure as a need' as the main rationale for public expenditure on leisure. The relatively small and rare areas of growth in public sector leisure spending have been in budgets allocated for specific purposes eg urban programme, Sports Council grants for urban deprivation, areas of special need, football in the community and Action Sport initiatives. This enhances provision for the more volatile, potentially disruptive groups (in particular young, male, unemployed, inner city residents, often from specific ethnic groups) but erodes or ignores the position of other recreationally disadvantaged groups (eg the elderly, the handicapped, housebound mothers etc.) neglect of whom is unlikely to generate other costs in areas such as law and order.

The financial stringency model incorporates, therefore, a range of concepts of leisure need − from the 'democratisation of culture' sought by conservatives in sport and arts (though where possible without direct state intervention) to the pragmatic cost-benefit analysis of social democracy with its emphasis on certain types of recreational disadvantage. The response by the public sector over recent years to this particular blend of ideas about how to meet needs, has been the growth of 'community recreation'.

'Community recreation' has become an amorphous all-purpose term for non-standard, non-facility − based forms of provision. Perhaps three common strands can be identified in the family of services and policies to which the term is generally applied. The first is decentralisation, an approach to provision through small scale, relatively self-contained units in order to overcome some of the dysfunctions of large scale bureaucracies. The second common theme is a concern predominantly for disadvantaged groups. The third is an emphasis on community self-determination, a greater say for the community in terms of which services should be provided and how they should be delivered. These three conceptions of community recreation are evidenced in each of the models of local authority activity, in direct provision (eg small-scale, community sports/leisure centres), in acting as a catalyst (eg action sport/ community development initiatives), and in grant aid to community groups. It seems likely that under financial stringency the community recreation approach would continue to receive support because it addresses the need of priority groups, circumvents some of the problems of local government bureaucracy, making organisations more responsive to local needs, and in some instances shifts the burden of provision towards the voluntary and commercial sectors.

The development of community recreation policy and provision has considerable implications in terms of the skills required of recreation managers in the public sector. Traditional curriculum concerns have been dominated by 'technical' matters (water treatment, soil science, facility design etc.) and to a lesser degree by generic managerial skills (financial management, marketing, personnel management etc.). The area of neglect in these curricula has been that of understanding the social context of leisure policy, the nature and dynamics of communities and the roles which leisure can play.

The community recreation approach implies some devolution of power to communities and community groups which conflicts with the strategy of professionalisation which has been adopted by leisure services staff particularly in the public sector. When occupational groups seek to attain the status and recognition of 'profession' a number of claims about the nature of their work are normally made including the notion that the 'professionals' are experts in defining and meeting the needs of the community. For this reason it seems unlikely that the new, unified professional body (the Institute for Leisure and Amenity Management) will give prominence to community recreation policy in the syllabi of its membership examinations, despite the emphasis placed on community recreation policies by local government.

It is important to stress that community recreation is not simply to be seen as a pragmatic response to financial constraint. This may for some be the critical factor in opting for community recreation approaches; but for others the community recreation approach is valued in its own right as a means of overcoming fundamental problems of community alienation from service provision and the dysfunctions of large scale bureaucracies. Furthermore 'one-nation' Conservatives may well *oppose* community recreation initiatives since they are associated not simply with voluntarism but also with community development, which may imply political activism. Since traditional Conservatism is anti-adversarial in philosophy the benefits of voluntarism may well be sacrificed to the goal of consensual administration. There are therefore tensions or ambiguities which attach to the promotion of community recreation as a policy goal. This is reflected in the fact that community recreation is described as a feature of both this model of local government and the 'post-industrial' model discussed below.

There is a further tension apparent within the financial stringency model in terms of the skills required by managers. While social skills are given primary emphasis in community recreation work, financial and entrepreneurial skills are also required if income is to be generated by services. Although maximisation of income and of community participation and satisfaction are not necessarily mutually exclusive, there are clearly situations in which such goals are incompatible, and managers are therefore likely to experience frustration in attempting to meet or trade off incompatible goals.

Inherent within this model of local government with its emphasis on service provision for volatile, disadvantaged groups, is a concern with averting certain forms of social and financial crisis. Traditional, bureaucratic local government structures are however ill-suited to the immediate and imaginative responses required to deal with urgent and intractable problems in a fast-changing situation. New organisational structures are therefore required and a number of local authorities (particularly in inner city locations) have set up special measures teams, sometimes with executive power to deal with issues such as unemployment and ethnic minority needs. This trend seems likely to continue in the absence of any fundamental reorganisation of local government structures since it circumvents the 'democratic' but slow process of the committee cycle. It should be noted however that such arrangements tend to concentrate power in the hands of leading politicians and key officers.

2.2.5 The financial characteristics of local authority leisure services under the financial stringency model

Because of the structure of local authority finance in this country, and the fact that most capital expenditure is financed through loans, capital commitments place a considerable burden on revenue expenditure. Debt charges accounted for as much as 19.6% of all local authority revenue spending in 1970, and although interest rates have been somewhat lower in the recent past the figure was still 11.6% in 1983. The difficulty of making savings from revenue budgets has therefore been exacerbated by the size of debt charges and other 'committed' revenue expenditure. For this reason Central Government has made considerable efforts to discourage capital spending since the mid 1970's and such a strategy is likely to continue.

In addition leisure, (under the general heading 'other environmental services') has been identified in successive Public Expenditure White Papers, by both Labour and Conservative governments, as a service area which should be encouraged to generate higher incomes in the form of fees and charges to off-set revenue losses (Hamilton 1983). This also seems likely to continue as an integral element in the financial stringency approach. (It is also a central feature of the present Government's approach to the public library service and sports and leisure facilities – although their overall approach is closer to contract management rather than purely financial stringency). Little is known about the income elasticity of service pricing however, and even though greater revenues may be forthcoming from charging for previously free services, or from raising prices, there seems likely to be a disproportionate effect for low income groups. (Of course revenue might be increased in some cases by lowering the price and generating greater up-take of the service, though current practice under financial stringency does not provide many examples of this).

2.2.6 The context of local authority leisure services under financial stringency

The pressure to reduce net expenditure which local government has been experiencing since the mid-1970s has had an inevitable effect on the balance of provision between public and commercial sectors. Forms or categories of privatisation experienced within local authority leisure services and now reinforced by the Government's treasurers for compulsory competitive tendering include the following:

Privatisation of the production and management of services eg contracting in firms to manage not simply ancillary services such as catering but also primary services such as the operation of sports centres and ski slopes.

Selling off resources to the private sector eg the sale of plant, buildings and in particular playing fields which may or may not continue to be used as leisure resources.

Liberalisation of existing contracts eg where resources such as a golf course have been operated by a commercial concern through a management agreement, permission to increase charges, or to reduce opening hours, has been granted in order to lower the cost to the local authority, or to increase its income from profits.

Clearly arguments raised in relation to the contract management model (see Section 2.1.6) have some application here, particularly those concerning the structure of the commercial leisure industries, and potential effects on disadvantaged groups. In common with the contract management approach also, financial stringency in general might be said to reduce the influence of politicians and professionals by reducing the size and scope of local government. There are two caveats however in relation to this last argument. Firstly, politicians and professionals may still be very influential in deciding from which service areas savings are to be made. Secondly, members and officers associated with innovatory organisational structures (such as special measures teams) which are designed to increase responsiveness but will also decrease accountability, are likely to gain greater autonomy. However, such special measures teams are perhaps marginal to the activities of local government and generally have authority to make limited financial or policy commitments without reference to (or with the full powers of) the Council.

Unlike contract management the values underpinning the financial stringency approach do not imply an opposition in principal to quangos as a vehcile for state involvement. Indeed the arms length principle is consistent with allaying Tory concerns about state involvement in leisure. Conservatism, unlike neo-liberalism, involves a commitment to notions of shared cultural heritage (incorporating both sport and the arts) and therefore the co-ordinating role undertaken by the quangos in this respect is viewed as valuable. Nevertheless there has been concern expressed about the number of quangos. Phillip Holland, MP, for example, questions the need for national Sports Councils for Northern Ireland, Wales and Scotland. Others have criticised the profligacy of such organisations and their clients. On the whole, however, the financial stringency model implies a squeezed but still quangoid set of institutions in the public sector.

2.3 The Keynesian model

Keynesian economic management dominated post-war government policy until the early 1970s. In basic terms the Keynesian approach sees the economy as an equilibrium between demand and supply; the higher the demand for goods and services, the higher will be the supply of economic investment and therefore of people in employment. Unemployment occurs when an equilibrium is reached below the full potential of supply (ie below the level of relatively full employment). In such circumstances Keynesian economists have argued that governments should stimulate demand by investing public money in the purchase of goods and services. Such investments can take the form of employing more people directly in public services, or of contracting work out to the commercial sector. In both cases greater numbers of people in employment increase the level of demand for other goods and services since these newly employed people have increased spending power. Inflation is recognised as an unfortunate consequence of increasing public expenditure but, all other things being equal, Keynesians argue that a trade-off can be maintained between inflation and unemployment.

The 'Keynesian' model of local government reflects the strategic role which local government can play in Keynesian policy as a generator of local economic demand, stimulating the local economy by investing in local services and in local capital projects. Such an approach is invariably associated with expanding public sector employment, though increased local government spending may in many instances involve the contracting of goods and services from the commercial sector.

2.3.1 The ideological preconditions of Keynesian local government

Keynesian economic policies have been associated in the post war period with governments of both major parties. Neo-liberals however have never been happy with a growing public sector, and while traditional Conservatives were willing to adopt such policies in order to reinforce social cohesion in times of economic expansion, there is a resistance to increases in public expenditure in a recession, and a concern about the expanding influence of the state. While neo-liberalism and conservatism want the market to play the major part in the allocation and maximization of welfare, the left stresses that collective action is a necessary corrective to the inequalities generated by the market. Some forms of socialism stress the role which the state can play in a mixed economy in improving incrementally the position of the disadvantaged. Other strands within socialism promote the view that collective ownership and control of private industry (though not always ownership and control by the state) is a necessary condition for the erosion of inequalities.

This fundamental distinction within socialist thought is elaborated for example in Cole's (1976)[9] differentiation of utopian and scientific socialism. The former offers a vision of society based on mutual cooperation, equality and social justice. The latter provides a Marxist analysis of class society and class oppression which results in class politics and class struggle. Both versions are clearly anti-laissez faire, but both offer very different analyses of society, the economy and the state.

Utopian socialism (or Fabianism) sees the function of the state as producing welfare and reducing inequalities by redistributing resources via reforming legislation and services. Scientific socialists see socialism being achieved not simply through the welfare state and Parliament, but by the industrial mobilisation of trade unions and by a revolutionary Party leading working class action. The Fabian approach is perhaps most clearly articulated by Crosland (1956)[10] with his prescription for the reduction of welfare inequalities through economic growth.

For scientific socialists, this Fabian approach is doomed to fail because it fails to recognise the role of the state as an instrument of class domination. Even the welfare 'gains' of 1945–51 are seen as marginal since they leave the fundamental inequalities of class relations untouched. With ownership and control of production in private sector hands there is no possibility of real concessions being obtained in terms of welfare and the redistribution of resources. Such concessions can only be obtained by class struggle. For some scientific Marxists the state (and particularly the local state) can be a venue for class struggle, but for others it is unlikely to prove successful battleground if only because it is dominated by the professional middle classes which administer its services (Cockburn 1977).

Keynesian policies of reflation through state spending are therefore associated predominantly with utopian or Fabian socialism since they are premised upon the ability of the state to act in the interests (though not the exclusive interests) of its needy citizens.

2.3.2 *The economic preconditions of the Keynesian model of local government*

The fundamental principle of Keynesian economics, the notion of a trade-off between inflation and unemployment, provides the key to understanding when such policies might receive support. Keynesian policies were abandoned when stagflation took hold of the British economy in the early 1970's. Unemployment and inflation were rising. However, a number of economists have argued that the circumstances surrounding this period were unique. The oil crisis, Common Market entry, floating of major currencies etc were related and non-recurrent crises, and had Keynesianism been sustained it might have played a part in regenerating the economy. These advocates conclude that Keynesian solutions were not tried for long enough or with enough vigour. A reversion to greater strategic state spending (perhaps in partnership with other Western governments) would, in their view, restore business confidence, stimulate business activity and generate higher rates of economic growth, and employment.

High unemployment rates, low inflation and nil or low economic growth represent therefore the classic preconditions of Keynesian state spending. The form which such spending takes is not necessarily prescribed, though capital projects have the advantage of stimulating private sector activity while improving the infrastructure (social or economic) for which the public sector is responsible. Labour's publication *Jobs and Industry* (1985)[18] is a fairly typical Keynesian formula, advocating expansion of public sector employment and services, but also emphasising the need for public subsidy of traditional industries. The logic (though not necessarily the rhetoric) of this type of argument is that unemployment is primarily caused by a crisis of confidence on the part of investors which has starved traditional industries of investment, resulting in economic restructuring in the form of a reduction of primary and secondary industries. Fundamental structural changes in industry are seen as a consequence rather than a cause of Britain's economic problems. This point (though made in the context of an 'ideal-type' characterisation of the Keynesian approach) is the crucial difference between the kinds of public investment advocated under this model of local government, and that advocated under the 'post-industrial model' discussed below.

2.3.3 The political preconditions of the Keynesian approach to local government

The Labour Party's campaigns often focus on the three-fold aims of rebuilding industries, financing building construction programmes and capital projects, and improving public services. This suggests that the return of a Labour government is likely to be associated with a return to Keynesian policies. Two qualifications must be made here. Firstly, unless Labour resorts to legislation to require all local authorities to spend more on building and services then it seems possible that reflation through local government spending might be resisted in Tory controlled local authorities. Secondly, this Keynesian strategy assumes a right wing or centre-right Labour Government (or a coalition perhaps with Social Democratic centre parties.) A Labour Government dominated by the left might not be satisfied with Keynesian reflationary measures, and might want to move towards more radical forms of intervention in the economy.

2.3.4 The nature of leisure service organisation and delivery under Keynesian local government

Public service planning in general, and leisure planning in particular, grew in importance in the expansionary period of the late 1960's to the early 1970's, only to virtually disappear in the period of severe restraint which followed. Proactive planning of this nature, whether it was corporate or single service, promoted the importance of the professional whose 'expert' judgement was required to identify how services should be expanded. This growth in the importance of public sector professionals took place in spite of attempts to generate greater citizen participation, for example in town planning following the Skeffington Report.

Many local authorities have been trying to address the problem of how members of the community and users of services might be able to participate more fully in the decision making process. The fact that decisions in the current climate are now not so much about which new services should be added, but about which should be curtailed, makes the issue if anything more, rather than less, significant. However Keynesian expansion of local authority spending would require a swift response from local government organisations, minimising the opportunity (or at least offering an excuse for minimising the opportunity) for public consultation. In addition the burgeoning of local government activity, implied by the Keynesian model, suggests that the relative influence of full-time professionals in the determination of local policy would continue to be considerable, with largely part-time local politicians operating at a disadvantage in understanding and controlling the activities of the authority.

The concept of need which informs leisure policy in this professionally dominated model of local government is one of 'expert' assessments of the latent needs of the community. This contrasts with the concern for community self-determination implied by the concept of community recreation, under the financial stringency model discussed earlier.

Expansion of services within the existing organisational framework of local government may promote bigger and more powerful leisure departments. Regeneration of the public sector without some strategy to counter the problems of large-scale bureaucracy would simply reinforce the problems experienced in the post-1974 reorganisation period.

The Keynesian model of local government encourages more than a simple expansion of service provision. It also specifically promotes higher levels of capital investment and improvement of the environment. This would provide an opportunity to promote amenity provision (particularly in urban parks and inner city areas which have characteristically experienced neglect during the recession) and to upgrade existing built facilities by replacing the old, and expanding the overused, stock of recreation buildings and plant.

2.3.5 The financial characteristics of local government leisure services under the Keynesian model

When in the mid-1970's the Labour Government sought to reduce local government expenditure, its initial strictures concerned capital spending. Although leisure was freed from its subordinate status in the capital programme as 'non-key sector' expenditure, nevertheless it became evident (from published out-turns) that local authorities were finding it very difficult to give priority to leisure capital spending over other claims on their capital allocation. The present government's attempts to further control local authority capital spending means that capital investment in total, and on leisure projects in particular, has not grown.

One of the changes characteristic of Keynesian local government might therefore be an increase in the capital/revenue ratio for public sector leisure investment, and this despite a significant increase also in leisure revenue expenditure. A further characteristic change would be an increase in the cost income ratio which would follow from greater revenue investment, and a lesser emphasis on income targets.

2.3.6 The context of local authority leisure services under the Keynesian model of local government

The post-war Keynesian policies of Labour and Conservative governments were founded not simply on a theory of the way the economy should be managed, but also on the notion that economic and social policy decisions were largely a matter of the application of rational principles to achieve agreed goals. As this chapter has already argued such a position yields power and influence to those technocrats with specialist skills in applying such rational planning and management techniques. Such thinking also legitimates the role of the leisure quangos as panels of technical experts providing neutral advice on how to maximise welfare and other leisure goals.

However given the recent conflict-ridden nature of British politics (which is reflected in the 'politicisation' of the activities of the leisure quangos; cf Hargreaves 1984[14], Hutcheson 1982[16]) it seems doubtful whether the notion of ideological neutrality can easily be restored. Any Labour government, pursuing Keynesian policies, is likely to be opposed on ideological grounds by the right, even if its economic policies meet with some success. It is perhaps because of the rejection of the view of quangos as neutral, and also because of the failure of the leisure quangos to date to serve a truly representative cross-section of the population, that the Labour Party has declared its intention of promoting a new Ministry of Leisure to oversee policy in this area.

The effect on the commercial sector of a growing public sector investment in leisure under a Keynesian model of local government might be to push commercial leisure firms towards the exclusive, high price segments in leisure service markets, or indeed towards the high cost non-local facility which may be beyond the scope of most local authorities.

2.4 The post-industrial model
The projected role of local authorities for 'post-industrial' theorists is similar in some respects to that portrayed in the last model. It certainly involves the expansion of local authority services to reduce social inequalities, and the investment of public funds to stimulate economic activity. However, there are crucial differences, both in the rationale for government intervention, and in the industries and services which post industrialists would wish to see funded.

Keynesians, it has been argued, describe Britain's present economic difficulties as the result of a crisis of confidence in the Western economies on the part of investors. Local authorities are therefore to be employed as agents of regeneration, contributing to a strategy of reflation of the (traditional) economy. For post industrialists however, the root cause of Britain's problems is that the economy is undergoing a metamorphosis, a structural shift analogous to that experienced in the industrial revolution. Whereas the 'growing pains' experienced in the eighteenth and early nineteenth century were associated with the transition from a rural, agrarian, mercantilist system to an urban, industrial, capitalist society, the present frictions arise from the superseding of that industrial system by a new transnational information-based, institutionally controlled economic order.

The kinds of change that British industry has experienced are seen by post-industrialists as permanent. Large-scale multinational corporations when they seek to maintain or extend profits basically have only three options open to them (when their markets are nearing saturation at a given price level). They can seek to reduce wage bills either by transferring production from a high to a low wage economy, or by automation, or they may seek to find cheaper raw materials. The first two options have been experienced in this country with attendant job loss while the third option (in the form of North Sea oil and gas) has only partially mitigated this process. For the post industrialist there is little point in providing government subsidy for traditional manufacturing industries, such as textiles, where jobs and investment have been transferred to the third world. Government subsidy should be aimed at facilitating rather than opposing the structural changes taking place. This facilitating role takes on a number of forms:

- investment in what Stonier (1983) has called the new 'knowledge based' industries, and other growth areas (such as tourism); fiscal incentives for private investment might also be provided;
- provision of an infrastructure, specifically in the fields of education and research, which will service the needs of such industries;
- alleviation of the social costs of the economic restructuring process by providing employment and services for displaced employees.

Within this overall role for the state, local government is seen as undertaking some element of all three sets of tasks.

2.4.1 The ideological preconditions of the post industrial model
In ideological terms this model of local government is a variant of the social democratic approach traditionally associated with post-war Keynesianism. Post-industrial policy prescriptions are consistent with 'one-nation conservatism' in their concern for the state's role in maintaining social stability in troubled times, as well as with utopian or Fabian socialism, which sees the state as a vehicle for improving the quality of life of the disadvantaged.

2.4.2 The economic preconditions of the post industrial model
Perhaps the major difference between this model and those of the Keynesian scenario lies in their assumptions about the rate of economic growth. Whereas Keynesian policies might be seen to be a reaction to slow economic growth, the post industrial presumption is that the high technology industries will flourish, generating increasing rates of economic growth but employing fewer and fewer people. Inflation would be held at a steady and acceptable level.

One might also expect some evidence of social unrest as a precursor to increased government intervention since the gap between rich and poor, those in work in the 'sunrise' industries and those unemployed, or in low-paid peripheral employment, is likely to grow, as workers reap the economic rewards of the rapid expansion of their high technology industries. Government intervention in such circumstances would be required in order to reduce such iniquities and ensure social stability.

2.4.3 The political preconditions of post industrial local government

The political values which are consonant with this level of state intervention would seem to require a central government controlled by, or at least heavily influenced by, 'moderates' in either of the two major parties or by social democratic centre parties. A mixed economy is implied here, with a far greater proportion of GNP going through government hands than is currently the case, thus alienating the new right. However the approach stops well short of government (or worker) control of industry and thus will not meet the demands of scientific socialists. The post war British experience has however illustrated how in times of relative affluence political militancy is considerably reduced within the mainstream parliamentary groups.

Given the climate of moderate political opinion indicated here, there is likely to be some convergence in the policies adopted by both Labour and Conservative controlled local authorities. Spending patterns and levels of service provision are therefore unlikely to be markedly different across authorities of a given type. Nor under such circumstances, would central government be required to place statutory controls on local government spending levels.

2.4.4 The nature of leisure service organisation and delivery under the post industrial approach

In the same way as the post industrial approach to public sector economics is more specific than its Keynesian alternative, in terms of the kinds of industry to be supported, so the post industrial model carries with it a more specific prescription for leisure services than simply a generalised Keynesian plan of expansion. The post-industrial model implies the demise of the work ethic in post industrial societies, to be replaced not so much by a 'leisure ethic' (however that might be defined) but rather by a set of values focused on 'service'. Social status under such a system of values is to be derived not from accumulation of wealth through hard work, but from a demonstration of one's worth to the community through work, certainly, but also through the acquisition and application of socially useful skills. Although therefore the post industrial explanation predicts extended periods of 'leisure' in the normal life-pattern, such periods are likely to be taken up in personal development through (a very broadly based liberal) education, and through work with and for people.

Education in particular performs a pivotal role in the social system of the future for post-industrialists. The skills required of individuals in work are likely to change rapidly as technological change accelerates, and therefore vocationally oriented training and education are likely to be required at more regular intervals across the life-span of each individual. Furthermore with increased auto-mation and job-sharing the time available to the individual for self-fulfilment in non-work pursuits will expand, generating increased demand for opportunities for personal development across the whole range of non-vocational interests. Life-long education is seen by many post-industrialists (cf. Best and Stern 1978; Stonier 1983) as providing a solution to such problems. The education system is portrayed in such accounts as making the opportunity for self fulfilment universally available. Although this is contrasted with education for work it is not the antithesis of this approach, and it is certainly not simply education for leisure. Perhaps a more appropriate banner might be 'education for self fulfilment' – such a title gives an indication of the utopian flavour of post industrial accounts.

Clearly what both Best and Stonier have in mind when they refer to expansion of the education system incorporates aspects of traditional leisure services. Self actualisation for many is after all achieved through sports, the arts, hobbies, etc. The post industrial model therefore incorporates a much more pro active approach, on the part of the providers of services. Traditional 'caretaking and maintenance of plant' roles in the leisure service would be super-seded by those with an emphasis on interpersonal skills.

Freedom from long hours of work is also seen by post industrial theorists as providing a stimulus for greater participation in local and national affairs. This has consequences for the way that leisure services are delivered. It implies both decentralisation of provision and self determination on the part of the community. In addition, given the social democratic ideology which is expected to pre-dominate, there will be emphasis placed on the needs of dis-advantaged groups. These three criteria – decentralisation, self-determination and a concern for the leisure needs of the dis-advantaged – have been identified above as the key characteristics of the community recreation approach to service delivery, and this approach is therefore likely to receive greater emphasis within the post industrial local authority.

Organisation theorists have argued that traditional bureaucratic structures are inappropriate to the dynamic and changing environment of a high technology society. Local authorities can therefore expect to experience some of the changes anticipated for work organisation in an unstable environment, with work groups formed around particular types of task, membership of these groups being decided on the ability and skills of the individual rather than her or his formal position within the organisation.

Public sector organisations are also likely to be required to promote the notion of job sharing as a social responsibility, in order to aid the process of the redistribution of work.

A number of local authorities are currently attempting to promote this practice though admittedly on a fairly small scale. It seems likely that this practice would be expanded as under this model local government adopts a position of moral leadership. Values will have to change if individuals are to be persuaded that it is anti-social to consume a full-time post. Such a state of affairs is not inconceivable given for example that over-time work is considered anti-social in certain industries. However, it may require the full force of legislation, rather than moral leadership alone, to impose a maximum working week.

Investment in tourism by local government (for economic rather than social purposes) is promoted by Stonier (1983) in order to foster an important post-industrial growth area. Indeed it is our industrial heritage that provides one of the most important advantages for the UK over competing tourist destinations. Tourism is after all an ideal buffer against the effects of poor national economic performance since a weak pound stimulates trade. Local government will have a key role in coordinating and stimulating local tourist and heritage industries.

2.4.5 The financial characteristics of local government leisure services under the post industrial model

The kind of expansion of services prefigured here presupposes a considerable expansion in the taxation base which funds such provision. This is in part to be funded by an expansion of the economy as the new industries generate higher levels of profit. However, this scenario also presumes a growth in the proportion of GDP taken up in government spending. It would have been inconceivable at the beginning of the Industrial Revolution that government should 'consume' approximately 40% of GDP in taxation. Nevertheless in a period of industrial and economic growth, government spending has increased disproportionately and it is only recently that some economic theorists have been able to argue that the balance between public and private sector spending (or spending on marketable and non-marketable sectors) has resulted in negative effects for the economy as a whole. In contrast to the Bacon and Eltis thesis post industrial theorists argue that public spending is essential to the growth of the economy, and can only be viewed in a negative light if consideration is limited to its effects on traditional, ailing industries. These industries are failing to stimulate growth despite rather than because of public spending. Their failure is to be attributed to the realignment of world trade; the newly emerging international division of labour and this failure is therefore inevitable.

The growth in public sector leisure spending is likely to take the form predominantly of increased numbers of employees dealing face to face with clients rather than of massive investment in the hardware of leisure services. This reflects a major claim of post industrial theorists that although industrial jobs may disappear (or drastically reduce) because of advances in technology especially in robotics, there will be an increased demand for the kinds of human services which cannot be provided by machines. Such a scenario implies a considerable expansion of revenue budgets for leisure related services in the public sector.

2.4.6 The context of local government leisure services in the post industrial local authority

As has already been noted, this scenario presumes a greater opportunity for citizen involvement in decision making, and a 'service ethic' which implies greater concern for matters of local and public significance. People with more time and greater exposure to education might be expected to make a more significant input into the affairs of the local and national state. However, experience of the period of expansion of the 1960's and 1970's seems to suggest that increasing the size and complexity of the public sector militates against public participation, and would reinforce the position of the professional. It remains to be seen therefore whether professional power would be eroded in favour of client involvement in decision-making about services. This will represent a crucial issue for public sector services generally. Community recreation and other related decentralisation movements are at least partly anti-professional and a reaction against the failure of service professionals to meet the needs of what have ostensibly been priority groups. This major tension is therefore likely to be reproduced in the post indus-trial model.

The role of the leisure quangos under the post-industrial model is difficult to identify because of the same tension between enhanced professional activity and the increasing value placed on public participation. This may be resolved to some degree by promoting a more democratic structure for the quangos with representation drawn from local elected representatives, the unions, professionals and leisure interest groups as well as central government appointments. Such a pattern of membership is similar to that advocated by the TUC (1977)[22] in its consultative document *The Working Party Report on the Arts.*

The retention of quangos is consistent with the post industrial theorists' promotion of the notion of consensual government. Quangos are therefore seen as promoting shared social and economic goals through strategic grant aid and advice, and central government influence of local government leisure policy is likely to be limited to that exercised via the relatively 'neutral' and 'independent' quangos.

2.5 The municipal socialist model

This final model of local government encompasses an approach to public sector intervention which goes beyond any of the other models described. Investment is undertaken either via loan or equity through an arms-length Enterprise Board (or via directly controlled municipal enterprises) in spheres which have traditionally been the preserve of commercial sector organisations. The aim is only partly to generate surpluses to subsidise redistributive services funded by the local authority. The underlying aim is to bring local economic development more directly under the control or influence of an elected representative body, acting on behalf of the community as a whole.

2.5.1 The ideological preconditions of the municipal socialist model

In section 2.3.1 above, the distinction between utopian and scientific socialism was employed to identify the political values underpinning the Keynesian model. The values consistent with the municipal socialist model derive from the scientific socialist arguments in that section.

A further distinction within scientific socialism is important in understanding the ideological foundations of this model. Scientific socialists argue that Labour governments have proved ineffective in acheiving real working class gains in part because the Labour Party parliamentary hierarchy is insulated from grass roots pressures and therefore is able to pursue compromise policies; and in part also because the state is an instrument of class domination or, at least, itself, a battleground between competing class interests. This leads some hard-line 'anti-statist' theorists to advocate economic and industrial class struggle as the only way of achieving socialist gains. However, other scientific socialist thinkers advocate a dual approach of industrial action together with attempts to control the local state.

They argue that local socialism is more readily achievable because in its decentralised form the state (and the Labour Party) can be more readily controlled. This dual thrust, promoting struggle over work place issues and around collective consumption issues, represents an extended form of syndicalism.

2.5.2 The economic preconditions of the municipal socialist model

The impetus for the kinds of radical change implied in this model is likely to come from adverse economic and social conditions – high levels of unemployment, low or negative economic growth, and attendant social disorder.

The left's analysis of the current economic crisis, is similar to that of the right in many ways. Both argue that taxation to provide public sector services is an increasing and eventually intolerable burden for private industry. However, whereas economists such as Bacon and Eltis argue that what is required to restore economic growth and therefore social stability is a reduction in state spending, the left (cf Castells 1978[7]) interprets such a policy as equally disastrous for both capital and labour in the final analysis. This is because collective consumption services such as education, housing and leisure are essential elements of the capitalist economy since they are part of the social infrastructure on which industry depends – it requires a fit, healthy, receptive, educated workforce in order to function profitably. This then represents one of the 'contradictions of capitalism' which generates fiscal crisis and which under this model is likely to be resolved only through socialist transformation.

2.5.3 The political preconditions of the municipal socialist model

The current polarised economic situation has already generated radicalism at local level in urban areas which are experiencing the worst difficulties – Sheffield, Liverpool and the London Boroughs for example. However, the freedom of action of local authorities is severely curtailed by the present central government's legislation. The political preconditions for the adoption of the municipal socialist approach to local government are likely to be the return of a Labour Government dominated by the left of the Party and with the political will to enact the legislation required to give local government significant powers of intervention. This model goes beyond public investment in industry as carried out by existing regional and local Enterprise Boards; it extends to new forms of municipal ownership or intervention in local industry and the labour market. Such a strategy would exceed the powers currently vested in local authorities.

2.5.4 The nature of leisure service organisation and delivery under the municipal socialist approach

One of the fundamental problems for scientific socialists in respect of leisure provision is defining the leisure needs of the community. Leisure is seen by some Marxist thinkers as an area in which false needs have been generated.

The role of competitive sport, for example, is viewed critically by Brohm (1976) and Hargreaves (1984) in that it encapsulates and reinforces capitalist values, through its apparent structure of goal orientated, meritocratic activity, involving the division of labour, specialism of task and winning and losing. Indeed for a short period in post-revolutionary Russia attempts were made to ban such activity. The high arts similarly are seen by some socialist thinkers (cf. Bourdieu and Parsovan 1977[5]) predominately as vehicles for conferral of status in a hierarchical society.

However, though some scientific socialists take the view that leisure needs are not real needs in that they are socially constructed in the interests of capitalism, other commentators, such as Whannel (1983[23]), take the view that leisure is an appropriate area of social policy in which to pursue egalitarian goals.

Municipal investment and intervention in private industry would have considerable effects on local leisure provision given the relatively larger commercial sector which currently exists. Leisure industries are certainly one area of the economy which are generating profits. Even in the most run down and neglected inner city areas or housing estates, the pub and the betting shop are generating sufficient revenue to maintain a presence. Municipal betting shops and municipal pubs would allow such profits (if they could be maintained) to be ploughed back into the community rather than be redistributed to share-holders.

Leisure clothing and equipment are areas of high turnover and profit in recent years. One local authority in West Yorkshire recently considered a report advocating the establishment of a municipal enterprise in this area together with a launching of sports and interest holidays for overseas visitors. Though the report was not acted upon, these are examples of activities within the leisure sector which a municipal socialist local authority might wish to pursue.

The traditional public sector leisure services would not however remain unaffected. Socialist writers have stressed the need to allow greater worker user representation in the organisation of services, and have emphasised also those whose needs are not being met in the present system. The skill requirements for professionals operating in the municipal socialist context include greater political awareness (to appreciate the political goals of the council) and a balance between entrepreneurial skills (to generate successful innovative projects) and the predominantly interpersonal skills of the community recreation worker.

Finally, the kinds of sporting and cultural activity to be promoted and supported by the public sector might change under a municipal socialist approach. As Whannel (1983) points out support for boxing is questionable. Municipal socialist leisure strategies might be sceptical about glorifying the ability to batter a fellow human being, however skilfully. Fishing and fox hunting may also be questioned. Any concern for gender equality is also likely to necessitate the restructuring of service provision. Community arts are also likely to be promoted by municipal socialists as a means of generating working class consciousness and culture.

2.5.5   The financial characteristics of leisure services in the municipal socialist authority

The most significant financial feature of this model is the increased volume of public sector led activity which the expansion of local government implies. The growth in volume of business, together with socialist concerns about large scale state bodies, might suggest a reorganisation at the local level into geographically smaller, more easily controlled local bodies with decentralised budgets. To maintain existing local authority boundaries and structures might hamper the ability of the local community and its elected representatives to impose radical change on this tier of government.

2.5.6   The context of leisure services in the municipal socialist local authority

Given the socialist concern that workers, members of the community and/or their representatives be more closely involved in decision making, there is little doubt that this model of local government would carry with it a reform of the make-up and role of the quangos to make them more democratically accountable.

The rejection by scientific socialists of the argument that high arts are more important than, or aesthetically superior to, other community-based art forms might also lead to a shift in priorities and perhaps even the radical reform of the Art Council's areas of concern. However, the role of the arts in stimulating tourism would seem likely to ensure that they are given prominence in leisure strategy.

Unlike utopian socialists, the promoters of municipal socialism would probably reject the creation of an over-arching Ministry of Leisure since this would run counter to their concern for decentralisation and local autonomy. One suspects that Dennis Howell's proposal for such a new ministry (which was accepted by the 1984 Labour Party Conference) would have attracted greater opposition had leisure been perceived as a more crucial policy issue by local party activists.

3. Conclusions

The primary aim of this chapter has been to outline the diverse responses that might be expected from local government leisure policymakers, to changes in the environment within which this tier of government operates. That local government in this country is experiencing crisis has become something of a cliché Critics from both the political left and right advocate its radical restructuring. The crisis has perhaps six dimensions. Local government faces a fiscal crisis, as the resource base (in terms of income both from central government and local rates) is eroded and the funding of traditional services become problematic. It faces a social crisis, with an increasing gap between the 'haves' and 'have-nots' within the local authority population, and increasing proportion dependent upon welfare services. It faces an economic crisis, as local government struggles to tackle high levels of unemployment, to stimulate skill-training and job creation, and to foster economic development in the face of increasing pressures on traditional industries. It faces a physical crisis with the decay of the environment and infrastructure particularly of the inner city. It faces a political crisis with polarisation creating inter and intra party conflict, as well as conflict between local government professionals, their clients and political representatives. Finally, it faces an ideological crisis as the consensus over the role which local government should play has disintegrated, to be replaced by a range of competing prescriptions for this tier of the state.

The alternative models of local government discussed in this chapter are presented in terms of ideal types, and as such their adequacy is to be assessed both in terms of their internal coherence and of their usefulness in explaining the changes and challenges facing local government. Although it does not advocate one form of local government in preference to any other, the chapter itself does constitute a species of rational planning, with all the attendant problems of assessing the actual consequences of change in a complex environment. To deny these problems would be foolish. It is in part for this reason that ideal types rather than prediction of alternative scenarios for local government are employed. Whatever the limitations of the methodology, hopefully the chapter will serve to illuminate some of the profound issues facing local government leisure services, and to emphasise the need for informed choices to be made.

Table 9.1 – Summary of the arguments

Preconditions required for each type of local authority				Consequences for leisure services of each type of local authority
Local government type and role	Dominant ideological position	Economic conditions	Political conditions	
Contract management – provider of last resort	Neo-liberalism	High inflation, growing unemployment, low economic growth	Radical conservative government, with large majority. Local autonomy challenged and restricted	a Leisure needs to be identified and supplied through free market b Government to provide only those activities where market imperfections occur and then use private sector contractors c Leisure quangos disbanded; 'essential' tasks (eg tourism; anti-vandalism measures) go to central government d Leisure professional's skills: appraisal and monitoring of contractors work e Growth in role of commercial leisure sector, through privatisation
Financial stringency – manager of shrinking resources	One-nation conservatism, or a form of social democracy	High inflation, growing unemployment, low economic growth	Conservative government with small majority or conservative led coalition. Local autonomy low	a Leisure needs recognised but not necessarily met through state b Priority within shrinking local government provision given to meeting needs of 'disruptive' elements and the disadvantaged c Emphasis on cost-cutting and generating-revenue through charges and sales d Quangos retained as 'neutral' planning bodies e Professional's skills: financial (cost-control), interpersonal/social (community recreation) f Significant role for commercial leisure sector through contracting of services
Keynesian – manager of expanding resources	Utopian socialism or social democracy	Low inflation, low economic growth, high unemployment	Labour government dominated by the right, or coalition government. Local autonomy high	a Expansion of public leisure services as consequence of policy of reflation b Leisure needs identified by professionals – new provision to meet latent needs c Emphasis on positive benefits of public sector expenditure on leisure (new capital projects) d Quangos drawn into new Ministry of Leisure e Leisure professional: traditional skills of manager and social planner, with new emphasis on interpersonal skills f Public sector "competing with" commercial sector in many fields of leisure
Post-industrial-facilitator of citizen involvement and the ethic of service	One-nation conservatism, utopian socialism, or social democracy	High level economic growth, high unemployment, low inflation	'Moderate' Labour or Conservative Govts, or coalition. Local autonomy high	a Leisure need is seen as an aspect of need for personal development b Public sector expenditure on leisure seen as part of a positive commitment to education for self-fulfilment c Flexible, non-bureaucratic organisation structures d Quangos democratised e Professional skills – community development, educationalist counsellor f Public sector support for tourism and high-tech industries
Municipal socialist – active intervention to counteract the private market	Scientific socialism	Low economic growth, high unemployment, high inflation, social disorder	Labour government dominated by left, with large majority. Local autonomy high	a Leisure need seen in terms of equality of opportunity b Municipalisation of commercial leisure sector to generate revenue (eg, municipal pubs and betting shops) c Selective support of sport and arts (eg, anti-boxing, pro-community arts)

References

1 Amis, K. (1979) *An Art Policy?* Policy Studies Institute.
2 Bacon, R. and Eltis, W. (1978), *Britain's Economic Problem: too few producers,* Macmillan.
3 Barratt-Brown, M. (1984), *Models in Political Economy,* Pelican.
4 Benington, J. (1975), Local Government Becomes Big Business, CD Publications.
5 Best, F. and Stern, B. (1978), 'Lifetime Distribution of Education, Work and Leisure', *Review of Sport and Leisure,* Vol 3, No 1.
6 Bourdieu, P. and Passeron, P. (1977), *Reproduction in Education, Society and Culture,* Sage.
7 Brohm, J. M. (1978), *Sport; A Prison of Measured Time,* Ink Links.
8 Castells, M. (1977), *The Urban Question: A Marxist Approach,* Edward Arnold.
9 Cockburn, C. (1977), *The Local State,* Pluto Press.
10 Cole, G. (1976), 'What is Socialism?', in *Ideologies of Politics* (eds) de Crispigny, A. & Cronin, M., Open Univ. Press.
11 Crosland, A. (1956), *The Future of Socialism,* Jonathan Cape.
12 Dearlove, J. (1973), The Politics of Policy in Local Government, CUP.
13 Friedman, M. (1962), *Capitalism and Freedom,* Chicago Univ Press.
14 Hamilton, D. (1983), *Public Expenditure and Leisure: A Study of Central- Local Government Relations,* Papers in Leisure Studies No 8, Polytechnic of North London.
15 Hargreaves, J. (1984), 'State Intervention in Sport and Hegemony in Britain', paper to the Leisure Studies Conference *Leisure: Politics, Planning and People,* University of Sussex.
16 Hayek, F. A. (1944), *The Road to Serfdom,* Routledge, London.
17 Hutcheson, R. (1982), *The Politics of the Arts Council,* Sinclair Brown.
18 Kogan, D. and Kogan, M. (1982), *Battle for the Labour Party,* Kogan Page.
19 Labour Party (1985), *Jobs and Industry,* Labour Party.
20 Newton, K. and Karren, T. (1985), *The Politics of Local Expenditure,* Macmillan.
21 Scruton, R. (1980) *The Meaning of Conservatism,* Pelican.
22 Stonier, T. (1983), *The Wealth of Information; a profile of the post industrial economy,* Methuen.
23 Torkildsen, G. (1983), *Leisure Services Management,* Spon.
24 TUC (1977), *The Working Party Report on the Arts,* TUC.
25 Whannel, G. (1983), *Blowing the Whistle: the Politics of Sport,* Pluto Press.

10 The need for a new strategic vision for leisure services

John Benington and Judy White

Public leisure services now face three simultaneous challenges:

(i) changes on the demand side (eg growth of unemployment and ageing;

(ii) changes on the supply side (eg 'commercialisation' of the private leisure industries); and

(iii) changes in central government policy (eg contraction of resources and the introduction of compulsory competitive tendering).

Local government, like leisure, is facing a crossroads in its history and development. It faces rapidly changing and increasing needs; fundamental changes in its operating environment; contracting resources; and a profound challenge to its basic value-system. The 'new right' has questioned and challenged not only the fiscal burden of public services, but more fundamentally the whole post-war consensus in support of a welfare state based on collective solutions to needs. It is thus a challenge not only to the efficiency but also the legitimacy of local government. Their alternative is the meeting of individual needs through the purchasing of goods and services in the private market, or through self-help and the nuclear family. Public services are to be privatised wherever possible, or exposed to the competitive discipline of the market, and contracted out.

It therefore seems increasingly unlikely that public sector policy or expenditure will be restored and uplifted to the levels necessary to sustain comprehensive leisure services. However, there is also great doubt whether the private market or the voluntary sector can by themselves provide leisure services of the kind and quality necessary to match the challenges of the next decade. The demographic and socio-economic changes (which together mean that a high proportion of the population may be elderly, unemployed, under-employed or otherwise unwaged) will result in a new set of leisure needs and priorities among a population with less resources to pay for them. Privatised or contracted out services are not likely to respond to the leisure needs of those without the purchasing power to express them in the market. They depend upon the public sector to collectivise and organise such areas of unmet need, in preparation for their putting out to tender as viable contracts. The private sector also requires some kind of framework for planning and co-ordination to tackle the inter-relationships between different kinds of leisure needs and problems, or even to avoid the most wasteful forms of duplication or competition. Competition within the commercial sector can often produce innovation and cost efficiency; but it is less capable of producing an overall strategy for meeting leisure needs, or consistent quality standards. The private sector cannot operate in a vacuum. It depends upon an infrastructure provided by the public sector.

The challenge to local government, therefore, when faced with commercialisation, privatisation or compulsory competitive tendering, is not to retreat passively into acting as a residuary body, (merely administering the letting of contracts to the private sector) but to take on an even more pro-active leadership role, generating a strategic vision and framework for the whole sphere of leisure, public and private.

Local government has three potential sources of power and authority in the community, which can enable it to give this important leadership:

(i) A social role – identifying needs and priorities within the community, and developing and distributing services to meet those needs;

(ii) An economic role – using its position as an important employer, purchaser, and economic agent within the local community to influence patterns of investment, job creation and training within the area;

(iii) An ideological and political role – using its authority as the (only) body with an electoral mandate to represent the needs and values not just of one interest group, but of the community as a whole (the employed as well as the unemployed; old as well as young; women as well as men; black people as well as white; management and labour; future generations as well as the present population).

The three sources of potential power identified above provide the basis for the strategies which local authorities can adopt in the field of leisure. Each will be discussed in turn.

The need for a clear redistributive social strategy

Over the past decade, local authorities have taken the lead in opening up access to leisure facilities by a wider class of users. Sports like golf, squash and sailing, which used to be associated with elite groups, and restricted membership clubs, have been "popularised" and made available to a much wider range of people through municipal golf courses, sports centres and water sports facilities. The same is true of publicly subsidised theatre, opera, ballet and music. However local authorities will have to go further than this if they are to meet the challenge of the unwaged over the next decade. Evidence seems to suggest that, in many areas of public leisure provision, facilities are still used disproportionately by professional, managerial and skilled workers, and under-used by the unemployed, the elderly, women with dependents, and the lower socio-economic groups – the very sections of the population which are increasing as priority categories for the future.

To simply maintain current policies and practices in the face of increasing and intensifying needs can only mean a further widening of inequalities in leisure between the better off and the already disadvantaged. The current pattern of supply-side subsidy (that reduces prices for everybody using public sector leisure facilities) has in practice turned out to be mainly a subsidy to the better-off. To encourage increased use specifically by lower-income and priority groups might suggest a subsidy on the demand side ie to the specific categories of potential users which have been targeted as priorities. There are enormous logistical problems with such an approach, plus all the dangers of a stigmatisation which are associated with other forms of means-teasting. However, many local authorities have been experimenting with various kinds of voucher scheme (often called Passport to Leisure), to direct the subsidy to particular groups like the unemployed. Others have reduced charges at off-peak times to increase take-up by the unwaged. In some cases these measures have been successful in increasing the usage of a narrow band of facilities by targeting groups. However the evidence suggested that cost is only one of the barriers to participation in a broader type of leisure activity. In sport and recreation, libraries, and arts there are (not surprisingly) significant differences in the leisure and cultural preferences expressed by different socio-economic classes, age-groups, sexes and ethnic groups. What is more surprising is the disparity in the distribution of public sector subsidies. This is most true in the arts (where subsidies have traditionally gone to "High" culture rather than to more popular, community-based forms). In the recreation field too, special government subsidies have tended to go towards programmes for the potentially disruptive groups (eg youth), rather than the elderly, the housebound, women with dependents etc.

If the public sector is to even begin to respond to the rapidly growing leisure needs of the unwaged sector of the population and other priority groups it cannot rely simply on the manipulation of subsidies and charges (or even better marketing) to attract these new groups into its traditional building-based facilities – whether these be libraries, sports centres, theatres, museums, swimming baths or parks. A quite different orientation is required which reaches out into the community, to identify the specific needs and preferences and personalities of the target group, and then develops programmes of activity to match those needs, and stimulate the active participation of the users.

It is clear that many local authorities have already begun to develop this kind of outreach towards special needs groups (eg specialist programmes for ethnic minorities or the physically handicapped). But it is important to emphasise that the priority groups we have identified are by no means a minority. Over the next decade they may well in fact constitute a majority of the population. The kind of re-orientation towards the community which is required, therefore, is not just for special projects at the field level. A comprehensive community development strategy of this kind is made even more, rather than less, necessary by the Government's proposals for compulsory competitive tendering and contracting out of services. Whether or not the local authority is directly responsible for the delivery of particular leisure services, it nevertheless has an extremely important role in:

- identifying and articulating leisure needs, particularly among those sections of the population lacking the resources to express their needs through the private market;
- developing a clear but broad-based leisure strategy for the area, in dialogue with other providers (voluntary and commercial) and users of services;
- stimulating other agencies and organisations to direct their resources behind an agreed set of objectives and targets and to harness their energies and efforts behind a common strategy;
- networking and negotiating with other organisations to gain their commitment to joint ventures, or to specific sub-contracted activities, within the framework of an overall leisure plan, and to agreed quality standards.

These roles as catalyst, enabler, and coalition-builder (rather than direct provider of services) may be unfamiliar to some in local government, but they are a necessary part of the repertoire for local government policymakers and managers in the public leisure service of the future. The local authority may have a smaller role in direct service-delivery than in the past; but it could have a much more important role in providing vision, direction, strategy and standards for all providers of leisure, whether they be in the public, private or voluntary sectors.

The need for a local economic and employment strategy

The significance of leisure goods and services for the UK economy in general, and for jobs in particular, has been recognised for some time. However, the potential for local government to have some influence on these factors has been explored only more recently.[1]

The starting point for many local authorities is the awareness that the commercial leisure industries are important sectors within their local economies as well as at the national level. For example, the GLC calculated that printing and publishing were London's biggest manufacturing sector, employing 112,000 people; that a further 50,000 were employed in the audio and audio-visual industries, and another 30,000 in the music industry.[2] Liverpool City Council has estimated that the arts employ about 17,000 people in their area.

The leisure (and particularly the cultural) industries are therefore seen by several local authorities as an important part of their economic development strategy – as an opportunity for investment and intervention to support local industry and employment. The GLC, before its abolition, carried out quite a lot of explanatory work in this field and included the cultural industries as an important section of its London Industrial Strategy report.[3] Subsequently a coalition of local authorities in the South East (SEEDS) commissioned a leisure sector study, leading to a report proposing a local authority led 'strategy for leisure and choice' in each area[4]. The Centre for Local Economic Strategies (CLES) has also developed work with several other local authorities under the theme of 'cultural industries and urban regeneration'.

The approach adopted by these local authorities tends to have several common features:

- priority support is given to 'popular' culture rather than traditional 'elite' culture; support is targeted at independent small-scale producers, and multi-cultural or indigenous art forms;
- support takes the form of equity investment or loan, rather than the more traditional subsidy or grant. The argument for this is that it avoids some of the dangers of patronage, and over-dependence of cultural producers upon their sponsors' tastes rather than their consumers' preferences.
- the strategy often involves trying to intervene in the distribution circuits for leisure and cultural products and services. The argument here is that popular forms of culture (eg indigenous, multi-cultural or minority theatre, art, music, literature, dance, film, video etc) are often excluded from access to wider markets, or can only get such access if taken over by the big business distributors, with a consequent loss of autonomy.
- in an increasing number of cases the local authority initiative is not limited to support for commercial or independent cultural industries, but

extends to direct municipal enterprise. For example, Sheffield has pioneered a 'cultural industries quarter' in the city-centre, which includes the Red Tape Recording studios, an audio-visual enterprise centre, a photographic gallery, the Leadmill music and arts centre, and workshop space. Several other cities like Liverpool, Birmingham, Bradford, and Glasgow are developing similar cultural and media initiatives. They are seen as an opportunity not only to support indigenious and locally controlled cultural enterprises, and local employment, but also to regenerate older buildings and the environment of the inner city.[5]

The above examples are relatively small initiatives in themselves. However they are prototypes for much wider-scale involvement by local government. A PSI report on The Economic Importance of the Arts in Britain concluded that the arts form "a significant economic sector in their own right" with an annual turnover of £10 billion; but that government, the local authorities and business organisations are failing to exploit fully this economic value and potential.[6]

At a more immediate level, local authorities can influence jobs in the leisure sector by their own employment policies. The leisure sector as a whole now employs more women than men. However, full time female jobs in leisure have been steadily falling, while part-time female jobs have been expanding. By 1983 bearly a third of the total leisure workforce consisted of *part-time* women workers. These patterns are replicated in the local authority leisure sector. While leisure services employment represents a fairly constant share of total local authority employment, (about 6.5% of full-time jobs) the proportion of part-time leisure jobs is increasing.[7] Local authority leisure policies can therefore have an important effect not just upon the services available to the public, but also upon the number and pattern of jobs available in the locality, particularly for women. Any local authority strategy for leisure should therefore consciously include this economic dimension – its impact upon the quality and quantity of employment in the local labour market.

The need for leadership in values and ideology

One of the key themes within this book is that some of the basic values which have been implicit in the public leisure service may now be threatened by the "commercialisation" of leisure by big business, and by the moves towards compulsory competitive tendering. One of the ways in which local authorities can offer leadership, therefore, during this period of fundamental change, is to try to make these values *explicit* rather than implicit, and (if necessary) to rework and restate them in the light of the changing circumstances.

The basis on which local government can undertake such an important ideological role is that it is the only body with a democratic mandate to represent the needs of the whole community rather than any one of the constituent parts or interest groups. This does not necessarily imply that the local authoritiy's role is to find a consensus between competing interests and ideologies. In fact one of its functions may be to make conflicts of interest explicit and to subject them to open democratic enquiry and debate. This is the effect of the public enquiry and planning system in articulating and resolving conflicts of interest in relation to land-use issues. However land-use planning operates within a framework of public values which to a great extent have been articulated and embodied in legislation and in case-law. Public leisure is different in the sense that many of its underlying values seem to have remained unexpressed. This may be because the values of the public leisure service therefore lie in a set of assumptionss about universal services provided as of right, financed collectively through a redistributive tax system, and made available freely or at subsidised rates (eg. libraries, art galleries, museums, swimming baths, sports centres etc.) In spite of much discussion about charging, and about targeting of services, the basic values within the public leisure sector are still those of collective provision of services as of right.

It is precisely these values which are being challenged explicity by the new right and implicity by the commercial leisure business. Their alternative model for society is a market of consumers purchasing individual services, according to ability to pay, rather than a community of citizens making collective provision for their needs through the State.

Leisure is thus at the centre of a very profound battle of ideas, interests and values about the future of the welfare state itself, and about the whole relationship between the public and the private spheres. It is essential that these issues are brought out into the open and worked through democratically. Local authorities have both the opportunity and the responsibility to articulate and to advocate the values they stand for in the field of leisure and culture and to provide a vision and a sense of direction for their future development in this time of fundamental change.

Conclusion

The challenge to the public sector (and to local government in particular) over the next decade, therefore, is to help identify and articulate the basic values which should inform the development of leisure services during this period of profound change. Its mandate for leadership derives from its unique position as a body elected to present the interests of the whole community. Local authorities will clearly not be in a position to provide all the necessary leisure facilities and services, directly, by themselves. It is certainly not realistic to imagine that public sector expenditure will be raised to the levels which would be necessary to transform the existing, colourful but uneven patchwork of local authority leisure services into a universal social service. However local authorities are in a position to provide the kind of imaginative leadership which would allow them to orchestrate a wide range of leisure facilities and services which are not all under their direct control – creating a lively framework of ideas, values, strategies, plans and programmes which would effectively harness the energies of many different agencies (public, voluntary and private) behind a common vision and sense of direction for leisure services for the whole community. This would involve a very much more outgoing, entrepreneurial, catalytic and interventionist role for local authorities than is traditional; a commitment not just to provide high quality services to those who come to use them but also to reach out into the community to identify unmet need; to develop solutions in dialogue with the potential users of services, and in conjunction with other agencies. This new kind of role for the local authority has implications not just for service-delivery at the field level, but also for strategic planning and resource-management and organisation at the corporate level. It means active and imaginative local government, committed to the highest standards of quality in its service for the public.

References

1 Myerscough, John (1988): *The Economic Importance of the Arts in Britain*, Policy Studies Institute.
2 Greater London Enterprise Board (1985), *The London Industrial Strategy: The Cultural Industries*, London: GLEB/GLC.
3 *Ibid.*
4 South East Economic Development Strategy (SEEDS) (1987): *On the Town: A Strategy for Leisure and Choice.*
5 McKeller Stuart (1988): *The Enterprise of Culture in Local Work*, The Centre for Local Economic Strategies, (CLES).
6 Myerscough, John (1988): *op cit.*
7 Gratton, Chris and Taylor, Peter (1987): *Leisure in Britain*, Leisure Publications (Letchworth) Ltd.

Appendix: The view from the field

(Analysis of questionnaires to chief leisure officers of the changing roles of the leisure service)
Judy White

VIEWS AND ATTITUDES OF CHIEF LEISURE OFFICERS TOWARDS THE PUBLIC LEISURE SERVICE

Introduction

This appendix is a brief discussion of the responses received from the circulation of about sixty chief leisure services officers in local authorities, who were asked a set of questions about their services. The authorities were chosen in accordance to the proportion of each authority in each category in 1985/1986:

	total	consulted	responses
metropolitan districts	36	5	2
non-metropolitan districts	333	42	14
GLC and other metropolitan counties	6	3	2
shire counties	47	6	3
London boroughs	33	8	3

The chief officers were asked to reply to a set of semi-structured questions which covered four areas:

1 the suppliers of leisure goods and services;
2 the users and consumers of leisure goods and services;
3 the impact of economic, social and political change over the next decade;

4 the major changes in resources and organisational structures.

The responses varied enormously between the different tiers. Those from the shire districts were particularly disappointing; of the 45 sent invitations to help, 15 did not reply, 13 apologised for not being able to respond due to lack of time, lack of staff, or because they were in the process of reorganisation, leaving 14 district councils who replied with varying degrees of frankness and fullness, 5 of which were subsequently interviewed. Two metropolitan districts gave interviews and responses, as did 3 London boroughs, the GLC, and 3 shire counties.

The appendix is laid out following the four headings under which officers were asked for information and opinions. It attempts to reflect the flavour and attitudes of the respondents in the hope that this will provide indicators of the strengths and weaknesses in the service which policy makers and politicians might want to pursue.

PART 1 – THE SUPPLIERS OF LEISURE GOODS AND SERVICES

The most important factors in the development of the present pattern of leisure provision in the public and private sectors in the past two decades, and the ones which will continue to be important over the next two decades;

Other factors which will become more influential.

It was somewhat of a surprise to discover that only a minority of respondents mentioned local government reorganisation as being an important factor in the development of provision in the past. This may be because most were more concerned with taking a more global overview of *leisure* and attempted to discern trends which affected and will affect provision. Hence replies were mainly concerned with the following issues:

1 increased amount and distribution of leisure *time*, due either to changes in working conditions, or to unemployment, or to earlier retirement;

2 increased disposable income for those in work to spend on leisure pursuits;

3 increased awareness of the multiplicity of ways in which increased income can be spent for example – through fitness and health; through participating in 'new' types of sport generally promoted commercially or via TV (eg snooker, fishing, basketball); or 'fun' activities, especially those

associated with sponsorship for charity, such as marathons, fun runs; through new technological developments eg computers and videotapes; through membership of conservation bodies;

4 increased awareness by local government of the economic potential of leisure and tourism provision, and of the need to be 'economic' and 'efficient'; as defined by central government.

It was indicated by many that these trends had been accelerating at a time when local authority lesiure was beginning to exercise more professional and political clout. Reorganisation brought with it a short time of significant spending on such provision as sports and leisure halls, swimming pools and specialised museums. This was replaced by a more considered and measured period when financial restrictions forced reappraisals – although in many places the maintenance of the large prestige projects militated against the development of smaller neighbourhood projects, or dual use or joint provision facilities. Respondents felt that the primary role of being leisure providers for majority participation will continue – but the methods by which this will be done will change. For example, with the expectation that high levels of unemployment are a permanent feature, many authorities foresee a trend towards voluntary labour and self help which will need a different attitude and training to the existing professionals. Whether the apparent increased political will in some authorities to be key providers (which arose to some extent as a result of the withdrawal of political momentum in the more traditional areas of operation such as housing) will continue might depend on the quality of marketing which is developed. Marketing leisure products and improving financial and personnel management are considered to be factors which *must* become more influential if public leisure services are not to become pale shadows of the commercial sector. The optimists look to a swing towards a more caring society, and even the emergence of a 'leisure society', but these views are not general.

Factors directly influencing the direction of leisure services are however generally agreed, especially finance and increasing drives toward contracting out and privatisation. Accelerating factors in society for which local authorities need to be forearmed include:

1 changing mobility patterns – linked to national and regional variations in availability of public transport and adequacy of road systems; to travel costs; and effects of violence and terrorism;

2 reduction in the retirement age; increases in job sharing and job splitting; retraining for new and increasingly changing skills;

3 impacts of new technology (eg cable TV);

4 emergence of even more sophisticated leisure publics and the political debates over redistribution of wealth and the quality of life;

5 increases in unemployment amongst 18 to 30 year olds;

6 increases in the old and very old (over 85).

The levels of capital and revenue expenditure: past, present and future

A common pattern emerging from budgets submitted was that after reorganisation in 1974, there was a steadily rising revenue expenditure, both in real terms and as a percentage of total authority spending. Capital expenditure rose in the late 1970s, peaking by the early 1980s, since when it has declined very rapidly.

The general tenor of the responses to the future direction of budgets was far from optimistic. There was resignation and occasionally depression evident in the apparent current need identified in most to minimise capital expenditure *and* revenue expenditure, so that authorities do not become victims of centrally imposed revenue target systems. Whichever system is in operation now, past capital expenditures have affected present revenue budgets, and in many authorities there is a struggle to contain the lesiure revenue budget below the inflation rate. The problem will centre on revenue as costs of maintaining and operating increasingly ageing plant will increase, despite energy saving schemes. Many authorities are also concerned about facilities developed and run by charitable trusts whose revenue budgets rely heavily on public subsidies, unless they can reduce their labour costs and use more voluntary labour.

If capital expenditure remains low (as most seemed to expect), many major new initiatives will have to be funded from other public or commercial sources, which will also have to be prepared to become long term revenue funders. Even now, many new leisure related projects rely on specialist public agency funding, such as Inner City Partnership and Urban Aid grants. Whether community management of projects is more cost effective was contentious. The degree of partnership with the private sector considered desirable was also a matter for disagreement. One respondent favoured a radical solution whereby the private sector becomes more involved in both provision and management, and hence making 'more realistic charging policies', and transferring capital and revenue expenditure to that sector. The same respondent presented 4 alternative pricing and management structures for the next decade:

1 co-operatives being formed from existing local authority management staff who would tender for concessions;

2 partnership with the private sector on a management fee basis whereby the private managing agency decides on the viable charge per facility, and the local authority pays the difference between viability and the charge agreed as acceptable for its social objectives;

3 private sector managing without social objectives subsidies in 'hard line' areas;

4 the odd local authority continuing to operate 'in house' if they allow

managers to manage with adequate and appropriate delegation to be entrepreneurial.

The structure of ownership, financing and control in leisure provision

Most authorities returned answers which indicated that they were owners of the full range of leisure related facilities, and in the majority of cases were also directly concerned with their management and control. They appeared to be the bread and butter providers (apart from the necessary statutory provision of libraries) for basic leisure needs – swimming pools, sports facilities, visitor centres and museums, community centres, public halls, play facilities, parks, and open spaces. Most also ran some facilities such as arts and community centres or theatres either in partnership with a trust or with a management board, whilst retaining overall ownership and control. Others, particularly those with catering and tourism responsibilities, put all or some of their activities such as town hall catering or sea front amenities, out to concession.

All authorities subsidised voluntary sector owned and/or managed provision, in a variety of ways – either as a straight grant, partnership and joint management agreements, through infrastructure work, or low cost leases. Many voluntary sector provisions seem to supplement the basic local authority provisions – neighbourhood leisure and community centres, sports clubs, play provision, and sometimes museum trusts.

There does not appear to be any easily defined boundaries between the groups, and it is difficult to generalise about funding and control arrangements. Many felt that the system and arrangements would become increasingly complex, with more joint boards, trusts, and committees being established. Although this multi-funding process is far from efficient, it is effective in fund raising as organisations are played off against each other.

Existing commercial provision varies much more, both in quality and quantity, between authorities, than does the public set of provisions. This is partly a result of location (eg suburban authorities on the boundaries of metropolitan districts tend to be less well served by commercial provision than shire districts with large freestanding towns) but also of the perception of the market from a commercial standpoint. At present, many authorities either subsidise or have many equitable partnership arrangements with providers on the fringes of the voluntary/commercial sectors who are providing an activity not otherwise available or only to those with high incomes – eg golf courses and squash courts. It appears to most respondents that that situation will become more commonplace.

Most metropolitan areas reported a well established network of industrial sports clubs and working mens clubs, but the former were rapidly being closed and often land sold off for development, whilst the latter were sometimes running into financial difficulties, reflecting perhaps overall industrial decline as well as changing leisure habits. The other main commercial providers tend to be in either the entertainment or sports and health sectors; everyone noted the need to be increasingly aware of the potential for sponsorship – particularly from locally based enterprises – and for partnership. One respondent was clear that local authorities must identify the market(s) for which they are aiming, its potential for income, and 'must decide whether or not it forms part of a fully comprehensive leisure service or sets out to directly compete with the private sector'. No other respondent put the choice so starkly or even hinted that these choices were being contemplated.

Staffing: existing and future

The structure of staffing has changed quite radically over the past decade, as more professionally trained employees have been taken on at higher grades at the expense of manual workers. However, this situation is not considered to be static, and there were indications in responses of the overall need for flexibility. Some foresee the reduction in paid full time professional officers being inevitable as the availability of 'professional' volunteers increases. Many mentioned job sharing increasing alongside an increased use of part time labour.

All agreed that pay, working conditions, job security and trade union organisation will very much depend on national and local politics over the next two decades. The debate on manual worker pay is underway, and it appears that the emphasis will increasingly be on local authorities achieving a greater degree of flexibility from the workforce and a dismantling of the existing rigid pay structures. Shift work, weekend enhancements, etc. will be progressively phased out in lieu of an inclusive salary which takes account of the special circumstances operating in employment in the leisure field. There was certainly a general feeling that the *forced* onset of privatisation, contracting out and value for money exercises will remove job security from many parts of the service.

Some felt the increased flexibility would involve quite radical changes in contracts and in management style, such as management by results or target management providing incentive based incomes – so that manual workers as well as middle and top managers would leave the ranks of the lower paid.

Variations in opinions over the future role of trade unions was considerable, probably reflecting individual chief officer's own experience. Some felt trade union organisation would disappear with the closed shop, whilst others anticipate that it will be re-organised and re-developed to take account of changing conditions.

The leisure services profession

1 'The leisure "profession" embraces many areas of activity which are professions in their own right with individual aims, interests and values. Common to all these activities are the principles of identifying, anticipating and satisfying customer requirements and community needs. The process also takes account of educational requirements that maximise the benefit to the customer or community, and the current financial climate which necessarily influence priorities';
and
2 'Leisure is an integral part of living a full and rounded life. Leisure must not be seen therefore as an appendage in the context of local authority service – indeed, it is being increasingly regarded as a respectable and essential service. Leisure provision is resource intensive – return is measured not so much at the box office as in the physical and mental well being of the individual user and of the community at large. Leisure services corporately are a significant employer, an important element in the development of tourism and in many respects are becoming an essential part of the local economic development strategy'.

These two statements are representative of the views expressed of the interests and values of the leisure profession. Most respondents were keen to specify that their primary interests lay in serving the community, but there was also an awareness that as leisure is a mutli-disciplinary service, it affects considerably organisational structures and the significance of resource allocation to meet the conflicting demands of professional aspirations. There was no general agreement as to whether ILAM and CLOA were appropriate bodies to deal most effectively with these dilemmas, or how a corporate approach to leisure provision might be managed.

The key aims of the profession were also not totally agreed on. They varied from a desire 'to supply as much leisure provision as possible within the finances of the Council, and to assist and encourage provision by the commercial and voluntary sector', to:

'to be cost effective; to ensure value for money, and the highest quality of life for *all* sectors of the community; to provide the broadest possible programme mix for all aspects of the leisure industry; to promote, publicise and market the products.'

Most officers seemed overburdened with the restrictions which they felt were placed on them in finance and budgeting which left them with little room for manoeuvre to develop their primary aims relating to the community's quality of life. Further, the onset of privatisation and more political and financial constraints could put these values and ethics under pressure. The ability to play a full part in the provision of integrated leisure service depends also on the local politicians and officers being willing to raise the profile of leisure provision and become more politically oriented but few discussed how this might affect the roles of and relationships between members and officers. Some were critical of the increasing professionalism of members which made the officers traditional role more difficult to sustain. Although many stressed the need for more innovation, greater management efficiency, and meeting community needs, few spoke of how they might be opinion leaders, standard setters, or opportunity promoters within their community. Whether this was any more than modesty is difficult to surmise!

Few commented on management training *per se*; but those who did were unanimous: managers in the leisure service in the next two decades will have to be far more astute, more business minded, and far better trained.

PART 2 – THE USERS AND CONSUMERS OF LEISURE GOODS AND SERVICES

The present patterns of use of local authority leisure services and the gaps in provision and access problems

There is some overall agreement on the present patterns of use between authorities, although the variations in responses to this question only allows a discussion of the trends which were identified in common.

Present patterns show a steadily increasing interest in a widening range of activities, although few authorities claimed to be particularly different or innovative, confessing instead to their formal and traditional approach. But this is being overtaken as services for particular targets and market segments are identified in an effort to boost attendances and attract grant from Quangos. At the same time, there is a conscious move toward self help, informal activities developing community meeting places, and increasing local control, underlying the notion that leisure services must become a community service and a facilitating agency rather than a simple provider.

Traditional provision – swimming pools, leisure centres, libraries, parks – continue to be used by small cross-sections of the community, although at least three authorities admitted that they could not accurately describe the patterns of use as they did not keep appropriate data; even more (seven), said they had no more than hunches about who the non-users might be. 'Suspicions' of gaps in user take up of services and facility managers' experiences are commonly used to justify positive action to encourage family groups and unemployed people. Most targetted campaigns appear to have had some success in introducing new long-term users, except those for the unemployed, who need 'a much more concerned and objective attack to deal with their enforced leisure predicament'.

Councils in large conurbations confessed also that they had not responded effectively to particular ethnic community needs. The shire counties with large rural populations were worried about rural deprivation associated with decreasing access from cuts in transport services, which affected groups already deprived in other senses eg the elderly. The metro counties were plainly worried that their strategic role and identification of policy lacunae would die when the counties were abolished. All authorities felt that if the inference from central government that admission prices were to increase to make the leisure service self supporting was turned into a statutory obligation, their present worries about increasing overall use and access would pale into insignificance: they would be forced into competitive targetting rather than social targetting. They felt that they should not be forced into such a drastic either/or situation; both types of targetting are usually required, as some parts of leisure services are, and will remain, social services, and should be so treated.

Strategies for equalising access

Most authorities felt that the recreationally illiterate (the non-users) tend to be those who are heavily dependent on other local authority social services and central government funded support: the young unemployed, especially ethnic minorities; the poorly housed; single parent, more particularly but not exclusively the single mother; and the single elderly. All of these are on low fixed incomes. It should not be too difficult for leisure services to liaise with other social services departments to encourage greater participation in such groups or to discover what sort of provision would be most appropriate. This seems to be rare amongst our sample.

'Strategies' were rarely coherent within a department and none mentioned active strategic co-operation with other departments. 'Affirmative action' targetted at ethnic minorities, women, children, unemployed was generally through special events, campaigns, and cheap access to leisure service facilities. The ethos of helping as many as possible is strong:

> 'No strategies, but we try to help everyone, no matter what interests or subcultures, but this is difficult when we lack so many basic facilities';

'The very broad programme mix, the frequency of changes, the sponsorship that enables a reduced charge to be made whilst still meeting social objectives, ensures that the widest possible cross section of and members from the community are given opportunities in leisure participation';

'No strategies at present: waiting for trends to become more obvious, and for clarification of present political ambiguity.'

Should leisure services wait? Should they be more innovative and intrusive? And more interactive?

PART 3 – THE IMPACT OF ECONOMIC, SOCIAL AND POLITICAL CHANGE OVER THE NEXT DECADE

The sections dealing with impacts of change – economic, technological, political – provided a great variation in opinion and crystal gazing.

Assessments of the likely effects of economic restructuring on the leisure service included the belief that as the service is substantially free or at a minimal cost to the user and is likely to remain so, there will be little effect: the users will continue to enjoy what they have already begun to take for granted. Others were concerned that the users will change and so will inevitably affect the service. The emergence of a two class society was a common theme: economic restructuring will create a two class society in the short term, with 'so called middle class leisure activities being used by those in employment or with pensions – with those in unemployment or with fixed incomes being ignored'. There was not much support for the belief that there will be 'a more altruistic approach to wealth' – ie that those who are fortunate enough to work *must* recognise their good fortune and must accept responsibility for 'sharing' that earned wealth with the unemployed.

There was considerable agreement over the longer term effects of economic restructuring on the leisure service: it is likely to put it under more pressure, due to the absolute increase in leisure time amongst those in work as well as many more with enforced leisure time. This increased pressure will also result from overall increases in unemployment, about which there was significantly more – and more diverse – comment. There was not much hope, but a lot of desire, that continuing unemployment would lead to a change of attitude towards *work*, whilst it was more widely felt that many more would be demanding a more satisfying 'leisure life', whether or not they had a satisfying 'work life':

> 'there will be increasing demands for satisfying leisure activity';
> 'one of the roles of leisure services will be to provide the support through which interest in "life" will be developed and maintained'.

Problems over the role of the service have become centred on issues such as unemployment; this was evident from the anguish expressed in some comments:

> 'unemployment currently means hardship; leisure is often associated with costs. The psychological effects of unemployment shouldn't be ignored – for example, the failure of projects designed specifically for such people and the implied apathy the situation causes';
> 'as unemployment is reduced over the next 20 years by subsidised initiatives (job sharing, work rationing, community enterprises), it will lead to a need for a radical and entirely new resolve by central government backed by popular opinion, aroused by escalating law and order problems and apathy. It is entirely speculative to argue whether the 'public' or 'private' leisure service will be the stronger force in meeting the obvious challenge.'

Speculation is popular however: if it is agreed that within a mixed economy, there is a degree of inter-dependence between sectors, it can be argued that a strong financial and economic situation is necessary to enable leisure services to survive, and that much of this strength will come from economic revival fuelled through private enterprise. But public leisure services need to be maintained in the era of uncertainty due to their increased role in 'preventive social work' (eg vandalism). How can this role be dovetailed with the increasing pressures on local authorities to become more cost effective and show commercial rates of return on capital investment unless there is some financial recognition of the social benefits of leisure provision?

Most respondents felt that on the whole private leisure provision will remain profit centred, whilst the social benefit of public provision *will* be recognised by central government and be given financial support, by the end of the century. The underlying disquiet remains that in the short term whilst the need for leisure services will increase as unemployment increases, the demand may not increase – partly as a consequence of the cost barriers, unless financial and pricing strategies recognise these barriers.

The impact of technological change in the manufacturing and services sectors on the need for and delivery of services

This question evoked answers which indicated that most officers have not been able to envisage more than incremental change to the existing patterns – for example, computers bringing new uses to television sets. The few who recognised the possibilities of more fundamental change identified the role of leisure in alleviating the *results* of technological change – such as stress, diminution of skills acquired and used in the work place, whether physical or other; and passivity from 'screen related' occupations and interests.

The benefits of technology in freeing up types of provision were not noted by many. There was some mention of the potential for improved efficiency of operation which might free staff to develop more 'people based skills' which could be vital in a community orientated service. The improved operational efficiency would itself make leisure services more accessible to more customers: 'networking will enable us to book facilities at a wider range of venues, and should eventually bring the booking of all services to our doorstep'; and some hinted at a unique role for public leisure:

> 'where public leisure will score will be in areas of therapy and re-cuperation, since the boredom of the new technology will eventually produce the demands for much-reduced work time and the concentration of human effort in re-creational and recuperative leisure pastimes: "Education for Leisure" will feature strongly in this context.'

Political change

Views on the most important areas of political change likely to impinge on developments in the leisure field appeared to be more closely conditioned by the officers' immediate and current preoccupations and conceptions than other responses. But perhaps a representative summary would be:

> 'Rate capping may mean that local authorities will not be able to afford to offer services at a level which the authority wishes and the public expects; whether a change in central government would alter this is now somewhat debatable. But to privatise leisure is to alter its overall objective of breaking down barriers, since the objective of the private sector is to make money – and prices charged would be prohibitive to most people'.

Most emphasis in most replies was placed on short term scenarios in which the present government is likely to remain in office for the next two years and and there might be a change of government after that. The policies of central government will exacerbate the local authorities' abilities to meet rising needs, and they will be forced to look increasingly at schemes which are sanctioned or encouraged by central government through partnership funding or private sponsorship, and which have economic objectives. A majority decided that there will be increasing interference from central government over the short term which will not only reduce the autonomy of local authorities, but also introduce some arbitrary controls – such as compulsory tendering in some sections of the service.

Those respondents who were prepared to crystal gaze and contemplate change beyond the 1980s felt, not surprisingly, that the key lay in the type of government which might be in power. A three-party 'hung' government could mean that initiative was not encouraged, and safety and predictability would be the order of the day. It was not felt that such a government would be able to distribute the common wealth more equitably, and so it would be difficult for policies which recognised the dependence of the improvement of the quality of life on such equitability, to be propounded. A Labour government might be more concerned with developing a leisure service as a social and community service, whilst not discouraging public and private enterprise working together as it does now in some authorities.

PART 4 – CHANGES IN RESOURCES AND ORGANISATIONAL STRUCTURES

The most likely and most significant changes in the next 10 years in the ways in which central government directly and indirectly finances/subsidises leisure and leisure related activities

'Central government may have to be dragged screaming into providing greater awareness and finance for a more fulfilling leisure time. Bored, disgruntled people become dangerous. The present government's attitude, which appears to be "if you can't pay, you can't have", will have to change. I do believe, whichever party is in power, leisure may have to pay its way to a greater extent than previously. However, as leisure provision is costly, governments will have to help.'

This (more than slightly) worried statement reflects a fairly widely articulated feeling about the uncertainty of the change which might occur between tiers of government as a result of financial policies. It underscores the effect that financial policies can have on the whole of the relationship and on the ensuing attitudes to provision.

Few respondents, however, were willing or able to be very specific about the detail of the likely changes in financing, although clearly they were troubled about the possible implications of any change or of a continuation of the present situation. But there was little consensus. Views included:

1 the belief that there will be a increase in direct resources for leisure from central government, principally through the creation of a Ministry of Leisure with advisory bodies constructed for many disciplines, and with the abolition of many quangos;

2 central government will maintain its present subsidy to local authorities via the Rate Support Grant and leisure related quangos (Sports Council, Arts Council etc);

3 central government will reduce its present direct support – but 'football disasters and riots may force an increase in indirect funding'. But this might not be sufficient or applicable to maintaining facilities, many of which cannot be maintained from revenue, and so standards could fall if revenue cannot be increased;

4 the situation depends on which political party is in office. 'Conservatives will continue to push for the private sector control of all our services under the misapprehension that they are efficient. RSG will possibly be phased out in favour of some other form of local government financing (for whatever services remain in local government control)'.

Others felt that a change of government might do little more than decelerate trends already underway – and that there is little hope of reversing them. The most optimistic view stabilised local government's role through the development of better developed and managed partnership arrangements – due not least to the realisation by the private sector that it must cater for wider market sectors than hitherto. Government inducements might be involved here:

'the government might allow certain subsidies to be passed over to the private sector to cater for the lower paid while still maintaining a charging policy for those who can well afford. Although there might possibly be a growth in the country club set at the expense of the poor, this will result in urban unrest, riot, etc.'

There were a few specific techniques and mechanisms suggested which might alleviate local authorities' financial position. Tourism was felt to be the most likely candidate for increased intervention and financial incentives by central government owing to its perceived ability to be a significant earner for invisible exports. Changes in VAT laws could recognise the improved status of leisure and either reduce, eliminate or earmark the revenue for the leisure industry. Some respondents felt that one of the most significant actions which government could carry out would be to improve the incentives to companies to sponsor events or buildings by easing the tax laws. A beginning has been made in the 1986 Budget with easing the ability of companies to donate to charitable organisations.

Changes in the relationship between central government funding and local authority budgetting which will affect the ways in which services are provided

Responses to this seemed to link with answers to the previous question, and provided more evidence of the overall disquiet felt by authorities with their financial situation and their abilities to change it. Whilst one was moved to comment that 'forecasting of changes are unpredictable', more shared the hunch that with even tighter controls of local government spending and increasing uncertainties, planning for leisure will become even more difficult. This will be exacerbated whilst government is so unspecific in its aims toward leisure and it remains a non-statutory function.

Overwhelmingly it seemed that the only pattern which local authorities can foresee is that of local differences: even more than now, each authority will be forced to make local decisions on the way in which costs should be split between ratepayers and service users – which will have decisive impacts on provision. Thus each individual authority will have to face decisions on the *type* of service it provides and *how* it provides it – a service for all or for a few? Many worried that these decisions, difficult in themselves, are likely to be made without any strategic planning framework at regional or national level which incorporates detailed financial planning – hence encouraging a return to the opportunistic approach, from which some have been struggling to escape.

The sceptre of 'haphazard, unco-ordinated and piecemeal expansion' was well summarised by one response, which predicted 'vital gaps' in the service. He suggested some solutions and strategies to compensate for this might include:

- the increasing use of MSC schemes to supplement – for example, community programmes, merging of interests, community health/leisure/education to maximise resources, manpower, buildings etc;
- squeeze on all overheads to release 'sharp end' moneys;
- use of grant, funny money etc. to achieve service needs.

Equally, local authorities may be forced to rely increasingly on the voluntary and commercial sectors to provide some services – which could mean diminishing standards. Some went so far as to say that *any* new developments will only be those made by commercial concerns and be commercially viable – thus making the social welfare function of local authorities increasingly central. There were only a few dissenters. A continuing Conservative government may reduce grant, but it will want to retain control over strategic development in some spheres and so continue to encourage matching expenditure formulae. Some looked to the introduction of local income tax to improve local financial control and increase independence. More yearned for a Labour administration and Labour local government alert to the importance of widespread provision based on analysis of need – but warn of the consequences if this is not matched by sympathetic, sharp and professional management.

Despite secret fantasies hinted at, clearly few respondents really felt that radical change is likely to occur. They will have to content themselves with increasing their abilities to manage flexibly and responsively and being prepared to understand and predict the reasons for incremental changes in policy in the central government plethora of agencies.

Changes in the relationships between private and public sector investment and pricing policies, and their implications for provision

This question gave respondents the opportunity to expand on their rationale for provision and associated pricing policies. It provided one of the most interesting sets of responses – and a surprising amount of unanimity:

> 'local authorities will need to co-ordinate and harness the resources of all providers and managers of facilities to ensure that duplication of provision is avoided and that any available finance is widely used. However, co-ordination of the private sector may be difficult to exert, except through any procedures for financial assistance.'

The private sector is expected to continue to invest in areas of leisure provision which are 'commercially viable', 'where there is sufficient financial return', but might also move increasingly into particular specialised areas such as exclusive facilities for sports such as snooker and squash, and the much more broadly based 'leisure clubs' centred on country hotels designed to attract affluent middle class upwardly mobile families. Inner cities and suburbs may also be the sites of development deals which include sports facility provision.

The public sector picture is much muddier – due to the recurring problems of conflicting objectives, restrictions on capital expenditure, and tight control on revenue. A consensus emerged indicating that there are more likely to be schemes concerned with rehabilitation and refurbishments to minimise capital expenditure, whilst efforts to reduce costs will inevitably lead to the examination of alternatives such as community management, selling off assets, joint management, and partnership arrangements.

In reality, many of the public sector decisions are concerned with closing the gap between private and public provision – but not necessarily resolving the problem of incompatible objectives. Whether joint partnership arrangements can be for the mutual benefit of private developers and local authorities in a wider range of facilities remains to be seen. The long term effects on local authorities of increasing infiltration of private developers on one side and increasing central control of powers and finance on the other are not regarded with much enthusiasm. Will local authorities still have the skills and the morale 'to co-ordinate and harness the resources of all managers and providers of facilities to ensure that duplication of provision is avoided and that any available finance is wisely used'? The only way forward may be improved co-operation between the public and private sector through joint provision, sponsorship, consultation, agreed pricing policies; but do leisure services have these skills? If community management is adopted, are the relevant skills available to be nurtured and developed?

The probable impacts of the changing consumer's attitudes to leisure related expenditure on the patterns of provision

'The public's expectations of leisure provision has increased considerably over the past decade and this will continue. Individuals, while spending more, will be looking for a wider range of facilities, higher standards, and value for money.'

This quote reflects the overall conclusion from the replies. Increased participation will not discriminate over the sector which it uses; it will continue to use facilities and participate in activities which meets its needs most closely. Local authorities have traditionally tended to react to rather than mould need, but this is changing as they have realised both the direct costs (in capital expenditure on short lived schemes) and indirect ones (of alienating rather than encouraging users) are too high. More are beginning to recognise the validity of their role as facilitators, of helping others to organise and run facilities which they have provided, but are constrained by their requirements to maximise income received from facilities.

There seemed to be some dissension over the ways in which consumers' attitudes to leisure might change, but this might be as much to do with the constituency being considered as real differences. Some felt that the key variable is the net disposable income of the individual. 'Expenditure on leisure is one of the first to go when this net level falls', and with rising unemployment, this is not likely to change significantly – so local authorities need to be aware of the dangers of pricing their service out of the market.

This calls for much clearer analysis of needs, provision, use, and price structures – linked with objectives – according to a majority of respondents. Others were more confident of the growth in self reliance:

'I believe that with greater leisure time people will, in general, somehow find the money to use facilities to greater effect. Their attitude to leisure will be one of self help or voluntary assistance, as well as being partakers of leisure on their own account.'

The most realistic options for organisational structures for the planning and delivery of leisure services; the implications for present structures; and the changes which need to be made

'In a word – flexibility'
'Undoubtedly, this is the most important, and most controversial question of the lot'.

Being the most important and controversial, it was also the most difficult to answer – and did not generally provide much that was striking or original. The overall feeling that flexibility is essential did not get to the root of how this might take place and who might be involved. The options for organisational change which were offered were very much reflections of the existing power base and tier of local government in which the respondent is presently situated.

A typical response from a county was very forceful in its belief that co-ordinating between tiers is vital, as all have a responsibility for the provision and management of some leisure facilities – but many individual authorities prefer to act in isolation, some proceed un-ilaterally, with complete disregard for what their neighbouring authorities might be doing, or have done. Some felt this situation was becoming more common, often occurring as a direct result of disagreements among individual members of neighbouring councils.

Leisure service departments should not operate in isolation but too often they do: many departments in local government provide and manage facilities which contribute to overall leisure in an area – and the work of these departments should be more closely co-ordinated.

It seemed that many districts would be happy to see local government re-organised so that more power resides at local level. They argued that this would make it more straightforward to co-ordinate all those elements which have some leisure interests, and to break down artifical barriers between professions, to encourage the total community concept. Unitary authorities concerned with a whole community concept 'will require an entirely new attitude in leisure management, new skills and provisions and a level of tolerance to consumer and public reaction not very prevalent at the moment'.

The local conclusion of this attitude is envisaged as a 'Programme Development' system (rather than departmental-orienated committee structures) in which all functional resources are co-ordinated to deliver a given policy/strategy/action plan. But there is little optimism that the kind of leaders needed to develop this approach are available: where will they be found?

Some officers felt that a first step might be further back in the process: 'the most realistic options available for organisational structures are for the authorities to recognise the importance of leisure time and use and to appoint directors or chief officers with representations on the council's management team'. At member level, leisure committees should be given more authority in ensuring that the council's overall leisure strategy is carried out, whilst officers should be given greater delegation of powers. They might then be able to encourage reorganisations which include fewer administrators and more servers in departments which are increasingly centralised and management by generalists (rather than specialists, which seems to be a current trend). Serving, animating, and helping people to help themselves are not skills particular to specialist managers; they are associated with managers concerned with delivering needed services who are attuned to the local users, and to the voluntary and commercial sectors.

Within a flexible organisation, local authorities need to be more responsive to changes in the market – which will require a much more central role for financial and marketing functions. Few respondents actually examined realistic options for service delivery in detail. Some looked at the requirements of partnership with the commercial sector in which local authorities buy land on which the commercial sector builds and manages facilities, based on a competitive approach.

A 'service approach' to service delivery involves direct provision based on need, requiring personnel working as animateurs, on outreach; as well as social pricing policies, community provision and recognition of leisure as a necessary service.

An approach, already mentioned above, which attempted to integrate leisure objectives between departments, could be formalised through joint policy, or even one service department 'providing personnel services to the community, destroying the box approach of traditional public service provision'.

The approach akin to the DLO philosophy in which the organisation takes on a quasi commercial company approach 'using commercial techniques of pricing', 'production marketing' to the exclusion of social considerations was also suggested. The implication of this approach would be 'a small central core of managers, client orientated and handling the social/political end'. This may be the current favourite in possible organisational change in central government but it was generally felt that most changes will be much more fudged and incomplete. Financing and marketing will be central to any change, however, as more examinations are made of the costs and overheads of service and of central departments, and cost centres more clearly defined. All this will necessitate adaptable and skilful management and communication – and huge commitment. A huge challenge for leisure service management to which these officers are seemingly prepared to respond.